MW00852790

BARK!

Praise for *Bark!*

"Zazie Todd knows what it's like to have a fearful or reactive dog, and in *Bark!* she brings her kind, science-based approach to our shy, timid, and terrified canine friends. This book is packed with tips based on Todd's own expertise and insights from interviews with dog trainers, scientists, and veterinarians. *Bark!* is a fun, enjoyable, and eminently practical read."

DR. MARTY BECKER, America's Veterinarian and founder of Fear Free

"Full of practical solutions and tips for even the most fearful of canines, all backed by extensive research, witty personal stories, and Todd's own beloved animals."

KELLY S. THOMPSON, national bestselling author of *Still, I Cannot Save You*

"Rarely do you come across an author who writes with real academic authority, but who is also accessible to a wide audience... *Bark!* would be at home on the bookshelf of any professional trainer, experienced dog parent, or new adopter. It's an extraordinarily informative read from cover to cover as well as an almost encyclopaedic 'dip in, dip out' resource. If the dog world is to make the science of animal behavior commonplace in the way we all think about dogs, this book will lead the way."

SI WOOLER, acclaimed dog trainer

"Packed full of practical and useful advice. I will definitely be recommending this book to my clients."

NICK HONOR, CTC, clinical animal behaviourist and chair of the Canine Behaviour and Training Society

"As the guardian of one dog rescued from an animal testing laboratory and another rescued from the dog meat trade in China, I needed this book! *Bark! The Science of Helping Your Anxious, Fearful, or Reactive Dog* is clear, concise, and convincing. I immediately put the advice to use, making life better for me and my dogs. This insightful book gave me, a lifetime dog guardian with a passion for all things dog, much to think about. I'll be referring to it often!"

TERESA J. RHYNE, #1 *New York Times* bestselling author of *The Dog Lived (and So Will I)* and *Poppy in the Wild*

Praise for *Wag*

"Using the latest canine science, Zazie Todd gives us a clear
and compassionate guide to bringing out the best in your dog."

GREGORY BERNS, *New York Times* bestselling author of *How Dogs Love Us*

"*Wag* is a must-read for all dog lovers. An amazing, well-written book
that makes canine science easy to understand and apply in a useful
manner to improve dogs' lives and the relationship we have with them.
The anecdotes about Dr. Todd's dogs are the highlight of the book."

DR. WAILANI SUNG, board-certified veterinary behaviorist, San Francisco SPCA

"Zazie Todd does dogs the immeasurably good favor of taking their happiness seriously. Todd is dialed in to the science of dogs and a thoughtful
trainer of dogs. Everything she writes about, you want to know. *Wag* is a
welcome addition to the books geared to helping you help your dog."

ALEXANDRA HOROWITZ, author of *Our Dogs, Ourselves: The Story of a Singular
Bond,* and *Inside of a Dog: What Dogs See, Smell, and Know*

"If you care about your dog, you need this book. It's packed
with insights from the latest canine science, and loads of advice
on how you can give your dog the happiest possible life."

DR. JOHN BRADSHAW, author of *Dog Sense: How the New Science of
Dog Behavior Can Make You a Better Friend to Your Pet* (*In Defence of Dogs:
Why Dogs Need Our Understanding* in the UK)

"Love dogs? Then you'll love *Wag*! Dr. Todd skillfully translates dozens of
recent scientific studies into practical recommendations for all of us who
strive to reciprocate the joy our dogs provide us so often and so well."

KATHY SDAO, applied animal behaviorist and author of *Plenty in Life Is Free:
Reflections on Dogs, Training and Finding Grace*

"Beautifully written and meticulously researched, *Wag* brings the latest
and best science on dog welfare, behavior, training, and health to bear
on the paramount topic for all of us interested in dogs: their happiness.
Required reading."

JEAN DONALDSON, the Academy for Dog Trainers

ZAZIE TODD

Foreword by **CAT WARREN**

Bark!

THE SCIENCE OF HELPING YOUR ANXIOUS, FEARFUL, OR REACTIVE DOG

GREYSTONE BOOKS

Vancouver/Berkeley/London

Greystone Books Ltd.
greystonebooks.com

Cataloguing data available from Library and Archives Canada
ISBN 978-1-77840-136-7 (cloth)
ISBN 978-1-77840-137-4 (epub)

Editing by Lucy Kenward
Copy editing by Brian Lynch
Proofreading by Jennifer Stewart
Indexing by Stephen Ullstrom
Jacket design by Belle Wuthrich and Fiona Siu
Text design by Fiona Siu
Jacket photograph by Lyly/iStock.com

Printed and bound in Canada on FSC® certified paper at Friesens. The FSC® label means that materials used for the product have been responsibly sourced.

Greystone Books thanks the Canada Council for the Arts, the British Columbia Arts Council, the Province of British Columbia through the Book Publishing Tax Credit, and the Government of Canada for supporting our publishing activities.

Canada

Greystone Books gratefully acknowledges the xʷməθkʷəy̓əm (Musqueam), Sḵwx̱wú7mesh (Squamish), and səlilwətaɬ (Tsleil-Waututh) peoples on whose land our Vancouver head office is located.

For Roy and Frankie

CONTENTS

PART 3: HOW AND WHERE TO GET HELP

FOREWORD

FOR THOSE OF US who have lived with fearful or reactive dogs—
and I'm raising my hand here not once, but twice—it can
sometimes feel as though there's no light at the end of the
tunnel. Your dreams of romping slow motion through a field of
buttercups with your confident and carefree canine have been
crushed. Or perhaps you envisioned your dog relaxed under a
café table on the sidewalk in spring, grinning happily, while you
sipped cappuccino and chatted with friends. That's a nope.

Instead, from now till eternity, all that faces you is a dark
maze of dog management and embarrassed apologies and lots of
bad advice from well-meaning strangers. And close calls. Lots of
heart-pounding, frightening close calls.

Okay, maybe that's not you, but that was certainly me. More
than once. And I'm here to say that *Bark!* can help you.

My first reactive (but still handsome and funny) German Shepherd pup arrived when the majority of bestselling dog training
books and misguided trainers were explaining helpfully—and
erroneously—that my problem was that I needed to be a better
"pack leader." My male German Shepherd was clearly trying to
dominate me. I should "muzzle wrap" him, pin him down with
an "alpha roll." Never let him go out the door first. Make sure I
could grab his bowl of food or marrow bone any time I pleased.
Those essential skills would keep me happy—and keep him in his
proper doggy place.

It took me time to understand that Solo's aggression towards other dogs didn't stem from overconfidence, but instead from unease. As an only pup in a litter of one, he couldn't easily learn how dogs communicate with each other. For the first time in my dog-obsessed life, I had a "difficult" dog.

We flunked out of puppy classes because Solo was growling, fur raised, barking frantically at other pups the moment we entered a training building. One vet told me my 10-week-old pup, when he was older, would inevitably attack someone and come to a very bad end. Part of the problem, she explained, was that by giving him treats on the exam table I was "coddling him," rewarding his bad attitude. I turned down offers of doggy playdates. I obsessed about where and when we might walk in my neighborhood because I didn't want us to encounter other people walking their dogs who wanted our two dogs to meet and greet.

And, of course, I got the ultimate grim, fairy tale warning: never, ever, let a dog like him play tug with you . . .

BACK THEN, I would have benefited enormously—and saved time, money, and lakes of tears—if I had had a guide exactly like the one you are reading now. *Bark!: The Science of Helping Your Anxious, Fearful, or Reactive Dog* is psychologist and animal lover Zazie Todd's latest contribution to creating happy canines and happy owners. *Bark!* is packed with wise advice and plenty of sympathy. Nowhere in this book does that smug, unhelpful dog training aphorism appear: "You don't get the dog you want. You get the dog you need."

Bark! is backed by the best science, clearly explained. We've learned a lot since the pack-leader school of training. *Bark!* gives every worried dog owner numerous road maps to follow and solutions to ponder. All the road maps have one thing in common: kind and effective training approaches.

Zazie doesn't minimize the problems that an anxious, fearful, or reactive dog can bring to a household. (Early on, before I fell entirely in love with him, I compared Solo to Stephen King's monstrous Cujo.)

Bark! is filled with thoughtful exercises a caring pet owner can follow. And Zazie has words of comfort for the dog owner who is feeling frustrated and exhausted, sad and inadequate. She gets it. She's been there.

You are not alone if you struggle with a dog you can't take for a walk because she's trembling or trying to pull out of her harness as you leave your home. Or if you have a dog who explodes in alarm, barking every time a car drives by. Or one who growls and creeps under the couch when your overly enthusiastic neighbor with a booming voice wants to pet her. There are so many of us. This book is for you. And me. And especially for our dogs.

You may find that dipping in and out of *Bark!*, reading a few pages at a time, is your best method. You can sample just a few tidbits on your first foray, such as "It's okay to comfort a fearful dog" or "Dog training involves treats." That advice will make you feel better, nourish you, and help you help your dog. Or you might learn that pain may well be an underlying factor in your dog's reactions. It's much more common than people realize. Our spicy Spaniel, Brio, who was asleep on the couch, growled at our mellow Shepherd the other night when he nudged him walking past the couch. Instead of immediately scolding Brio, I realized he was probably in pain from overdoing a recent nose-work search. I gave him an anti-inflammatory in a pill pocket—and praised sweet Rev for not taking Brio's growl personally.

Part of what makes *Bark!* so helpful is that Zazie, who also wrote *Wag: The Science of Making Your Dog Happy*, doesn't condescend, or judge, or promise miracles. She doesn't minimize the commitment of time, patience, and creativity it takes to help your dog become the best version of themselves. You probably won't have a perfect dog in thirty days. You won't be a perfect dog trainer in thirty days. But *Bark!* can be the start of understanding more about your dog, about their fears and anxieties, and how to assuage them.

After much trial and error (and yes, flailing and frustration), I finally learned how to understand and work with Solo. He became the best dog ever. Not the most obedient. Never fully comfortable around strange dogs. Not a dog who liked to lie under an outside table at a coffee shop. But a dog I loved with all my being. Who played long, enthusiastic games of tug with me. And sometimes went out the door first. And who expanded my idea of what a dog could be, and who I could be.

And by the time a second German Shepherd puppy came into our lives who was anxious and worried about the world, Zazie Todd and other savvy positive trainers were there to help.

I hope you find happy surprises and solace in these pages and out in the wide world with your dog. I did.

CAT WARREN, author of *What the Dog Knows*

HOW TO USE THIS BOOK

I F YOU'RE READING THIS BOOK, it's probably because your dog is somewhere between a little shy and terrified. You're not alone; up to 75 percent of dogs have some kind of fear or anxiety, so there are a lot of fearful and anxious dogs out there. Sometimes we call them shy, sensitive, reserved, or reactive. Many cases of aggression in dogs are also the result of fear or anxiety. It can be hard to feel empathy for a dog who is growling and showing their teeth at you, but understanding that fear is the root cause can be helpful when dealing with these dogs.

This book is designed to help you understand how you can help your dog. It's based on the best available science, and I only recommend kind and humane methods. We'll begin, in Part 1, by looking at what you can do to start making a difference right away. This section also answers common questions about shy and fearful dogs and explains the techniques we will use to help. It's essential reading before Part 2, which looks at different types of fears and how to tailor the techniques to an individual dog. Finally, in Part 3, we'll look at where to get help. And because some people learn so much from helping their fearful dog that they are motivated to learn more, we'll look at additional resources you might find helpful, and how to learn more about dog training. There's a summary of the most important tips to help your fearful dog at the end of the book.

If your dog is not fearful, you will still learn a lot from this book, especially from the first and last parts. You'll learn the two ways dogs learn (by association and by consequence) that we use in dog training, why it's so important to stick to reward-based methods, how to choose treats for different training tasks, the most important skills to teach your dog, how to build a training plan, and what to look for in a dog trainer. The chapters in Part 2 will give you tips on preventing those fears and anxieties.

This book is not a substitute for consulting your dog's veterinarian and/or a suitably qualified dog trainer, behaviorist, or veterinary behaviorist. If you have any concerns about your dog, see a professional.

PART
1

HOW TO START MAKING A DIFFERENCE RIGHT AWAY

UNDERSTANDING YOUR FEARFUL DOG

．．．．．．．．．．．．．．．．．

DIDN'T GROW UP WITH DOGS. It's kind of assumed that all dog people had a family dog and loved dogs all their lives, so it surprises people to hear that about me. But it's worse than that: as a child and young person, I was terrified of dogs. It was only as a young adult that I got over that fear and understood just what great friends dogs can be. And then I was smitten. These days, I feel a particular affinity for fearful dogs. It doesn't take a psychologist to say that may have something to do with the roundabout way my friendship with dogs finally blossomed.

I know what it feels like to be terrified of something that everyone else thinks is fine. But when it comes down to it, so do many of us: there are spider phobias and fears of public speaking, people who jump on a table and shriek at the sight of a mouse, people who faint at the sight of a needle or blood, people who are terrified of flying, being in an enclosed space, or leaving the house. Having a dog who is fearful or shy is in some ways the same and in other ways very different. This book aims to explore what we can do to help fearful dogs and how the science of fear—which is based largely on studies of humans and rodents—can help us understand fearful dogs better.

A number of words are sometimes used to describe the fearful dog: *shy*, *fearful*, *nervous*, *anxious*, *reactive*, *stubborn*, *stupid*, *dominant*, and so on. Some of these terms are more helpful than others. Those with a judgment attached (for example, *stubborn*, *stupid*) often show a lack of understanding that the dog is actually feeling nervous or afraid. It's not helpful to assign blame to a dog who is, in fact, simply struggling. When we describe a dog's behavior through human terms, it's called anthropomorphism. Sometimes anthropomorphism can get in the way of understanding our dog, such as when we assign higher-order emotions to dogs and say they are jealous, spiteful, or guilty. So far, there's no evidence that dogs can experience these specific emotions, which require a certain level of cognitive processing. Since dogs experience the world differently from us, these labels are probably not appropriate. But at other times, anthropomorphism can help us understand what it must be like for our dogs, such as how they feel in a situation when they are scared.

We all have things we're afraid of and can think of specific times when we were scared. For me, there was the time when a car came over the brow of a hill on the wrong side of the road, and I had to do an emergency stop to prevent a collision. And when, as a young person, I was walking home from a nightclub with a friend and realized that the man following us was the same man the bouncers had thrown out a couple of hours earlier for harassing me. Or when an angry momma bear escorted me, my husband, and our two dogs down a mountain, huffing and puffing in the trees just to the side of the gravel road for the longest ten minutes of my life. Different situations, but all with a heart-stopping moment of terror.

THE DIFFERENCE BETWEEN FEAR AND ANXIETY

IN SCIENTIFIC TERMS, *fear* and *anxiety* have slightly different meanings. Fear is something dogs (and humans) feel in response to a specific stimulus or event that is potentially dangerous. In many cases, it's a sensible response that will start a fight-or-flight reaction to help keep us safe in the presence of something or someone that might hurt us. The examples I just gave were real dangers: the oncoming car might have hit me; the man might have attacked; the momma bear was afraid that we posed a danger to her cub, and so we, ourselves, were in danger.

In contrast, anxiety is a more generalized emotional response that is not tied to something specific; anxiety is a feeling that may nag at a dog (or us) over a period of time. Anxiety can often feel quite vague. In human terms, an example might be the feeling we get before an exam, when thinking, "What if I don't know the answers?" There is no actual danger in not knowing every answer, so it's an anxiety rather than a fear, but nonetheless it's an unpleasant emotional feeling. Anxiety may be associated with depression and can be long-lasting. Although fear and anxiety can be very useful to keep us safe, when anxiety becomes chronic it can have serious effects on our health.

In practice, many people use the terms *fear* and *anxiety* interchangeably in everyday life. In terms of the brain structures involved, these are not two completely separate circuits; everything is interconnected, after all.[1] From a practical standpoint, since we cannot tell exactly what is going on in our dog's mind, it can be hard to tell fear and anxiety apart. As a dog's guardian, you can leave the question of which it is to your veterinarian and simply focus on doing the things that will help your dog feel better.

Of course, fear is not the root cause of all behavior issues in dogs, even if it accounts for quite a few of them. For example, a dog who jumps up to greet people, although perhaps annoying, is generally not afraid; usually, this is a sociable behavior from a friendly dog who is excited to see people. A dog who chews the remote control or digs up your favorite plants is exhibiting normal dog behaviors of chewing and digging. It's best to give your dog options to do those behaviors in ways that aren't annoying to you—for example, by providing chew toys or a specific space where they are allowed to dig.

As for anxiety, sometimes a dog who appears to be anxious turns out to actually be frustrated. This distinction can be a bit tricky, but I'll get to it in sections of the book where it's especially relevant, as in cases where dogs who are reactive to other dogs on-leash are not actually afraid (see Chapter 8), or where dogs who are left alone and misbehave aren't actually afraid to be on their own (see Chapter 11). Behavior issues that don't have a component of fear are not covered in this book, although you will still find the training sections helpful because the general principles of training and management are the same no matter why you are using them. It also helps to know how to prevent fears from occurring in the first place.

THE RISE OF FEAR

IF ANYTHING, we could say there is an epidemic of fear. According to one study, 72.5 percent of dogs have some kind of fear or anxiety.[2] The most common is sensitivity to noises (32%), especially fear of fireworks (26%); the second most common is fear (29%), which includes being afraid of other dogs (17%), of strangers (15%), and of new experiences (11%). A fear of surfaces (like slippery floors) and heights affects 23.5 percent of dogs, while many dogs also have inattention (20%), compulsive behaviors (16%), and impulsivity (15%). Another study, this time of a representative sample of dog guardians in Denmark, found that a third of dogs (34%) have a behavior issue, with the most common being fear and disobedience (such as jumping up or not coming when called).[3]

Dogs' fears and anxieties may have become worse as a result of the COVID-19 pandemic. During the worst times, people could not take their pup to puppy class and could not attempt to make up for that socialization in other ways; and dogs got used to their guardians being around almost all the time. But it's not like fear in dogs is anything new. We already know that behavior issues are the leading cause of death in dogs under 3 years of age, and many of those issues are because of lack of socialization and the resulting fear and aggression.[4] For dogs of all ages, undesirable behaviors are one of the most common reasons for euthanasia (with old age and poor quality of life being other common reasons).[5]

The trouble with fear is that it's very easy to create, as we know from human psychology. John Watson's 1920 demonstration of inducing fear in an infant, Little Albert, is one of the classic studies. Watson was already an accomplished psychologist when he did this experiment; his PhD research had shown that rats were able to form associations—that is, to learn things—which at that time many scientists thought only some kinds of animals could do.[6]

Almost everyone who's taken an introductory psychology class will have heard of Little Albert. Watson had learned of the work of Russian physiologist Ivan Pavlov, who had found that his laboratory dogs salivated when they heard a signal that food was coming. This is known as a classically conditioned response. At this time, only one of Pavlov's lectures was available in English (his book, *Conditioned Reflexes*, was not translated to English until 1927).[7] Watson wanted to know if the same kind of thing could be done in humans, and together with his graduate student Rosalie Rayner he conducted an experiment on an infant, Little Albert.

After a pre-test when Little Albert was 9 months old, the experiment began when he was 11 months. When Watson showed him a rat (the conditioned stimulus, or CS), Rayner was behind him, ready to hit a metal bar with a hammer and make a loud, clattering noise. They already knew that this noise made Little Albert startle and cry. After more than one session of showing the rat and banging the bar, Little Albert became afraid of the rat (a conditioned response, or CR): he cried when he saw it and crawled away quickly. Later, he showed signs of generalizing this fear to a rabbit, a fur coat, and a mask with a long nose and unruly hair.[8]

Over the years, there's been a lot of debate about this study, including about who Little Albert was, and whether the fear really was a conditioned response or if there is another explanation.[9] The study of Little Albert marked the start of experimental psychology, but would not be allowed today because of ethical issues. It illustrates that fear can be acquired from bad experiences. "The Greatest Enemy of Babies Is Fear" says the headline of an article about the Little Albert study in a 1922 issue of the *Morning Oregonian*, reproduced in the *Journal of the History of the Behavioral Sciences*.[10]

From an evolutionary perspective, however, fear has its uses to help us survive. It mobilizes our fight-or-flight response to keep us safe in the presence of a threat (more on that later). But when there isn't a real threat, as when a rat is not really something to be afraid of, fear and anxiety can be a problem. We'll look into the causes of fear and anxiety in more depth in Chapter 4, but first, it's important to know that many things people commonly say about fearful dogs are not helpful and may even be harmful.

THE FACTS ABOUT FEARFUL DOGS

MYTHS AND OUTDATED (but still common) narratives about fearful dogs, and dogs in general, can lead you astray. I want to dispel these myths, but since repeating myths can make them more salient, I'll stick to the truth. Here are a few important facts to bear in mind.

It's okay to comfort a fearful dog. For a long time, some trainers used to falsely say that you should not comfort a fearful dog. This isn't true. Your job, as your dog's guardian, is to protect them from fearful events and to provide comfort in stressful situations. You are a secure base from which your dog can explore and a safe haven for them to return to when things are stressful (see Chapter 3).[11] So if your dog is fearful and wants comfort, you should comfort them. But bear in mind that not all dogs want this, and that comfort will likely not be enough to resolve the situation.

Ditch the idea of dominance. Dominance is an outdated concept in dog training that comes from older studies of captive wolves. We now know much more about how wolves cooperate and work together. One of the big problems with dominance as it pertains to dogs is that it is associated with aversive approaches to dog training. And dominance is associated with some odd ideas about how you live with your dog too. Ditching this idea has many benefits, because it means you understand that it's okay to let your dog on the sofa or bed if you want, to go ahead of you on a walk, and to eat their meals in peace.

Dogs should be able to make choices and have control over their lives, as far as possible. Another drawback of old-fashioned ideas about dominance is that people expect their dog to always do as they're told. In fact, it's much better for your dog if you give them choices. That includes the choice of whether to be petted. (Do a consent test if you're not sure—pause and see if they ask for more or not.) It includes the choice of whether to take part in training. If they wander off from a training session, that's up to them. (It's your job to find ways to motivate them to enjoy taking part.)

Don't force your dog to face their fears. The technical term for this is *flooding*. In everyday language, you might use the expression "throwing them in the deep end." It doesn't help, and it's likely to make things worse. Instead, as you'll see from the rest of this book, it's important to protect your dog from things they are scared of. The way to resolve those fears involves gradual exposures and always helping the dog to feel safe.

Dogs don't need to be provoked to see how bad a problem is. Any dog can bite, and you shouldn't ever put a dog in a situation to see if they will do so. Since dog training isn't regulated, it's important to know that dog trainers should not provoke a dog either. The emphasis should be on helping the dog feel safe. Sometimes people will provoke a dog to get a bad reaction and then use that reaction to justify using harsh methods with the dog, but . . .

You don't need to use harsh methods just because the dog has behavior issues. Although harsh methods may suppress a behavior in the moment, ultimately they risk making the dog's behavior worse. Studies show that aversive methods like shock and prong collars, leash "corrections," yelling at the dog, and so on have risks that include increased aggression, anxiety, fear, pessimism, and stress, and a worse relationship with the people in the dog's life.[12] Some studies also find that these methods are less effective than reward-based training.[13]

Dogs do like treats. If your dog isn't interested in chicken or cheese or other treats in a particular situation, ask yourself if that situation is scary or difficult for them. Not taking treats is often a sign of fear. Take steps to make the situation less alarming. The other question to ask is: Are the treats good enough? For example, maybe your dog isn't interested in pieces of hot dog but would work for pieces of cheese, meatball, or roast beef. (Of course, if your dog really isn't interested in food, see your vet.)

It's the dog's perception that counts. It can be hard to understand why a dog is scared of something, but that fear doesn't have to make sense to us. Maybe a car once backfired loudly at the same time that your dog reached a gate, and now they are afraid of the gate. Maybe they have become afraid of the higher-pitched noises from the dishwasher. Maybe your newly adopted dog has never seen a door before, and the way it swings open and shut is alarming to them. It doesn't matter if the fear seems stupid; the point is that the dog is afraid. We should acknowledge that and figure out what to do about it. Ignoring it, just because the fear seems daft, is not a solution.

Dogs don't just grow out of fears. If your dog is afraid of something, it's likely that they will continue to be afraid—or get much worse—if you don't do something about it.

Even though the dog is fearful, training should be fun for them. Training should be done at a level where the dog is happy and relaxed. Sometimes people ask me how to know when they are doing "too much" or if they are "pushing too far" because they think training a fearful dog involves subjecting them to things they are afraid of. But as you'll see later in this book, you can find ways to train that keep the dog comfortable, and that's when the magic happens.

WORKING WITH FEAR AND ANXIETY

ONE OF THE KEY TOOLS that we use to work with fearful dogs, and also to understand fear itself, is classical or Pavlovian conditioning. In the classic example of Pavlov's dogs, which almost everyone knows, a bell was rung before the dogs were fed. Actually, there wasn't a bell; there were many studies with metronomes.[14] But the idea is the same: the bell was initially unimportant, but since it was always followed by food, which made the dogs salivate, over time they began to salivate as soon as they heard the bell.

The food is known as the unconditioned stimulus (US) because it's something that the dogs automatically responded to (the unconditioned response of salivation), and the bell is a conditioned stimulus (CS) because they were conditioned to salivate in response to it (a conditioned response, or CR). Conditioned responses can include salivation, an eye blink, a knee jerk, or a change in blood pressure, but in dog training the type of conditioned response we are looking for is a conditioned emotional response (CER), in which the dog now loves the thing they previously thought was scary.

In classical conditioning, the conditioned stimulus (CS) can be something relatively neutral, something fear-inducing (in fear conditioning, or learning a new fear), or something already considered scary that will become something to love (in counterconditioning). As far as dogs are concerned, in counterconditioning the thing that's considered scary is the CS. And to teach the dog to love it after all, it is usually paired with an unconditioned stimulus (US) that's some kind of yummy snack (see table for ideas). But there's more to classical conditioning than that. It is one of the ways we learn about the environment we live in: when one thing happens, another is likely to happen next. We are making these kinds of associations all the time, such as when we look out of the window at the sky, see dark clouds, and decide to take an umbrella when we go out for a walk.

Dog training involves treats and yummy snacks. Here are some ideas for foods you can use.

Treats of various kinds

- Cooked chicken
- Roast beef
- Meatballs
- Parmesan, cheddar, or other types of cheese
- Spray cheese
- Cat food
- Tuna, sardines, or other fish
- Scrambled egg
- Carrot
- Blueberry
- Zucchini
- Commercial treats that your dog loves

Remember to check the ingredients of prepared foods to make sure they are dog-safe (no onion, for example).

Classical conditioning (learning by association) and operant conditioning (learning by consequence) are parts of learning theory that tell us how animals learn. As behaviorism gave way to the cognitive revolution in psychology, interest in these processes waned. But the advent of affective neuroscience (which investigates the brain mechanisms involved in emotion) and work in comparative psychology brought a resurgence of interest in how fear, anxiety, and stress work. We have a much better understanding of how fear and anxiety develop, and what can be done about them when they are inappropriate and problematic. That includes new insights into how to use techniques based on desensitization and counterconditioning, which we'll learn about in Chapter 5.

Fearful dogs can still be wonderful pets. Life with a dog works best when the dog has been well socialized as a puppy, and when their new life has some similarities to their former one, whether they arrive at it at 8 weeks or 12 years. Responsible breeders and reputable shelters and rescues are the best sources of pets. Most people who adopt a shelter pet are very happy with the outcome, and shelter dogs are really not much different from dogs from other sources.[15] Even dogs from quite different environments—such as retired laboratory dogs, former street dogs, dogs from overseas rescues, and former breeding dogs from puppy mills (puppy farms)—are often said by their new people to be good family pets.[16]

Some dogs, whatever their source, need a lot of work to help them settle in and adapt to their new life. Even if you've done everything right, it's possible to end up with a fearful or anxious dog. Living with that fear and anxiety can be hard not only on the dog, but also on the humans.

THE IDEA OF HOPE

HAVING A FEARFUL OR ANXIOUS DOG can feel very tough. Your life with your dog is not what you expected when you got them. Maybe, instead of going on long hikes together on popular forest trails, you have to find quiet trails at unpopular times of day, or hike without them and feel guilty that they are left at home. Maybe you dreamed of having a friendly dog who would play with all the children who visit your house, and instead have to shut the dog away and keep a close eye to make sure nothing goes wrong. Whatever the challenges you face, it can be a big adjustment that leaves you needing to grieve the life—or expected life—that you've lost. The day-to-day difficulties of caring for a fearful dog can be stressful too, and may involve making big changes to your routine and getting other household members to agree to them. Aside from all that, it's simply tough to see a dog who should be happy and exuberant and joyful instead retreating from difficult situations or lunging and growling when something frightens them. If it provides any comfort at all, you're not the only one. People who are caring for dogs with undesirable behavior issues can suffer from caregiver burden, as can those whose dogs have a terminal illness or other health issue.[17]

Emily Priestley of Wild at Heart Dog Training on Vancouver Island, British Columbia, sees plenty of people who are struggling with their dog's behavior. "Many times, our clients, when they're working with these dogs," she said, "are doing everything they can within their abilities to protect their dogs, care for their dogs, make sure their dogs are okay. It comes with a lot of guilt. If something goes wrong, they feel terrible. All of these things can take a toll on us as guardians, and we do see caregivers who are struggling with things like caregiver burnout. We don't talk about that enough in the dog world."

An added challenge is the sheer number of self-appointed experts on dogs who want to give you unsolicited or incorrect advice. In part, the fact that we grow up with dogs means that we think we already know about them, so our knowledge can easily be out of date. Another issue is that, in most places, dog training is not regulated, meaning that anyone can call themselves a dog trainer and start dishing out advice—even if they have no training or education. (Chapter 14 will help you know what to look for in a qualified trainer.) And random strangers sometimes seem willing to offer unwanted advice or commentary on your dog when you're out in public, which can feel frustrating, anger-making, humiliating, or just plain annoying.

I asked Kristi Benson, my talented and witty cohost on *The Pawsitive Post in Conversation* podcast, about the time when she had a dog who was afraid of cameras, a very photogenic dog whom she wanted to take more photos of. Benson is an anthro-pologist and dog trainer in northern British Columbia who is also a staff member at the Academy for Dog Trainers. Even though she had a ton of experience of working with fearful dogs, she found that the process took longer than she thought.

"It was sort of eye-opening for me," she says. "I was essentially my own client, and I expected that to be a fifteen-minute proto-col to get my dog comfortable with the camera again, and in fact it took months. I ended up having to literally break the camera down into pieces and do desensitization and counterconditioning with the pieces of the camera, and then the whole camera, and then the action of me crouching down and taking a picture with it. I knew, theoretically, what it was like to work through a fear of something, but it reminded me of the actuality of just how slow it can be, and just how important the technical aspects of desensi-tization and counterconditioning really are."

She had to go slowly and be careful not to push too fast in the plan. This is an important message that you'll get throughout this book—you really have to work at the dog's pace, which can ini-tially be very slow. But it's worth it, just as Benson found.

"In the end, it was so gratifying," she says, "because I got a wonderful picture of him. And he was so keen on the camera by the end that he just had the biggest smiley, happy, conditioned-emotional-response face whenever the camera came out. It was essentially a recall cue if he saw the camera come out!"

My friend and colleague Bonnie Hartney of Ocean Park Dog Training in Surrey, British Columbia, is very experienced at working with fearful dogs. I have sometimes had the privilege of working with her, and so I have seen firsthand how patient and kind she is (and what lovely meatballs she uses to make friends with fearful dogs). Some years ago, she was asked to foster a puppy who was so terrified that no one could touch her. When she arrived at Hartney's house, Dixie took two days to even come out of her crate. After two and a half months of working with her, Dixie would come up to Hartney to eat peanut butter from her hand. Hartney decided to try clipping the leash on.

"She instantly flattened to the ground, and kind of alligator-rolled, and I got her outside and she lay on the grass. And it was something I've never seen before, and I hope I never see again. It was like she was out of her body. She didn't move at all. She didn't look at me. She just lay flat, like this is something so horrible... I was in tears, like I can't do this to her, and if this is a dog who never wants to have a leash on, that's just the way it's gonna be."

Hartney started to train for the leash, and six months after Dixie first came to stay at her house, she was able to take Dixie for a walk for the first time, along with her other dog. At a year, Dixie was still very fearful and Hartney adopted her. Now, looking back, she describes the progress that was made. "When you look at a fearful dog, and you look back over time, she was better at a year than she was when she came to us. She was better at 2 than 1, and honestly it keeps going like that. She's better at 9 than she was at 8, and she's better at 8 than she was at 7. It just keeps going on and on, and she keeps growing and changing and becoming more confident. I think that's really exciting." Looking at Dixie now, you would never know that she started out as such a fearful puppy.

If you're struggling with your dog, it's worth getting help. Dr. Claudia Richter of Pacific Veterinary Behavior Consulting in Vancouver, British Columbia, is a resident of the American College of Veterinary Behaviorists. She told me, "Get help from a qualified professional, either a trainer, veterinarian, or, if needed, a veterinary behaviorist or a veterinary behavior resident. Even if you are a professional yourself, still get help, because it's different when your own emotions are involved."

One of the things that dog trainers often say is that there are no guarantees with behavior. (If your dog trainer claims there are, it's not a good sign.) Many different factors go into creating the situation where your dog has behavior issues. But the thing is, there is a lot that you can do to help a fearful dog. And the more you are able to do those things, the more likely it is that you will see positive changes in your dog's behavior. We'll look at how dogs learn and some powerful techniques to change how they feel about things. Classical conditioning is how we learn about the world around us. Operant conditioning, also known as instrumental conditioning, is how we learn to operate in the world and do things. Both of these approaches can be used with a fearful dog, but they aren't the full story. Along the way, we'll learn about the importance of helping your dog feel safe, and where to get help when needed. And we'll consider the role of pain and other medical issues that may contribute to a dog feeling anxious or stressed.

Here are three tips to get started. You'll learn more as you read on. And you'll develop a better understanding of dogs and dog behavior, and how to help your anxious, fearful, or reactive dog.

- Your priority is to help your dog feel safe. Start by thinking about what you can do so that your dog does not have to face their fears. People's safety is important too, which might involve muzzle training your dog, using pet gates and doors to keep your dog and people (especially children) separate, and so on. (See Chapter 3, in particular.)

- Pick a treat that your dog really loves. If something scary starts to happen, give them that treat. (For more details and to refine your technique, see Chapter 5.)

- Think of an activity that you do with your dog that makes them happy and that you enjoy too. Make time to do more of it. (See Chapters 2 and 6.)

There is hope. Hold on to it. This book will give you lots of ideas to help you and your dog. But first, it's important to be able to recognize when a dog is afraid, so let's take a look at the signs.

"In the early days, the dog is trying to learn about their new environment. So giving time and space is really important, and thinking about: What do you want those first lessons to be for the dog? And for a fearful dog, you want it to be that you're a safe person, that you're not going to force them, that they can trust you, that you're going to advocate for their safety. Those are really important lessons. And it's not always for everybody. I think most people have the kindness in their heart to go at the dog's pace. But there's a grieving that goes along with it. When people bring their dogs home, they probably have an idea that they'd like to go hang out at Starbucks and have their dog lie at their feet, and they'd like to take them to backyard barbecues, or maybe go to the dog park. But sometimes with a fearful dog, that's just not going to be in the cards, at least for a really long time. I like to talk to my clients about that, because it is a sense of loss. But I also like to talk to them about all the celebrations and the joy and the rewards of having a fearful dog, so that they're thinking about whether they can go at that pace and whether it's for them."

—**BONNIE HARTNEY, CTC, Ocean Park Dog Training**

FEARFUL FIDO:
FEAR, ANXIETY, AND STRESS IN DOGS

. . . .

M Y HUSBAND AND I started to look for another dog in the difficult days of the pandemic, having lost Bodger, our beautiful 11-year-old Australian Shepherd, to cancer in early 2020. I was expecting to find a mid- to large-sized dog, and would have loved another Aussie, but the only criterion that mattered was that our new dog should get on with cats. We couldn't tolerate a dog who would be a hazard for our felines, Harley and Melina. But this was the time when the whole world was looking for a dog. Any dog, whatever size or breed and whatever issues they might have, seemed to go within moments of their listing being posted on the web. And those notices didn't contain the magic words *good with cats*.

Finally, after about six months, there was Pepper. I hadn't planned on getting a Shih Tzu or any kind of little dog, but Pepper's listing had those magic words: *good with cats*. He was a senior, had just had various medical issues treated, and seemed to love everyone. I showed his photo and bio to my husband and put our application in right away. Soon the call came to say that we could go and meet him.

Pepper was 10 years old when he came to live with us. We don't know much about his previous life, but it's clear that someone loved him very much, liked to have him sit on their knee, and fed him human foods. At first, he didn't do very much. And he was so quiet. "Aren't little dogs supposed to bark a lot?" I thought, but he made no sounds. Then, one day, there was an item on the local TV news about some dogs at the shelter we had adopted him from. We recognized the voices of staff members there—and so did he. He ran to the TV and made the strangest, most strangulated bark sounds I've ever heard. It was as if he was saying, "I'm here! I see you!!" to the people who had cared for him in the shelter, but the sounds just weren't coming out right.

All of a sudden, Pepper had found his voice. *Yap yap!* he went at dogs walking up the street. An urgent *yip yip yip!* when the black bear went through our yard. And little *grr grrr*s when he's playing tug.

So why was he so quiet when he first moved in? In fact, right at the beginning he didn't do very much of anything. You could have looked at him and said he was a very good dog. And you wouldn't be wrong, because he is a very good dog—but in reality, he was nervous, too nervous to do anything and make a sound. Of course, we did everything we could to make him feel at home and safe with us. But it was a big change in his life to come to a new home with new people. He had already spent a while getting used to the shelter and the foster home. Any change was bound to make him shy.

"Shut down" is what we call it when a dog is too scared to really do much, too frightened to do any behaviors. It's often mistaken for being a good dog, because the dog isn't misbehaving in any way. But they aren't happy or comfortable. It pays to practice reading dogs' body language so that you can recognize when they are fearful and do something about it.

A TUCKED TAIL AND A TIGHT JAW

MANY THINGS CAN BE SIGNS of fear, anxiety, and stress.

When you're trying to understand how your dog is feeling, look at all of their body parts. Take the context into account too. If it's a situation where you know your dog is sometimes stressed—or you know that many dogs are stressed—look a little harder for the signs. You can spot a happy dog in the joyful drawing below, while the fearful and worried drawings show different levels of stress. Both have a closed mouth, but while the worried dog does not look too tense and still has ears forward, the fearful dog has a lower posture, almost folded into themselves, as well as worried eyes and face, and the ears are back.

Fearful, worried, and joyful. ILLUSTRATIONS BY LIZZY FLANAGAN

Things like a dog's breed can affect what their body language looks like. Stumpy or corkscrew tails lack the full range of movement, making it hard or impossible to tuck them under, for example. A dog's face shape or fur that's too long can make it hard to see their eyes. Cropped ears and docked tails are harder to read, but luckily these procedures are now banned in many places.

Look at your dog when you know they are happy, just relaxing at home, so that you know what is a normal posture for them. A dog who is tense or stressed will often lower their posture. In extreme cases, they may even get low to the ground. I've seen dogs crouch down and crawl forward to get a treat, ears flat against their head, clearly terrified but wanting that treat at the same time. (Incidentally, it's best not to set up a situation like this; put the treats somewhere within reach of the dog so that they don't have such an approach-avoidance conflict.)

The tail is often a good indicator of how your dog is feeling. If the tail is upright and stiff, buzzing rapidly from side to side, that's a warning sign. A loose, wide wag, however, is a sign of a happy dog. Sometimes you'll see the whole body wiggling. When a dog is really unhappy or very scared, the tail is not so much down as completely tucked under them, between their back legs.

A loose, open mouth with the teeth showing is a sign of a happy dog. A closed mouth can be relaxed, but if the commissure (corners of the mouth) is pulled forward or back, that can be a sign the dog is feeling aggressive. Wrinkles around the mouth can be a sign of tension. There's a look called an appeasement grin, or submissive smile, with the lips pulled back to show the teeth; this is often mistaken for a snarl or sign of aggression, but it is a "nice" kind of smile, even if we don't fully understand why dogs do it. Maybe they are feeling a bit unsure and want to show they mean no harm. In a snarl, the teeth are showing because the lips are curled up, and it's often accompanied by ears that are back (or potentially forward) and a hard eye.

A hard eye is an unfriendly stare that might be accompanied by a freeze or by that stiff, narrow wag of an upright tail. "Whale eye" is the expression dog trainers use to describe those times when you can see the whites of the dog's eyes. Maybe they are just turned to the side, but it can be a sign that they are feeling a bit scared or unhappy. Squinting can be a sign that the dog is nervous. If you get used to noticing how your dog's eyes look when they are relaxed, it will help you spot the times when their eyes are telling you something else.

Ears forward are a sign of interest, which could be friendly or—especially if it's a hard forward—not friendly at all. If the dog's ears are relaxed, either up (if the dog has prick ears) or down (if the dog has floppy ears), that's a good sign that the dog is feeling relaxed too. Ears plastered against the side of the head can mean the dog is fearful or stressed. With some dogs, you will also see the ears back when they greet you.

A shiver, quiver, tremble, or shake is another sign of fear, as is a raised paw. These are very common with little dogs.

Stillness can mean the dog is shut-down, and is too afraid to do much. But stillness can also be fleeting, just a moment before the dog does something else—like lunge or bark or growl. Then we call it a freeze. A happy dog is usually in motion; stillness is a sign to pay attention, to consider what the dog doesn't like, maybe even to defuse the situation (which might be done with stillness of your own). In extreme cases, an animal can become so shut-down that they don't move and seem to be playing dead. This is especially common in prey animals such as rabbits, and is called tonic immobility. People can mistake it for the animal being calm or cooperative, when really they are terrified.

Some behaviors can be signs of stress, but should be considered in context. A lip lick is one of them: if you've got a treat in your hand and your dog knows they are likely to get it, the lip lick could be happy anticipation. But if not, then it's probably a sign of stress. Looking the other way, sniffing the ground, and grooming can all be what's called a displacement behavior—in other words, a sign of stress, as if the dog is saying "La la la, I can't see anything" and pretending something stressful isn't there. Pepper has learned that if I point my phone at him to take a photo, this will be followed by treats—which is why his tongue is coming out in the photo below.

Pepper's tongue is out because he's anticipating a treat. In the absence of food, a lip or nose lick can be a sign of stress. ZAZIE TODD

The photos of Dixie, Bonnie Hartney's dog whom we met in the last chapter, show a range of body language, from scared, when she first arrived at her new home, to very happy. Pay attention to the differences in her body posture, ears, tail, mouth, and eyes. If you want to get more practice reading dog body language, look closely at all the dogs you see in public and ask yourself "In this moment, is this dog happy—or not?" Another way to get practice is to watch videos of dogs on YouTube. Try turning the sound off so that you can focus on the visuals only. Unfortunately, once you know what signs you are looking for, you'll see that many photos and videos of dogs that people find cute are actually showing a stressed-out dog.

When you spot some of these body language signs or behaviors that show stress, you may feel sorry for the dog. But it's worth remembering that it's sometimes normal to feel a bit afraid. After all, a dog's growl, lunge, or air snap (snapping at the air) is designed to say "Back off." Dog trainer Lisa Skavienski of Dog Educated in Rochester, New York, finds people often understand when a dog is shaking, has a tucked tail, and is trying to hide. "But when fear or discomfort presents as freezing and hackles up and growls and showing teeth," she says, "for lots of reasons, people

First days with Dixie.

Dixie's first time on-leash.

Dixie with light on her face.

Happy Dixie, No. 2. *BONNIE HARTNEY*

find that is first of all frightening, and secondly, they look at it as disrespect. They look at it as the dog misbehaving or being bad. So I try to make sure that they understand that whether the dog is cowering and shaking or growling and showing their teeth, these are all signs of an upset dog."

The dog is not being bad, they are feeling bad.

The fact that these signs are there is a good thing. It means your dog has a way to communicate that they are stressed or afraid. In turn, that means you can do something about it. When you're trying to resolve a behavior issue that is due to fear, these signs are very helpful and indicate the likelihood of a better prognosis. Punishing dogs for growling or air snapping will stop them from showing these signals in future, but it won't resolve the underlying problem. You will then have a dog whose body language is much harder to read because some of those natural signals have been punished out.

Signs of Fear, Anxiety, and Stress in Dogs

- Low or tucked tail
- Ears back
- Low body posture
- Whale eye (wide eyes with visible whites)
- Licking the lips or nose
- Looking away
- Raising a paw
- Trembling, shaking
- Yawning
- Panting
- Grooming
- Sniffing
- Seeking out people
- Hiding
- A freeze or stillness
- Stiff posture and movements
- Peeing
- Pooping

RESPONDING TO STRESSORS

OUR BODY'S STRESS SYSTEM is designed to help us respond to threats—real ones or perceived ones—so that we survive. Although humans and dogs are very different in many ways, a lot is the same because of the way that we evolved. In all mammals, including humans and dogs, the main brain circuits that deal with fear are thought to be largely the same.[1]

Our stress system evolved to help us stay safe in response to unexpected events like seeing a tiger stalking us in the trees or spotting a grizzly bear in a mountain meadow. These days, some of the stressors we experience are very different from those our ancestors faced, but our stress system still helps our brain and body respond to stressful events. Our knowledge of the stress system is based not just on what we know about humans, but also on experimental work with rats and mice.

The fight-or-flight response was first described by physiologist Walter Bradford Cannon, who noticed that, in response to stress, some bodily systems that are usually working away become more strongly activated, while others rest.[2] When we perceive something stressful, the body activates the stress response system, which starts a range of processes in the body and brain. These processes help the animal (human or nonhuman) to respond and adapt, and ultimately return to a normal state after the danger has passed, potentially up to a few days later. Two main body systems are involved in the response to a stressor: the sympathetic-adrenomedullar axis (SAM axis), which activates quickly, and the hypothalamus-pituitary-adrenal axis (HPA axis), which is slightly slower. These axes are named after the main systems involved, and they work together. Physical stressors (like injury) and psychological stressors can activate different networks within the brain.[3]

When something stressful happens, the SAM system releases hormones—mainly produced by the adrenal glands—called catecholamines. These hormones are more commonly called epinephrine (also known as adrenaline) and norepinephrine. As they circulate through the body, they prepare it for that fight-or-flight reaction by increasing our alertness, preparing our body to burn energy rather than store it, speeding up breathing to make more oxygen available, making the heart beat faster, and affecting many other body systems. These changes happen very quickly, enabling you to take immediate action.

The HPA axis has a slower response that helps to regulate the stress response and return the body to normal after the stressful event is over. The most important parts of the HPA axis are the hypothalamus and the pituitary gland (both in the brain), and the adrenal glands. When the hypothalamus releases CRH (corticotrophin-releasing hormone), it makes the pituitary gland just underneath it release ACTH (adrenocorticotropic hormone). In turn, this travels through the blood to the kidneys, where it stimulates the release of cortisol from the adrenal glands. Cortisol makes sure there is enough energy available in the form of glucose to deal with the stressor. When the brain notices that high levels of cortisol are circulating, a negative feedback mechanism shuts off the production of more cortisol, ultimately returning levels to normal. Cortisol can stay high for some time: when dogs arrive at an animal shelter, it activates their HPA axis and results in higher cortisol levels for several days.[4]

Our fight-or-flight response was designed to deal with short-term dangers: in the past, our body would be highly activated while we fled our predator and then rest and return to normal later, when we were safe. Today, many of us find ourselves in fight-or-flight mode often and for long periods of time, not because of predators but because of time pressures, exposure to bright lights and loud noises, and the competing demands of work and family life. When we experience chronic stress, the HPA axis remains activated, and, instead of helping to cope with a stressor, it can have serious effects on the body. High levels of stress hormones can negatively affect memory and attention, increase our appetite, contribute to weight gain, damage the arteries, increase blood pressure, and increase the risk of heart attacks and strokes.

It's important to remember that fear and anxiety aren't necessarily a problem: sometimes they are adaptive. "Fear motivation may actually be completely normal and in context to the animal's perception of what's going on," says veterinary behaviorist Dr. Sarah Heath of Behavioural Referrals Veterinary Practice in northwest England. "It's our job to understand if fear is normal, how can we accommodate that individual so they can respond to it in a way that is helpful for them but not detrimental to us, so that they can learn to cope. Rather than think that fear is a bad thing and we should always get rid of it, think about 'Can we understand where it comes from and how we better accommodate individuals who have fear-related responses, and make their world easier for them to live in?'"

Mammals aren't born with a fully developed stress system, even though newborns can feel pain. For a short time after birth, there is a developmental period called the stress-hyporesponsive period (SHRP).[5] Although we don't know the full significance of this period, it's a time when the HPA axis is not yet developed. This SHRP is thought to help protect the developing brain from the effects of stress hormones at a time when young mammals are in the care of their mother, who can keep them safe from stressful events.[6] In rodents, this period is thought to be from 2 to 12 days old. In people, it may last up to five years.[7] And in dogs it seems to last up until 4 weeks of age.[8] Stress in early life can impact the SHRP, and potentially leads to early maturation of the stress system.[9] In people, adverse experiences in early life have a wide range of effects on the brain and bodily systems, and are a risk factor for some psychiatric diseases.

In dogs, when the stress system is activated, the fight option in fight-or-flight would involve biting. Luckily, puppies usually learn to inhibit the strength of their bites and have good control of their mouths, something called bite inhibition.

AN INHIBITED BITE

IN THE ROUGH-AND-TUMBLE of puppy play, a lot is going on. Puppies are learning appropriate social behavior for their species and practicing movements they will need throughout life. As they learn motor control, in those moments when they are off-balance they are also learning how to regulate their stress system. And as they mouth and bite each other, if they bite too hard, their play-mate yelps and runs off, and the play stops. If they want to keep playing, they have to play fair.[10] So they learn how to control their mouth and teeth and be gentle with them.

Play begins at 3 weeks of age and peaks in those first weeks, until about 8 or 9 weeks, which is typically when they go to their new home, although they will still be very playful. Puppies raised in barren environments, such as in small cages at puppy mills, may not have opportunities to play.[11] This poor environment is one of several reasons why puppies acquired from puppy mills are more likely to have behavior issues than those from responsible breeders.[12]

Because play is a learning opportunity, it's important for pup-pies to have opportunities to play—safely—with each other during puppy class. The dog trainer and their assistants should sepa-rate shy puppies from more boisterous ones and watch the play closely to ensure that all of the puppies are happy and no one is getting bullied. If in doubt, they will do a consent test, and should encourage you to ask for this any time you are concerned. A con-sent test involves separating the puppies and then giving the one who appeared to be on the "victim" side of things the choice of whether or not to go back into the play. Often, they will run back to resume the game and you'll know they were perfectly happy after all, but importantly you will have checked. At puppy class, all of the puppies have had their first vaccinations, the environ-ment is clean, and it's the safest way to give your puppy those playtimes. Because adult dogs may behave differently, don't let your puppy play with an adult dog unless you know they have had all of their vaccinations and are certain they will behave in a friendly way. Some dogs do not tolerate the bounciness of puppies, and the last thing you want is to give your puppy a bad experience.

Puppies have very sharp teeth and they like to use their mouths to explore things. So you and your family will probably be saying "Ouch" a lot in the first weeks of having a puppy in your home. This period gives you the opportunity to teach your puppy to be gentle. If you tell your puppy off every time they put teeth on you, they will learn not to put teeth on, but they won't learn to be gentle. You can have stages in which, at first, you tolerate a certain amount of pressure, but if they apply too much pressure, you briefly stop engaging with them. Don't expect children to do this training, as that's not fair; remember to use playpens and baby gates to keep children and dogs separate when you aren't there to supervise.

Good bite inhibition means that a dog has what dog trainers call a soft mouth, as opposed to a hard one that hurts. It is often the case that a dog with good bite inhibition will continue to have a soft mouth, at least for some time, but we lack research on this. Even if the dog knows how to be gentle with their mouth, additional factors such as being in pain or other stressful events happening at the same time (called trigger stacking) might mean that their mouth is less soft or even hard. Sometimes, when I'm working with a dog, one of the first signs that they aren't "under threshold" anymore is when they take the treats with a bit of a harder mouth instead of being gentle.

A classification system for dog bites was originally developed by Dr. Ian Dunbar and has subsequently been adapted, separately, by Dr. Sophia Yin, Jean Donaldson, and others.[13] It categorizes dog bites on a scale according to how severe they are. In the table below, you can see that the first level is not a bite, it's an air snap. This warning sign lets you know that the dog is upset and gives you the chance to resolve the situation, but doesn't tell you how hard a dog will bite. Level 2 bites involve the dog putting teeth on skin, but not breaking it; there's no puncture mark. A level 3 bite is not severe, but a doctor's visit may be needed for antibiotics and to check if you are up-to-date on vaccinations. If your dog bites at level 2 or 3 only, it's a good sign from a dog trainer's perspective. Levels 3.5 and up are severe. Dog bites are a serious issue; in the United States, they are the thirteenth most common cause of visits to the emergency department.[14] Young children are particularly at risk, but youths, seniors, and those with other vulnerabilities, such as learning difficulties or dementia, are most at risk of severe bites.[15]

Dog Bite Scale

A modified version of Dr. Ian Dunbar's dog bite scale.[16]

Level 1	An air snap or miss—teeth don't touch skin.	No information on bites.
Level 2	Teeth come into contact with skin but don't break it.	Dr. Sophia Yin called this a "near-bite." It counts as a "good" mouth.
Level 3	A single bite that results in one to four shallow punctures.	There may be some bruising, but there was no side-to-side shaking. More severe than level 2.
Level 3.5	Multiple level 3 bites.	This is now highly severe.
Level 4	A bite that results in one to four deep punctures.	Highly severe. There may be significant bruises and tears in skin, and the dog may have held on or shaken their head while biting.
Level 5	Multiple bites resulting in deep punctures.	This is a highly severe attack causing severe injuries.
Level 6	The attack results in death.	Luckily, such incidents are very rare: 25.6 per year in the US.[17]

It goes without saying that dog bites are best avoided. If your dog has ever bitten, even at the lowest levels, it's best to seek help. Your aim is to do everything you can to avoid putting your fearful dog in a situation where they might feel like they need to bite. This is obviously better for you and your family, because you don't get bitten. It's also better for the dog, because they don't bite and then suffer consequences, which may include being rehomed or euthanized. There's another important reason to avoid these situations: it helps protect your training. In fact, the most important thing you can do for a fearful dog is help them feel safe.

Your Dog's Superpower: Forming Associations (Both Good and Bad)

"Dogs have the rather remarkable ability to form associations. They quickly learn that when 'A' happens, 'B' follows. One obvious example you may have noticed is when your dog gets excited when you pull out their leash. It's not that they love their leash, but what the leash means: the chance to go for a walk. We can capitalize on this superpower by helping dogs form positive associations with things they previously considered scary. If the appearance of a bicycle always predicts the delivery of cheese, many dogs will (when properly taught and with some practice) start showing body language that indicates they are happy when a bike approaches. This superpower is also what can make basic training so effective: when 'Come!' is associated with hundreds of positive experiences, a solid association is developed that makes their return more likely the next time we call our dogs. Unfortunately, dogs can form negative associations just as quickly (and maybe even faster than they form positive associations). That's why protecting puppies from negative experiences before they've developed adequate padding from positive exposure to things is key."

—TIM STEELE, CTC, Behavior Matters Academy

SAFETY
(FOR YOU AND
YOUR DOG)

·················

WHEN I TAKE PEPPER for a walk, it's more like a meander. He's 13 years old now and has arthritis. I let him choose where to walk, which means following his nose and making sure he sniffs all the smells in our part of the street. When another dog has literally just walked by, he will happily follow their scent for half a block before turning to retrace our steps. Sometimes we go up and down and back again over the same 30 meters (100 feet) while he checks that he didn't miss anything. These "sniffaris," as I like to call them, are a great way to provide enrichment. Occasionally, something surprises Pepper: a bird flies right over his head, he hears a horse neigh, or he spots a neighbor's cat watching him from the bushes. When he's feeling unsure, he looks at me, eyes like saucers, waiting to see what I will do. He knows that if it was something he considers scary, my hand will go straight to my bait bag and treats will land on the ground. I love that he knows this and trusts me to make things better.

Helping your dog feel safe is one of the most important things you can do for them. In this chapter, we'll look at how to do that, as well as how to keep you and your family safe from bites. We'll also look at the role of training techniques and how you care for your dog in this.

The ease of instilling fear was shown in John Watson's experiment with Little Albert, mentioned in Chapter 1. This study sparked interest in what can be done to remove fear. The psychologist Mary Cover Jones was the first to demonstrate how to get rid of fears in children, in a study she conducted at a children's home.[1] Jones spent some time testing how the children reacted to different things, such as a rabbit, a frog, a loud noise, being left alone in the dark, and so on, to find out which children happened to be afraid of them. Then she brought those fearful children one at a time to a room where she tried one of several approaches to get rid of their fear. Many of the approaches—such as seeing if the child would simply get used to the thing they were afraid of—did not work, but two of the approaches showed promise. One was based on social input. She noticed that fear (of rats, for example) could be acquired from spending time with other children who were already afraid, and an existing fear could be lost by spending time with other children who were not afraid. But the more successful technique involved what we now call desensitization and counterconditioning. She used the case of Little Peter, who was afraid of a white rabbit, to illustrate the effectiveness of this technique in the paper that she published in 1924.

Over the course of seven weeks, Jones worked with Peter and the rabbit one to two times a day, pairing the rabbit's presence with candy. At first, the rabbit had to be 6 meters (20 feet) away for Peter to eat candy, but he was still unhappy about the animal's presence. By the end of this time, Peter was no longer afraid and was happy to pet the rabbit. Jones noted that linking the rabbit's presence to food had led to a positive reaction to the rabbit, but that if the positive associations were not made properly, it would be easy to accidentally cause the opposite effect of making the food something scary because it predicted the rabbit. There was never any follow-up to this study, so we don't know if Peter grew up loving rabbits or finding a career working with animals.

The training that can help a fearful dog uses methods very similar to those tested by Jones, and we'll look at that soon. But training isn't the only part of caring for a fearful dog. It's important to know how you can help your dog to feel safe, keep people safe, and create a positive relationship with your dog.

HOW TO HELP YOUR DOG FEEL SAFE

THE MOST IMPORTANT THING you can do for your fearful dog is help them feel safe. One thing to do right away is make a safe space for them, a place that they can choose to come and go from as they wish. That place may be a crate or kennel, a blanket or bed on the floor, or a settee in a spare room that isn't used much. A crate or spare room can make a great safe space so long as the door is always open. If your dog doesn't have freedom to come and go all the time, the space doesn't count as safe. For example, even if they love their crate, if they are going to be shut in there when you are out or when they travel, you should find a different space to be their safe haven. Using a towel or blanket on the floor means you can take it with you if you take the dog somewhere else, like to a friend's house or to the vet, but it doesn't separate the dog from other things going on, so the humans in the household have to learn to respect that safe space.

Daniel Mills, professor of veterinary behavioral medicine at the University of Lincoln in the United Kingdom, suggests establishing an exclusion zone of 60 to 90 cm (2 to 3 feet) around the dog's safe space, where no person is allowed. Anyone who can't be trusted to follow that rule, he says, can't be left alone with the dog. If you need to get your dog—it's mealtime or time for a walk, for example—then you should call them to you instead of going over to get them from the safe space. And the dog has the choice to say no and stay right where they are. In other words, the safe space is giving the dog control over a part of the environment that belongs to them, and the choice of when to go there and how long to stay is the dog's alone. Mills told me that sometimes simply creating and respecting this safe space is enough to resolve behavior issues in dogs over the space of three or four weeks.

It helps to give dogs choices in other parts of their lives too, so long as it is safe and reasonable to do so. This includes the choice to be petted or not. If you're not sure, do a consent test where you stop petting for a moment and see what happens. If the dog wants more petting, they will let you know! And if they don't, it's important to respect that choice. Being able to make choices and having control over the environment helps reduce stress in dogs.

You can start to offer those choices from the moment your fearful dog comes to live with you. In Surrey, British Columbia, Leila Kullar has fostered hundreds of dogs, some of them extremely fearful. "Once the dog has entered the home, I let the dog explore as much of the house as they want, and I ignore the dog," she says. "In other words, I don't follow the dog around, don't try to entice the dog to me, don't talk to the dog. If the dog comes to me and asks for attention (looks at me, not just sniffs me), then I will engage with them by giving them high-value treats like cooked meat."

Kullar lets the dog choose their own space to sleep or rest. "I give the dog lots of options by putting blankets or dog beds in rooms I think the dog may like," she says. "I also will put out a soft crate in case they like enclosed areas. If the dog wants to sleep on their own in a separate room or wants to sleep in my room on the bed, it's their choice. I let the dog choose where they feel safe. I have dogs sleep under my bed, sleep in the closet, and one who even liked the bathtub."

Avoiding the thing(s) the dog is scared of is very important. If that thing is avoidable, this might be all you need to do. For example, suppose your dog is afraid of horses, but you rarely see a horse, and when you do you can simply turn and go in the other direction, and your dog never has to see it. In that case, it's easy to avoid horses and you can leave it at that. On the other hand, if your dog is afraid of horses and you live right next door to a field where horses live, and every time you leave the house your dog sees horses running around in the field, it's not possible to avoid them. In that case, you would need to look for a solution; management would not be enough on its own.

Training a fearful dog involves working at what we call "under threshold"—namely, at a level where the dog is comfortable and happy. If you go "over threshold" and the dog gets scared, the training will take longer and may even make the dog more fearful and afraid. As well, they will get to practice behaviors like lunging and barking that you would probably prefer to see less of.

Management is the term that dog trainers use to describe making changes to the environment that will prevent an issue from occurring and/or, in the case of fearful dogs, help them feel safe. Management reduces exposure to the scary thing while you work on your dog's fears. It might involve putting a lot of distance between the dog and the thing they find scary, walking at times of day when it's not likely they'll see it, or avoiding the locations and situations where it might be. This isn't necessarily easy and can feel like effort on your part. Even if avoiding the fearful situation is the whole solution, it can feel like a loss—for example, if you have to leave your dog at home instead of taking them with you to a busy coffee shop patio. But if management keeps your dog happy, it's worth it. There are many different ways to keep a dog happy, and many different activities you can do together, so it's a question of finding what works for you both.

A consistent schedule is another way to help your dog feel safe, because it means that things are predictable. If mealtimes, walk-times, playtimes, and other activities can happen on a predictable schedule, then your dog knows when to expect them. Dogs seem to have pretty good internal clocks; if you want to make something a habit, like a time for training or for a walk, do it at the same time each day, and before long your dog will be nudging you to remind you.

Be consistent about house-training, as taking trips outside for toileting at regular times is another predictable part of your dog's schedule. When you have a puppy, you know that you need to house-train them; a new adult dog often needs to be house-trained too. Take them outside before they need to go, reward them for toileting outside, and, until you're sure that they are house-trained, don't give them free time in the house unless you know they are "empty." If they are not empty, keep them attached to you with a leash, on your lap, or in their crate if they are crate-trained. This is impossible with a fearful dog who isn't house-trained yet, and who you can't yet get on-leash. Then you need to either set up a toileting area in the house or decide to leave the house-training till later. Keep them in a part of the house where it's easy to clean up any messes. Some people like to use puppy pee pads or even establish a potty area in a shower that is not used, or in a corner of a room where the floor can easily be cleaned.

Kullar says: "If the dog is extremely fearful or anxious and is not house-trained, I don't house-train. I let the dog relieve themselves wherever they need to. Some of the dogs I foster are too anxious or fearful to be able to learn anything new. There is a lot to take in with their new environment, and, often, learning new things is something they can't do right away. So, if they 'go' in the house, that is okay. Eventually, they house-train themselves, just as Violet is doing now, my present anxious/fearful foster dog."

Never tell the dog off for going in the house; that's the opposite of house-training, since it just encourages the dog not to toilet while you are there, which you will ultimately want them to do outside. Instead, just clean up the mess promptly using enzyme cleaners to get rid of the smell.

Training methods matter

Another important way to help your dog feel safe is to never use aversive training methods. Harsh methods like these are bad for dogs' welfare. Amongst other things, studies show that dogs trained with aversive methods are more likely to show signs of fear, anxiety, and stress, so if your dog is already even somewhat fearful, it's easy to understand why you shouldn't make it worse with the dog training methods you employ.[2] As well, dogs may sometimes respond to these methods with aggression.[3]

Lisa Skavienski is a reward-based trainer with many clients who have previously gone to trainers who use force. Oftentimes, it is the former trainer (not the dog's guardian) who has done that training. I asked Skavienski about the fallout of using aversive training.

"The first thing I see, and it's very common," she says, "is that the dogs are already a little wary for the training setup. Even if they're taking treats from me while I'm chatting with the owners and they seem reasonably comfortable, and I'm tossing the treat or they're taking them from my hands and they seem pretty relaxed, the second I ask them for a simple behavior, a sit or something like that, you'll see them kind of freeze. You see the worried body language. And sometimes we even get a snap, or a low growl, and I need to back off right away. It's so common.

"Sometimes I won't know until I start to work with the dog. And it won't be until that point, when I try to interact with the dog a little bit, with very simple behaviors like a sit, that I see the dog change entirely. And I do think it's because of that learning history where any time there was a training interaction, they're anticipating something painful."

Skavienski's starting place with these dogs is often behind the dogs who have been trained with reward-based methods only. She has to get them used to the training setup, and maybe also to feeling comfortable with hands being near them. And as Skavienski has noticed, these methods affect the dog not only in the moment, but also in the long term. One long-term effect is making dogs more pessimistic, which scientists assess in the lab by training the dog that a bowl in one location always contains food and a bowl in another location never does. Once the dog has learned that, scientists put a bowl in an ambiguous location to see how the dog responds; a dog who is optimistic that the bowl contains food will get to it faster.

One study found that if dogs took a six-week training class that used (at least some) aversive methods, they were pessimistic compared with dogs who took a similar class that used only reward-based methods.[4] Another study found that when dogs' guardians used at least two types of aversive methods, their dogs were more pessimistic compared with dogs who were trained using only reward-based methods.[5] Another consideration is that some research has found that aversive methods simply don't work as well as reward-based methods.[6] There may be several reasons for this, including that people who use reward-based methods are more knowledgeable about dog behavior and therefore probably better at training, and that stress itself can affect how well animals learn.[7] People who attended obedience classes that used choke chains were less satisfied with their dog.[8] Another thing is that we get dogs for companionship and because we want to have a good relationship with them, but aversive methods damage that relationship.[9]

So, what is an aversive method? Put simply, it's a training method that relies on fear or pain. If you are someone who only uses food or play to train your dog, you might want to avert your eyes from the table that follows.

Aversive methods include but are not limited to:

- Using shock collars that deliver an electric shock to the dog's neck
- Using prong collars with spikes that dig into the neck
- Using choke collars that tighten and restrict the dog's breathing
- Using any kind of strangulation (such as "helicoptering" the dog—swinging them by the leash)
- Rolling the dog on their side and holding them there (a so-called "alpha roll")
- Pushing the dog down and holding them there (a so-called "dominance down")
- Yelling at the dog
- Hitting the dog with a hand or newspaper
- Popping the dog's leash (aka a leash "correction")
- Spraying the dog with water or citronella
- Shaking a can of pennies
- Making a sharp release of air, a hissing or *tssschh!* sound, or any other loud noise

Because dog training is not regulated, some trainers' websites are full of euphemisms, so read them carefully. See Chapter 14 for advice on choosing a trainer.

Unfortunately, many people have used aversive methods with their dog, often because they were told to by someone else, and in the mistaken belief that it would help. So you are not alone if it has happened to you. While you can't go back in time and undo it, you can do the next most important thing: promise your dog that you will never use aversive methods again—that from now on, you'll stick to reward-based methods.

While this section has been all about how to keep your dog feeling safe, there's another aspect of safety that's also very important: your own safety and the safety of everyone the dog interacts with.

HOW TO KEEP YOURSELF AND OTHER PEOPLE SAFE

KEEPING YOURSELF AND FAMILY MEMBERS safe around a dog can involve a combination of using pet gates and crates, training your dog to happily wear a muzzle, and being careful to avoid any interactions that may cause the dog to be worried. Management is not just for the dog's benefit; it's for your benefit too. Management puts the onus on you, as the dog's guardian, and everyone in your family to manage the situation to prevent issues. And with a fearful dog, management is also an important part of protecting the training that you do. So there's no getting round it: management is essential.

Using crates and x-pens

Just as it helps the dog to have a safe space to go to, using a baby gate, crates, pet pen, or doors can help to keep the dog separate from people. If there are children in the home, it's essential to keep dogs and children separate when you aren't there to supervise closely, even if the dog is super friendly. Young children, in particular, are at greater risk of a bite, and they are still developing and so find it harder to read dog body language. Babies and toddlers may accidentally be too rough if they reach out to the dog, because they are still learning how to control their arms properly.

A crate should be big enough that the dog can stand up and turn around. Sometimes people expect a dog to automatically like going in a crate, but it doesn't work like that. Put a nice bed in the crate to make it cozy. A blanket or sheet over the crate can help cut down on drafts and block out the sight of anything that might be disturbing or annoying. To train a dog to like a crate, use treats to teach them that when they go in there, they get many wonderful snacks. Use a lot more snacks than you think, because you want to build a strong association. Break the behavior down into steps, from partially going in, to fully going in while the door is wide open, to getting used to the door being closed for a very short time and then longer periods. You can also help build positive associations by feeding your dog in their crate. In a multi-dog household, using the crate at mealtimes can help to reduce worry (for the dog and for you) about conflict over food.

There's no specific research on how long a dog can stay in a crate, but a general rule is that for an adult dog, it should be no more than four hours. Of course, it may vary, depending on the dog. For puppies, it would be much less time, except overnight (but they need bathroom breaks in the night anyway). Even puppies have to be taught to love their crate; it really is a myth that dogs will automatically go in them. In some cases (such as separation-related issues), a crate seems to make things worse, so x-pens and baby gates may be a better solution for times when you need to keep the dog separate but still have visual contact with them.

Using a muzzle

If your dog has ever bitten someone, muzzle training is a must. Even if they haven't, it can come in very useful—for example, in case a muzzle is needed at the vet. Some dogs with a propensity to eat anything and everything they find on the floor also benefit from muzzle training, although of course that's not a fearful behavior, but a happy, seeking one. Just as you can't shove a dog in a crate and expect them to like it, you can't put a muzzle on a dog and expect them to tolerate it. It might happen as a necessary but temporary measure at the vet, but for everyday life you have to put time and effort into teaching them to like it.

For most dogs, it will be relatively easy to find a muzzle that fits, but sometimes it can be trickier—for example, if your dog is very flat-faced. If you're finding it hard to get a good fit, ask your dog trainer for advice. The dog should still be able to open their mouth enough that they can pant to help them regulate their body temperature, or have a drink if they are thirsty. To be comfortable, they also need a bit of space between the end of the nose and the muzzle.

One of the most common mistakes in muzzle training is to simply put it on the dog and expect them to get used to it, or to try to get them used to it in a very short time.[10] The result is a dog who tries to remove the muzzle by pawing at it or rubbing it on things, and who barks and whines when wearing it. Another mistake is to not use treats. We can use delicious treats to help dogs learn to like things, so be generous. If you're an ordinary person doing five to ten minutes' practice with the muzzle every day, it could take you six weeks to train your dog to love it. You can speed this up by following a plan (see Chapter 10). Set aside the time to do the job properly, as it will help your dog not only to tolerate wearing the muzzle, but to actually be happy doing so.

Forestalling bites

Any dog can bite. A bite is a normal response from a dog when they feel that their other signals of being unhappy have been ignored. Understanding the causes of bites can be tricky, and we're still a long way from being able to prevent them. What we do know is that children, youths, and seniors are at particular risk of dog bites. Responsible ownership is an important way to keep people safe, and breed bans don't help reduce bites.[11] It's hard to assess exactly how many people get bitten by dogs each year, as studies that rely on hospital records may substantially underestimate the number of bites. The number of bites may also change over time. For example, in Calgary (which emphasizes responsible dog ownership), the number of severe bites fell between 2012 and 2017 (although less severe bites increased).[12] In the UK, data from the National Health Service shows an increase in the number of hospital admissions for dog "bites and strikes" (a strike is an interaction that causes injury but does not involve a bite).[13]

Paying close attention to your dog's body language will help you recognize when they are uncomfortable, but there are also some things that you should know to do (or not do) around dogs. Never take your dog's food bowl away from them or take food from them; instead, train a "drop it" cue and, in an emergency, use a treat scatter as a distraction (see Chapter 12). Don't let small children walk or crawl up to a dog who is sitting or lying; instead, teach the child to call the dog to them *with your help*. Don't grab a dog by the collar (or grab any body part) when they are snarling, growling, lunging, or otherwise reacting to another dog or person; this would put you at risk of a redirected bite (see Chapter 8). Don't run away from a dog you don't know, or a dog you feel is a threat to you (and, especially, teach children not to do this). Don't reach out to pat a dog you don't know without asking the dog's guardian first, and without checking that the dog seems to want it. Don't do anything that you think might "bother" a dog.

If the dog does bite, get any necessary medical attention, and then make sure to assess what happened. Why did the dog bite? How severe is the injury? Were there any warning signs? How can you use this information to keep everyone safe in the future? If you're considering rehoming or euthanasia, don't rush; take your time to make a decision. Chapter 14 has advice on seeking help.

In addition to medical assistance, you might like to seek psychological help, especially to help children not to be afraid of dogs in future. The psychological effects of dog bites have not received as much attention as the physical effects. However, one study looked at thirty-four children who had attended an emergency department for a dog bite, and found that half of them had parents who felt, one month later, that their child could benefit from an intervention to help with fear of dogs.[14] A recent review says that the psychological effects of a dog bite on a child can last for some time, and recommends that parents be told that a normal reaction may include nightmares, fear of dogs, and behavior changes. The review suggests that parents should seek help if these reactions persist beyond a month after the bite.[15]

If you think a dog might be about to bite you, remember to be a tree. This is a technique we teach children, but it's helpful for adults to know it too. Basically, stand absolutely still, clasp your hands together or hold them at your sides, and look down. Don't stare at the dog, because that may feel threatening to them. Wait for help or call someone to help you.

HOW TO BE A SAFE PERSON TO YOUR DOG

WHEN WE THINK about our pet dogs, we think of how they greet us when we come home, how they seem to comfort us when we feel sad, how nice it feels to touch their fur or feel them lean on us. But how are these experiences from the dog's perspective? We assume that the feeling is mutual and that we get unconditional love. People who still believe in outdated dominance ideas seem to expect unconditional obedience too. You can't directly ask your dog how they feel about you. Probably, you see how they feel every day, from the way they nuzzle you awake in the morning to the way they lean on your leg as you pat them. Or the way they snuggle so close on the sofa that you can't move, because you can't disturb the dog... Scientists, however, can't easily measure the feelings dogs have.

One way that scientists look at the relationship between a dog and their human from the dog's point of view borrows a method from the psychology of human children. It's called the Strange Situation, and it was first developed by psychologist Mary Ainsworth.[16] It involves structured observations of how an infant interacts with their caregiver and a stranger in a series of encounters, separations, and reunions. In 1998, scientists at Eötvös Loránd University in Budapest, Hungary, published the results of a similar test on fifty-one dogs and their humans. They found that pet dogs display signs of attachment to their human guardians that are similar to those found between human infants and their caregivers.[17]

This finding is interesting because, in humans, attachment is important for regulating emotions, both as an infant and later in life. Infants who receive consistent care that is sensitive to their needs develop a secure attachment and know that their caregiver will help them if they are distressed. People who have a secure attachment style are more resilient, according to a meta-analysis (a systematic review) of thirty-three research studies.[18] They also have higher self-esteem, according to another meta-analysis of 116 studies (although attachment is likely not the only factor affecting self-esteem).[19] Children and adolescents with a poor attachment to their caregiver are more likely to be depressed.[20] Having an insecure attachment is linked to dysregulation of both the HPA and SAM stress systems (see Chapter 2), leading to an either over- or under-exaggerated response to stress.[21]

We have long believed that attachment is an innate ability that protects young creatures, as it keeps them close to the parent who is caring for them and helps them explore their environment and learn about it in a safe way. We don't yet know how dogs' ability to form attachments to people has evolved. One study of adult wolves brought up by humans and socialized in a very intensive program found that those wolves show some signs of attachment to their human caregivers, such as a secure base effect when they explore the environment more in the presence of their caregiver.[22] Hence, it's possible that the way wolves form relationships with other members of their pack helps provide an evolutionary explanation of how dogs developed the ability to form attachment bonds.

Several aspects of a secure attachment are relevant to a dog's relationship with their person.[23] Dogs like to be near a person they have an attachment to if something stressful happens. If their person is not there, the dog will sometimes experience distress due to the separation. From the dog's perspective, their person is a secure base from which they can explore, and a safe haven they can return to, whose presence will reduce feelings of stress. These are all similar to aspects of a child's attachment to their caregiver. Interestingly, there is now a theory that classical and operant conditioning may explain how different attachment bonds are formed.[24] The idea is that humans are born with the capacity to form attachments, but the type of attachment that is formed will vary depending on how the caregiver responds to the infant's needs.

While research on attachment in pet dogs is nowhere near as well developed as research on attachment in people, one study looked at the effect of training methods on attachment.[25] Scientists studied dogs who happened to be attending a six-week class with their guardians at one of six dog training schools in Lisbon, Portugal. Each dog and their person came to the lab to take part in a Strange Situation test. Dogs who had been trained only with reward-based methods played more and spent more time exploring the room when their guardian was present, compared with when a stranger was present. These dogs also greeted their guardian more enthusiastically when they came back into the room. When I think of how much I love Pepper's greeting when I come home, it pains me to think that in some dogs this reaction is subdued because of the training methods used. Anyway, the dogs in this study who were trained only with reward-based methods were showing signs of a secure base effect—in other words, a secure attachment to their guardian. In contrast, it's as if this attachment was damaged in the dogs trained with aversive methods. Another study found that after taking part in the Strange Situation procedure, dogs with an insecure attachment style had higher salivary cortisol levels and higher heart rates than those who had a secure attachment.[26] This finding suggests that a secure attachment helps moderate dogs' stress levels.

Other aspects of how people care for their pet, apart from the training methods they use, may also affect attachment in dogs. For example, when a dog's guardian scores high for warmth towards their dog, the dog is more likely to seek them out in a threatening situation.[27] With children, several general styles of parenting have been identified and linked to developmental outcomes. Some researchers have now turned their attention to whether these styles can also be found in dog guardians. Of course, caring for a dog is not the same as bringing up a child, but there may be similarities in, for example, the extent to which someone expects a child or a dog to behave well (demandingness), and to which they recognize and respond to the needs of a dog or child (responsiveness).

The parenting style that is widely seen as best for children is both having high expectations (being demanding) and taking account of the child's needs (being responsive). This is known as an authoritative parenting style. An authoritative parenting style means showing warmth towards the child, giving them choices (within reasonable bounds), being willing to discuss things and negotiate with the child. This style is associated with better outcomes for the child in terms of resilience, optimism, self-esteem, and educational outcomes.[28] Other common parenting styles are authoritarian (with strict rules, use of punishment, and little consideration of the child's needs), permissive (indulgent), and uninvolved (neglectful).

Whether or not you like to think of your relationship with your dog as being like a "dog mom," "dog dad," or "dog parent," it's still useful to think about parenting styles. An authoritative style is better for dogs. A study of 518 dog guardians in the Netherlands who were also parents identified two parenting styles for dogs, which correspond to two of the common parenting styles for children.[29] In this research, an authoritative parenting style for dogs turned out to have two main factors. One of these authoritative approaches was an intrinsic orientation towards the dog's needs and emotions, such as letting the dog make choices and comforting the dog if it seemed to be needed. The other authoritative approach was more focused on training, such as taking time to practice behaviors with the dog and using rewards to motivate them. This study also identified an authoritarian style, which included using "corrections" and physical force, and is thus similar to an authoritarian style of parenting children. It's been suggested that a person's pet-parenting style might also correlate with the way they feed their dog.[30] For example, someone who makes their pet wait for food and rarely gives treats would be considered authoritarian, and a permissive pet-parenting style correlates with dogs being overweight.[31]

Another study looked at the link between dog-parenting styles and the training methods that people use.[32] While walking with their dog past distractions, people with an authoritative dog-parenting style were more likely to praise their dog and less likely to tell their dog off, and had a loose leash, compared with those with an authoritarian style. This research suggests that it's important to pay attention to rewards and practice in training.

In a study from Dr. Carolyn Walsh's lab at Memorial University of Newfoundland, researchers looked at attachment and the stress response in dogs.[33] "We found that all twenty-six of our dog-guardian pairs had a secure attachment, based on the dog's behaviors in the test," Walsh says. "But within these securely attached pairs, there was still variation in their behaviors that correlated with some changes we detected in their salivary hormones—in particular, two that are related to stress responses (cortisol and chromogranin A, or CgA). In fact, there was some evidence for dogs and their guardians demonstrating some hormonal synchrony in response to the different parts of the test. So the attachment style is not necessarily the main driver of variation in how the dog/person responds to this stressor, but it certainly could influence this."

Another study tested dogs to see what kind of attachment they had to their guardian, how sociable they were with a stranger, and how well they solved the problem of getting a treat from a puzzle toy (with or without help from their guardian).[34] When people had an authoritative parenting style, their dogs were more likely to have a secure attachment to them, they were more social with the stranger, and they were more likely to solve the puzzle (in fact, no dogs from the other groups were able to do this). These results are similar to those found in children. One of the authors of the study, Dr. Monique Udell, said: "This is an important finding because it suggests that dog owners who take the time to understand and meet their dog's needs are more likely to end up with secure, resilient dogs."[35]

There are other ways to look at the relationship between person and dog. Some scientists use the concept of "dogmanship," which is similar to "horsemanship," to describe how someone trains their dog, as well as how they interact with them on a daily basis. Dogmanship may include a range of factors, including personality.[36] Good dogmanship includes how quickly a guardian delivers rewards and can get the dog's attention.[37] Other research has shown that certain kinds of people are more likely to use aversive training methods. Men are more likely to use some aversive methods and to use shock collars. In one study, men with depression were especially likely to use aversive methods.[38] This may, at least in part, reflect gender stereotypes, as "dominance" approaches to dog training seem to play into certain macho stereotypes, and the shift to reward-based training has been seen as a "feminization" of training methods.[39]

"Certainly, a secure attachment is seen as 'healthier' or more beneficial for the dog and the person (as it is for human children and their caregivers)," Walsh told me. "So doing things that promote a secure attachment with your dog is worthwhile. Most of these things are probably what we would consider to be 'good' dog guardianship behaviors anyways. However, there are many factors that can influence the type of attachment, and an insecure attachment shouldn't be seen as something that the guardian has failed at . . . While it is clear that neglect and inconsistency in meeting a human infant's needs often results in an insecure attachment, we don't really have the research for how the secure attachment between a person and their dog develops."

Sometimes people worry about whether their own worry will rub off on their dog. There is some evidence that dogs can detect human fear and anxiety. In one study, dogs acted differently when an odor dispenser had sweat from a person who was fearful, rather than sweat from a person who was happy, or no smell.[40] But I don't think this is a useful thing to worry about.

Although we are still learning about how human behaviors can help dogs be more resilient, it's clear that dogs are paying attention to how we behave. Overall, the research on attachment and parenting styles shows that your own personal relationship with your dog is affected by the training methods you use, as well as the extent to which you understand your dog's needs and respond to them. More experience and better knowledge of dog behavior can help. But before we can understand how to help dogs get over their fears and anxieties, it helps to know what causes them in the first place.

"If someone is getting angry at their scared dog for acting scared, a bit of anthropomorphism can help to show them that their dog is in fact motivated by real fear. I like to ask, 'When was the last time you were really scared? Have you looked up and seen your kids walking towards a busy road where they might get hit by a car? Have you been in a car accident where injury was possible?' This is the kind of experience that our dogs are likely having. They're not feeling petty emotions: they're worried for their lives. Anthropomorphism can be useful because humans also feel fear, and fear is terrible, and everybody would universally agree that living in a state of fear is not a good way to live.

The other side of the coin, though, is that humans have cognitive abilities that dogs don't have: we can use reason. So when a fearful dog is scared of something that isn't scary, it can be hard for us. We want to say, 'The vacuum cleaner is legitimately not scary. You don't need to be scared of it.' But in the end, saying 'You shouldn't feel scared' is not a useful framing. We need to pull away from the shared experiences that we have about fear in those cases and say, 'It doesn't matter that it's not scary. The dog is scared.'"

—**KRISTI BENSON, MA, CTC, northern anthropologist, dog trainer, and staff member at the Academy for Dog Trainers**

WHY IS MY DOG AFRAID?

·················

HAD BEEN STANDING in the back garden with Pepper for about five minutes when a sudden movement caught my eye. It was the flick of an ear, a big ear, and it was attached to a young stag with two velvety points on top of his head. He was lying on the ground at the edge of the trees and must have been watching us this whole time. Luckily, Pepper continued to sniff the grass thoroughly. Maybe he could smell where the stag had been, but he didn't know we were being watched. Now that I knew the stag was there, I could admire the beauty of this animal who, when motionless, completely blended into the background of trees and undergrowth. He was staring, and I don't think he found us beautiful. I encouraged Pepper to move and we made our way slowly to the back door under the watchful eye of the stag.

Deer freeze in response to something that startles them. It's a common response in the animal kingdom, and it makes perfect sense for animals who are hard to spot except when in motion. That freeze can keep them safe. It's a reminder that fear has an important role to play. Understanding the causes of fear can help us prevent new fears from arising or existing fears from getting worse. The study of Little Albert, mentioned in Chapter 1, showed just how easy it is to create a new fear, and was inspired by what scientists were learning from the research of Ivan Pavlov.

In 1890, Pavlov became the director of the physiology division of the Imperial Institute of Experimental Medicine in Saint Petersburg, where he researched the physiology of digestion.[1] Soon, he became known for his expertise at surgery. He used anesthetic and antiseptic, but still these experiments are hard to read about. You may wish to divert your eyes from the rest of this paragraph. Pavlov wanted to study digestive juices in a natural context, and so he operated on dogs. For example, he disconnected the mouth from the stomach so that the gastric juices would be excited but the food would fall out of a hole in the dog's neck back into the bowl and never reach the stomach. He also divided the stomach in two so that one section received food and the other had "pure" digestive juices that he could harvest and test. The dogs, such as the first one, named Druzhok, survived the surgery and were therefore useful for experiments. Meat, bread, milk, and sand were put in dogs' mouths to stimulate the salivary juices. Another set of dogs were kept as factory dogs and had their stomach juices harvested to be sold as a remedy to raise funds for the lab.

It was this kind of experiment that led to the discovery of classical conditioning. Two of Pavlov's team members, Sigizmund Vul'fson and Anton Snarskii, noticed that dogs would salivate in response to something associated with the food, instead of just the food itself.[2] But it was Pavlov who understood the significance of the discovery, and that the physiological reflex of salivation was "unconditional," while the "conditional reflex" was a psychic response to other things associated with the food. Because of Pavlov's discovery, classical conditioning is often called Pavlovian conditioning.

Over the years, Pavlov and the men and women on his team conducted many experiments to learn more about classical conditioning. For example, he used a metronome played at different speeds to show that dogs have a sense of time; only one particular speed was paired with food and not others, and the dogs could recognize which speed meant food. Classical conditioning has subsequently been used to investigate perception of color, distance, temperature, and so on. Interestingly, classical conditioning was also independently discovered by an American, Edwin Twitmyer, who used a bell to look at the knee-jerk reflex.[3]

Classical conditioning is a central part of everyday life. Michael Domjan is a professor of psychology at the University of Texas at Austin (and he has an excellent YouTube channel if you want to geek out about classical conditioning). He told me, "I like to emphasize that Pavlovian conditioning is not just a laboratory procedure. It occurs pervasively in the daily experiences of animals, including humans. Events in the environment do not occur randomly, but are ordered in time and by the causal structure of the environment. Some things cannot happen without certain precursors. Food, for example, does not randomly show up in your mouth. Before that can happen, the food has to be procured and processed. The squirrel has to discard the shell before it can eat a nut, for example. The precursors of a significant biological event like food in the mouth readily become associated with the food and thus come to serve as conditioned stimuli signaling the impending encounter with food."

Looking for food is an essential part of every creature's life and involves the emotional system called SEEKING that was identified by the neuroscientist Jaak Panksepp. He described seven emotional systems that are found in the brain of all mammals.[4]

We refer to them in capital letters to show that we are referring to the neurological system. They are SEEKING (such as foraging for food, finding shelter, and so on), RAGE (anger), LUST, CARE, GRIEF (formerly PANIC; it includes separation distress), PLAY, and FEAR (fear and anxiety). When the FEAR system is activated, we respond with a fight-or-flight response. This is an important response, and there are many potential causes of fear and anxiety.

THE MULTIPLE CAUSES OF FEAR AND ANXIETY

FEAR OF DOGS is commonly used in the psychological literature to show how fears develop. When someone gets bitten by a dog, it is an aversive and unpleasant experience, and so they learn to fear dogs. This is an example of fear conditioning. A child who is bitten by a dog may go on to develop a fear of dogs; in the terminology used in classical conditioning, the dog is the conditioned stimulus (CS) and the bite is the unconditioned stimulus (US).[5] However, this does not explain my own childhood fear of dogs. I was never bitten by a dog as a child (nor, luckily, have I been bitten since—unless you count a 6-week-old puppy chewing on my fingers with their needle-like teeth). I am hard-pressed to think of any interactions I had with dogs in my early childhood, never mind unpleasant ones. Maybe that's part of the issue. But it turns out that many people who were afraid of dogs as children do not know why they became afraid.[6]

There are multiple potential causes of fear, in dogs as well as in humans, and fear is hard to get rid of once acquired. Jean Donaldson of the Academy for Dog Trainers in San Francisco told me: "Fear is not at all difficult to inculcate into animals. Dogs acquire fear so readily, and they acquire it in myriad ways, independently and in conjunction with one another. How readily they get fear, but how hard it is to fix with the technology that we have . . . It is so important, because fear is so easy to acquire, that we prevent it, prevent it, prevent it, and avoid exacerbating it."

Often, when people talk to me about their fearful dog, they assume something has happened to the dog to make them afraid. This is especially the case when they are not the first home for the dog, and they think someone has mistreated the dog in the past. While that's possible, it's not necessarily the case. Some fears are due to lack of action rather than action. Some of the potential causes of fear in dogs go back to before the puppy was even born, and of course these causes may interact with each other too. We no longer talk about nature versus nurture, as it is recognized that the two are intertwined. As one example, we know that small dogs are more likely to be fearful or anxious, and this may reflect a genetic element.[7] At the same time, we know that people tend to treat small dogs differently from medium or large dogs, and this likely plays a role too.[8]

While different factors can help explain why a dog is fearful or anxious, it's important to know that those factors do not determine future outcomes. For example, even if the puppy's mother is stressed during pregnancy, good maternal care can significantly reduce any long-term effects. This means you can make a difference by providing appropriate training, enrichment, environment, and so on. And it also means that even if you have done everything right while raising your pup, they may still be fearful or anxious, because genetics and early life experiences play a role. So you should not feel guilty about your dog's behavior issues, as some of these factors are out of your control.

Genetic factors

Let's start with before the puppy is born. At the point of fertilization, the egg and sperm come together, bringing genes from both the mother and the father—the bitch and the sire, as we say when talking about dogs. Research shows that, to some extent, fear and anxiety may have a genetic component. For example, one study of German Shepherd dogs found that nonsocial fear has moderate heritability (as does human-directed playfulness).[9] Another study looked at pedigree and mixed-breed dogs and found ten genetic markers that were linked to fear and anxiety.[10] This study also found that nonsocial fears seem to group together with fear and aggression towards dogs and unfamiliar people, but that aggression towards the owner seemed to be more associated with anxiety. The fact that there is a genetic component to fear and anxiety suggests that breeders should not breed dogs who are fearful or aggressive. Puppy breeders who want more information to help with the physical and emotional health of puppies might like to check out the Functional Dog Collaborative, led by Dr. Jessica Hekman.

Gestational and maternal care factors

If the mom is well cared for when the pup is in utero, and has a relatively stress-free life with plenty to eat, and experiences no difficult circumstances, this is all good for the pup. On the other hand, if the mom is stressed-out, either by physical things like lack of food or space or by things that affect her mental health, then she will have stress hormones travelling through her body. Some of these will affect the developing pup. This makes sense from an environmental perspective, because if the puppy is going to be born into stressful circumstances, the stress hormones help to prepare them for a stressful life in which they have to be alert. But if life isn't going to be stressful, these changes are not a good fit for the pup's environment.

Good maternal care during the first weeks of a puppy's life will have a positive impact on their developing stress response. Puppies are born deaf and blind, and need care in order to survive. The mother's care includes making a nest before birth, giving birth, and then licking the pups to break the fetal membrane and guide them to her nipples to nurse. She nurses the puppies until they are weaned, grooms and licks them (including anogenital licking to stimulate them to pee and poop), and spends time in contact with them.[11] Her body heat keeps the puppies warm. In the first few weeks, the puppies sleep a lot in contact with her and the other pups, they nurse from her, and their heat-seeking reflex helps them find her and stay warm, because they are not yet able to regulate their own body temperature. Maternal behavior is affected by several factors, including which genes the mom has, whether it's her first birth, and how many puppies are born.[12]

Some bitches provide better care than others, and first-time moms lack experience. One study looked at ninety-eight potential guide-dog puppies and followed them until adulthood to see if they successfully entered the guide-dog program. Puppies were more likely to be successful as guide dogs if they had been nursed vertically, with mom standing rather than lying on her stomach.[13] When the mom lies on her stomach, nursing is easy for the pups; however, the pups who were nursed vertically benefited from the challenge. As well, the puppies of mothers who engaged in more maternal behaviors were less likely to succeed in the program. Dogs who left the guide-dog program were more anxious than dogs who succeeded in becoming guide dogs. We still don't know enough about the long-term effects of maternal care on puppies, and in particular we need more research on how breeders can help provide the best environment for this care.[14]

Socialization factors

Lack of socialization is another cause of fear. The sensitive period for socialization in puppies is from 3 weeks until about 12 to 14 weeks. We don't know precisely when this period ends, and it may be different for different breeds.[15] This period coincides in part with time spent at the breeder, meaning that it's crucial to ask a breeder what they do to socialize their puppies. If the breeder makes a good start on socialization, and then you build on it when you bring the puppy home, your puppy is more likely to grow up friendly and confident. During the sensitive period, puppies should meet and have positive experiences with everything that they will come across in later life—from different kinds of people to different situations (including visits to the veterinarian), other puppies, different sounds and surfaces, and so on. Difficult times during the sensitive period are linked to poorer executive function later in life, which refers to those brain processes involved in working memory, behavioral inhibition, and flexible thinking.[16] On the other hand, easy challenges and positive enrichment during the sensitive period are thought to lead to better executive function.

The best way to do a good job of exposing puppies to many experiences is to include a good puppy class as part of your socialization process. Unfortunately, around a third of puppy guardians don't do enough to socialize their puppy.[17] One survey found that dogs who are afraid of strangers and/or other dogs had much poorer socialization during the ages of 7 to 16 weeks.[18] This study took place in Finland, where dogs are typically weaned (and go to their new homes) at 7 or 8 weeks. Dogs who were rehomed later than that were more likely to be afraid of strangers, suggesting that breeders were not doing as good a job of socialization as a new home would.

More socialization is better. When Guide Dogs for the Blind in the UK tested a new socialization program, on top of their existing and already excellent one, they found that the puppies did even better when assessed at 8 months of age.[19] The extra socialization took five to fifteen minutes a day per puppy and involved extra interactions with people and animals, as well as more types of stimulation (such as investigating obstacles, having their teeth and ears looked at, or hearing a cellphone ring). A stimulating environment for a puppy may include stressors the puppy can easily cope with and have a positive experience with in terms of people and the environment. When socializing your puppy, pay close attention to their body language and make sure that you don't frighten them. Bad experiences at any age, but especially during the sensitive period, can cause fear. And having a bad experience during the dog's very first interaction with a particular thing can produce especially bad effects. In contrast, a history of positive experiences can help protect dogs from the effects of bad experiences.

If you have a puppy who is fearful but just outside the sensitive period, Jean Donaldson says: "Get yourself into the hands of a competent practitioner team. If the fear is severe, a veterinarian is probably a good idea to get the dog evaluated for potential medication. Whether or not it's severe, a competent trainer or behaviorist can set up a plan to get this improved." If the dog is a fearful puppy that's still in the socialization stage, she says: "Keep them in puppy class while working on their fear, let them play and do counterconditioning, because you can still get rapid improvement with a puppy."

Remember, the best window of opportunity for socializing puppies is between 3 and 12 to 14 weeks. "Now is the time to drop everything and get that puppy aggressively socialized," she says.

Bad experiences

As mentioned at the start of this chapter, a bad experience can result in the acquisition of fear. This is known as fear conditioning.

Preventing fears in the first place is the best strategy. "Whenever we have a fear case, or whenever we have a fearful dog ourselves," Donaldson tells me, "we renew our vow to be more aggressive in prevention." She says that many dogs who present as fearful seemed normal as puppies, and so it's important to do as much prevention as possible by socializing puppies very thoroughly, taking them to lots of places and making sure they get lots of treats in those places and from strangers. And she emphasizes that responsible breeders have a role in getting this socialization off to a flying start.

Developmental factors

We know more about early life experiences and less about later development. Behavior issues can change as dogs get older. Anecdotally, some people report having a tricky time as their dogs go through a "teenage phase" and are less likely to listen. Studying behavioral changes in potential guide dogs can help us understand more about them, because these dogs have similar upbringings with a standard socialization program. One study looked at adolescent guide dogs to see if they go through some changes similar to those experienced by adolescent humans.[20] Adolescent humans often go through a stage of increased conflict with their caregivers over relatively minor things. As well, when they enter puberty varies according to the degree of attachment to their caregiver: those with an insecure attachment start puberty earlier.

To assess the adolescent guide dogs' attachment to their caregivers, scientists used scores on a questionnaire called C-BARQ.

The questionnaire assessed behaviors related to two scales: one measuring attachment and attention-seeking, which looks at their attachment to their guardian, and another measuring separation distress, which looks at how they behave when separated from their guardian. The results were similar to findings about humans, namely that the dogs with poorer attachment tended to have their first estrus earlier than the average for their breed. To assess conflict with a caregiver, the scientists looked at how well dogs responded to a cue they knew well: "Sit," at both 5 and 8 months (that is, before and during adolescence). If the cue was given by a stranger, the dogs responded equally well both times; but if the cue was given by the caregiver, the dogs were less likely to respond at 8 months of age. This finding is consistent with the idea of a teenage phase. Separately, the guide dogs' caregivers rated their dogs as less trainable at 8 months than at 5 months, whereas the dogs' trainers reported the opposite. At 8 months of age, dogs with an insecure attachment were less likely to respond to cues from their caregivers. Although more research is needed, this study suggests that the quality of the relationship between the dog and their guardian is especially important during adolescence.

Another study looked at all the dogs who were withdrawn from Guide Dogs UK over twenty years—over seven thousand dogs.[21] Amongst those who were withdrawn because of behavior issues, fear and aggression was a more common reason in younger dogs (aged 3.5 years). Issues around training, such as being willing to work, were more common reasons in dogs just over 6 years old. This finding suggests that different behavior issues are likely to develop at different ages.

Most of the time, the circumstances in which the average dog is raised are fairly similar, but one recent event temporarily created very different conditions.

PANDEMIC PUPPIES

AS THE COVID-19 PANDEMIC SPREAD around the world in 2020, people rushed to buy puppies or to get rescue dogs. If you think about the potential causes of fear, several of these may apply to pandemic puppies. Whenever there is a great demand for puppies, like when a specific breed suddenly becomes popular, there is a gap in the market because responsible breeders will only breed a certain number of litters each year. People who run puppy mills can rush to fill that gap, which is likely what happened in some locations during the pandemic. That meant an increase in puppies whose mothers were likely stressed during pregnancy and who had poor early life experiences. Those early experiences may have included a long and unpleasant journey, as with puppies exported from one country to another.

While every country had its own pandemic experiences, many people who got a puppy at this time likely could not do a good job of socialization, and we would expect this to increase the risk of behavior issues. And because people were spending so much time at home during certain periods of the pandemic, puppies were not getting used to alone time either. Leaving puppies on their own for short periods, before they reach 16 weeks of age, is thought to be protective for separation-related issues, and is also recommended for newly adopted shelter dogs.

A study comparing people who got a puppy in the UK after the first pandemic lockdown with people who had got a puppy at the same time of year in 2019 revealed that people who became dog guardians during the pandemic were less likely to have seen their puppy at the breeder's home or with their littermates, and less likely to have chosen a breeder who did health checks on the breeding dogs.[22] They were more likely to meet someone outside to collect the puppy (a red flag). They were more likely to be first-time dog guardians and more likely to be families with children.

Pandemic puppies were less likely to meet visitors to the home, and less likely to go to puppy class, which is not surprising in the circumstances.[23] As well, pandemic puppies were less likely to be registered with the Kennel Club or to have a vet check. And they were more likely to be a "designer dog" (that is, a mixed breed with no oversight from the Kennel Club or a breeders' association—such as Cockapoos, Labradoodles, and Cavapoos). Pandemic pups in the UK were more likely to come with a pet passport, which signals that they probably came from a puppy mill abroad and had a long and stressful journey to get to the UK.

A large and sometimes illegal global pet trade has likely contributed to fear in dogs, and not just during the pandemic. In the UK, according to the charity Dogs Trust, ineffective controls at the border and a lack of enforcement mean that puppies are illegally smuggled into the country, at least 18 percent of them at an age when they are too young to legally receive a pet passport.[24] It's a lucrative trade, which means organized crime is likely involved.[25] Puppies may also be brought illegally into Canada and the US. In 2017, US officials started Operation Dog Catcher to address the arrival of illegal puppies at New York City's JFK International Airport.[26] In 2020, Canadian officials found five hundred French Bulldog puppies (thirty-eight of them dead) on a plane that arrived at Toronto's Pearson International Airport.[27] If you're looking for a puppy, being able to see them with their mom, ideally at more than one point in time, will help reassure you that your pup is coming from a good breeder rather than a puppy mill.

POTENTIAL MEDICAL ISSUES

NO MATTER WHAT your dog's age or provenance, whenever there's a sudden change in their behavior, it's important to see your vet in case there is a medical cause. But even if your dog's fears have always been there or have gradually increased, it can still be a good idea to visit your veterinarian. One thing we need to consider when we have a fearful dog is whether something medical, like pain, is contributing to their behavior.

As veterinary behaviorist Dr. Sarah Heath told me, "Pain is a very complex thing that has sensory and motor components, so that's the physical side of it, and then it also has emotional and cognitive components. In an emotional sense, pain is a subset of the FEAR ANXIETY motivational system, according to Panksepp. Panksepp talks about FEAR ANXIETY being the overall system, and pain is part of that in behavioral medicine. In behavioral medicine, we tend to talk about the pain system independently, but it is a subset of the FEAR ANXIETY system."

In Heath's behavioral science model—the Heath model—she uses the word *protective* rather than *negative*, so that caregivers can understand that this isn't an emotion they want to get rid of.

"You want these emotions to be present when they're needed, because they have a function to perform," she said. "And the same with pain. Pain is an emotion; it's a protective emotion when it is in the right place at the right time, which we would call acute pain. Then it is beneficial to the individual and protects them from harm and leads to a behavioral response to protect them. However, just like any emotion, it can also be maladaptive, and we call that chronic pain. When pain is chronic in nature, that is an abnormality; it's an abnormal form of pain. And that always needs some kind of intervention, both from the sensorimotor perspective that needs analgesic treatment, and also from an emotional perspective."

Heath also told me that there is an interplay between pain, fear, and anxiety. "When you are in a state of highly protective emotion—which could be fear, anxiety, or pain itself—that augments the perception of pain to that individual. And why that's important is that if you have an individual who has a more protective emotional bias, they may have exactly the same imaging results, for example of dysplastic hips. And you may take an image of two individuals whose hips have a level of dysplasia that is almost identical, but the relevance of that to the individual is not related to the X-ray findings."

In other words, the physical and emotional components of the pain may be increased by the individual's protective emotional bias.

One study of twelve aggressive dogs found that pain was a contributing factor to the aggression, and that osteoarthritis from hip dysplasia was a common cause of this pain.[28] It can be difficult to spot signs of pain, but when veterinary behaviorist Prof. Daniel Mills and his colleagues around the world looked at their client caseloads, they found that pain played a potential role in between 28 and 82 percent of the behavior cases they saw.[29] Mills said that the prevalence of pain as a contributor to behavior issues is likely much higher than people think. Essentially, we need to be more aware of the fact that pain can play a role in behavior issues such as fear and anxiety.

Pain can sometimes be a direct cause of behavior change. At other times, it may be a contributing factor, because the feeling of being in pain is using up the dog's emotional reserves and resilience, or limiting what they are able to do, and they have less capacity left to deal with other things. Other medical issues, including neurological ones, can also affect a dog's behavior.[30] A survey that compared healthy dogs with dogs suffering from canine atopic dermatitis found that those with itchy skin were more likely to have a range of behavior issues, including excitability, attention-seeking, chewing, and excessive groom-ing, and were considered to be less trainable.[31] The more severe the level of itchiness, the more behavior problems were found. No link was found between fear and anxiety and itchy skin. While these results are correlational and cannot show causality, they are in line with the suggestion that itchy skin is not caused by fear and anxiety, but that it may result in some degree of stress for the dog.

Heath says that there are four potential behavioral responses when you have any protective emotional motivation. Two of these are easily recognized: a dog who growls at you to prevent you from looking at a painful paw (a repelling behavior) or who moves away to prevent you from seeing it (avoidance). If the dog shows signs of inhibition, such as freezing or being passive, it may be hard to recognize pain because they appear calm. Finally, some dogs show signs of appeasement, such as leaning on or licking their guardian, which may be misinterpreted as clinginess but is in fact a sign of pain.

Bear in mind that medical issues may not only cause the onset of a new behavior, but also prevent the dog from doing their normal things. And even if a dog still does some of those normal things, like running when they are playing, it doesn't necessarily mean they don't feel pain. Even when in pain, they might feel motivated to do something they enjoy, like play; but they could be less motivated to do things they don't enjoy. I've noticed, for example, that Pepper has been much happier walk-ing in the rain since we made a change to his arthritis treatment at the recommendation of our vet. I asked Dr. Heath about this kind of situation, and she said that sometimes the seeking motivation of wanting to chase a ball can override the protective pain moti-vation. She points out that we experience this same overriding motivation when the desire to catch a bus causes us to run for it, despite the pain from a bad back.

Because recognizing the signs of pain in dogs is difficult, scientists are working on a grimace scale that would identify the signs of acute pain on a dog's face. Mills said that, surprisingly, this approach was easier with cats because, despite their furry faces and pretty markings, they don't have the wide range of head shapes that dogs do. (A feline grimace scale already exists to assess acute pain in cats.) Mills explained that although brachycephalic (flat-faced) dogs have many health issues, it seems people find it easier to read their faces than the faces of other dogs. The face of a brachycephalic dog is relaxed when they aren't in pain, and it's as if their whole face slides downwards.

Some high-tech tests to gauge pain in dogs are not yet available in general practice, but they show a lot of promise. Mills and his team in Lincoln put all dogs on a special runway with a pressure plate that assesses if their gait is uneven, and they use high-resolution thermographic imaging to look at the dogs' muscles. Again, the wide variability in dogs' conformation (body shape) is a challenge, as some breeds, like German Shepherds, are slanted to the back, while others are more even or slanted forwards. If there's an imbalance, it doesn't necessarily mean the animal is in pain—for example, tighter muscles may successfully compensate for an anatomical imbalance—but it is a hint to look more closely. "Obviously, dogs can't tell us how they feel," says Mills, "but these tests start to give us these measures and insights into what the dog is doing biomechanically to compensate for the discomfort." A recent survey found that some of the signs of chronic pain that guardians tend to notice include their dog's reluctance to go on walks or get up if lying down, stiffness when walking, difficulty turning over when lying down, licking a specific body part, and generally being less active.[32] As well, people noticed differences in the position of the ears and tail.

Some of the signs that you should see a vet are shown in the list on the next page. One sign that may lead a dog to be referred to Mills's clinic is that they aren't responding to behavioral treatment as expected.[33] "If you made an assessment of a dog and you start treatment and you're not making the progress you predict, then why not?" he says. "It's not usually because the owner isn't trying. It's very easy and tempting to blame the owner. It's often because something is holding the dog back, and usually what's holding the dog back is discomfort."

Mills goes on to say that he has some "impressive radiographs" of dogs who wouldn't sit when asked to in obedience class. "They had a bad sit, they took a long time to train, and basically you're asking the dog to dislocate his hips every time he sits." Other signs Mills mentions to look for are if the dog is not symmetrical, hopping on one leg, circling too many times before lying down, shaking themselves off a lot more than normal, seeming to withdraw from things, or doing anything in a strange way. If they do anything odd, recommends Mills, "instead of saying 'That's just him/her,' get them checked at the vet." If your vet agrees your dog is in pain, they will likely prescribe painkillers.

It can take a team approach to find out what the medical issue is, involving everyone from the dog's guardian to the vet and vet techs, the dog's trainer or behavior consultant, and potentially physiotherapists or anyone else involved in the dog's care. A referral to a veterinary behaviorist may also be useful. For joint pain, video of the dog walking, running, or going up and down stairs may be helpful, but of course other types of pain, such as dental pain or gut pain, are possible and won't show up on video.

Painkillers (and any needed medical treatment) aren't necessarily the end of the story. Mills points out that different painkillers work for different situations, and it may take trial and error to find the right one for your dog's pain. So bear with your veterinarian if the first painkiller has no effect and they want to try a different one. And although solving the pain may resolve the issue, some kind of behavioral treatment, typically involving counterconditioning (more on this in Chapter 5), will often be needed as well. Dogs who have experienced pain, especially ongoing pain, will have learned that certain situations are painful.

Signs you should see a vet

- The change in behavior is sudden and/or is rapidly getting worse.
- The training isn't progressing as you'd expect; you keep getting stuck or having regressions.
- The dog is sitting funny or walking funny.
- The dog is reluctant to go on walks, jump in the car, or walk on shiny floors.
- The signs seem to come and go, or occur after playtimes or walks.
- Something scary happened but the dog is generalizing that fear widely to other contexts.
- Your pet is getting older (you can't assume their symptoms are "just old age").
- You're just not sure and you want to rule out medical issues.

It's hard to predict how long it will take to treat a dog's fears, as many factors are involved. In some cases, the fear may resolve surprisingly quickly; at other times, fear and anxiety take a long time to resolve or will actually never fully resolve. The list below will give a rough idea, assuming any medical issues are taken care of.

Prognosis

The likelihood of a better outcome is higher if:

- Any bites are relatively minor, showing the dog has a good mouth
- The dog gives warning signs (for example, they growl)
- The dog is smaller
- The issue doesn't involve strangers
- The dog makes good progress once proper training starts
- You are willing and able to learn how to help your dog
- Everyone in the household sticks to the dog's treatment/behavior plan

TIPS TO PREVENT FEAR

AS JEAN DONALDSON REMINDED ME many times when I took her course at the Academy for Dog Trainers, fear is easy to instill and very hard to get rid of. That makes it imperative for us to avoid things that cause fear. For many of us, the trouble is that the most important things are behind us, as we can't go back in time—but they're still worth knowing about for next time. The best ways to prevent fear in dogs relate to choices you have already made when getting your dog and (if you got a puppy) socializing them.

I asked Donaldson about the common mistakes she sees when someone has a fearful dog. She says that some trainers have tended to try to prevent dogs from meeting and playing with other dogs. This can happen when they are concerned that the dog may show signs of fear, but it often backfires. She says that when the dog "wants to introduce themselves to everybody, and they want to jump on people, let's train the dog not to jump, which is the easiest thing in the world, but [some trainers'] solution to that is to create an asocial dog." Donaldson says that dogs have "a massive repertoire of skills to do with introducing themselves and investigating other dogs." Why would they have this repertoire, she says, if they weren't social creatures? "It's only dogs that you've sequestered that have a difficult time meeting other dogs."

Another common mistake, she says, is going too fast in training, which means people are basically flooding, forcing the dog to face their fears. And people also find it hard to tease apart whether the dog is afraid—for example, whether an aggressive dog is afraid of other dogs, or whether they are actually game and like fighting.

Here are some tips to help to prevent fear in dogs:

- When you're getting a puppy, always see the puppy with their mom. Check that the mom is friendly towards you (and the sire, if possible, but they are sometimes off-site). Keep an air of suspicion in order to avoid puppy mills. If anything seems too easy—they have just the puppy you want and they'll meet you at a convenient parking lot to show you the pup—then that's a red flag. Search the phone number, email, and photo associated with the puppy; if you find many other puppies linked to it, or the photo has been used before, that's a red flag. Be suspicious of any breeder or rescue that always has lots of different breeds of puppy available. A responsible breeder will ask you lots of questions to make sure that you are the right fit for one of their puppies, and will typically have a wait list.

- Choose a responsible breeder or rescue that has done a good job of early socialization of the puppies during the first part of the sensitive period. This increases the likelihood they will become friendly and confident adult dogs, and gives you a great base on which to build more socialization.

- Socialize the puppy as best you can. This is most easily done when a good puppy class is part of your socialization plan.

Always give the pup a choice when exposing them to new people/puppies/circumstances.

- Protect your dog from bad experiences (while still giving them opportunities to explore and be sociable). Give them choices when possible, so that they are never forced into an interaction they find scary.

- Be ready to take action if something bad does happen. Watch their body language—maybe they will be okay, in which case there's no need to do anything. Or maybe they will seem a bit stressed, in which case do some ad-hoc counterconditioning by giving some great treats and get them out of there.

- Teach your dog to come when called, keep doors and yards secure, and make sure they have identification (collar tag and microchip). This will help prevent them from getting lost and help reunite them with you if they do get lost.

- Stay up-to-date with vet visits and get any potential concerns looked at promptly, so that medical issues don't contribute to behavior issues.

- Get help for behavior issues promptly, so that the problem can be resolved sooner and not get much worse.

"No one gets a dog hoping to complicate their life. To be a good friend to someone with a fearful dog, please realize the emotions the dog and human are feeling are real. The dog is not trying to give their human a hard time, the dog is having a hard time. Just as the dog is struggling with their emotions, the people in the dog's life are also struggling. Everyone is doing the best they can with what they know.

Offer your friend support and understanding. Give them an opportunity to cry, and share their frustrations. Offer kind words such as 'I know this must be difficult for both you and your dog. I am sorry you're dealing with this.' While it is tempting to offer advice or to comment on the dog's seemingly unruly behavior, please do not. Instead, find a behavior to compliment: 'Wow, look at your dog's gorgeous smile' or 'Great job getting your dog out of that situation.'

Please respect and follow your friend's directions. Do not try to cajole, pet, or interact with the fearful dog without first discussing with your friend. The dog will also thank you for this. Your support and understanding can offer a much-needed lift to a person trying to navigate life with a fearful dog."

—**KATHLEEN MCCLURE**, CTC, CSAP-BC, FFCP-Trainer, founder of **The Happier Dog**

TRAINING A FEARFUL DOG

· · · · · · · · · · · · · · · · ·

SOMETIMES A SMALL CHANGE makes a difference you don't expect. Instead of making coffee when he wants it, my husband started setting the machine on an automatic timer. It was a great idea, except that when the machine turned on and started grinding the coffee, Pepper would leap up and run into the kitchen, looking scared. He didn't know the loud noise was just the grinding of coffee beans. So we decided to give him a treat whenever the machine made the noise. This was easy to do because we were always around when the coffee was being made. The treats helped enormously. Within days, Pepper was no longer running around terrified. Now, when he hears the noise, he looks expectantly for his treat. If he's in another room when the coffee machine starts, he comes running into the kitchen to get it.

In dog training, we take advantage of two ways that dogs learn. Dogs learn by association—that if one thing happens, then it is followed by something else. This is classical conditioning. Classical conditioning is a very powerful way to change how dogs (or other animals) feel about something. Dogs also learn by consequence— that if they do a certain behavior (like sit), then a particular consequence follows (like a treat). This is operant conditioning. In this chapter, we'll look at how you can use these types of training to help your fearful dog. The good news is that training is linked to improvement in dogs' fears.[1]

The training with Pepper in the kitchen with the coffee grinder is a type of classical conditioning called counterconditioning. The aim of counterconditioning is to teach the dog to love the thing they were previously scared of. This new, happy response is known as a conditioned emotional response (CER), in this case a positive one. We taught Pepper to like the sound of the coffee machine because it predicts nice food. The sound of the coffee machine becomes the conditioned stimulus (CS) that predicts the yummy snack of treats (the unconditioned stimulus, or US) and leads to his happy response (CER).

Conditioned responses aren't always positive. In fact, scientists test the development of fear (that is, fear conditioning) in humans and rodents by associating one stimulus (such as a sound, or a face or colored circle on a screen) with something negative, such as a mild electric shock.[2] For example, in studies with rats, the rat might hear a particular sound (like a beep or tone) and then receive an electric shock. After the rat hears the tone and receives the shock several times, they learn to associate the sound (CS) with the shock (US). And when they hear the sound, even if it's not followed by a shock, they still respond in a negative way, such as with a freeze or startle. The rat has been conditioned to fear the sound (the conditioned response, or CR).

Research on classical conditioning shows that fear conditioning parallels counterconditioning. That means we can draw on the science of both inducing fears and removing them to make sure we get classical conditioning right with our dogs.

We can also use operant conditioning to change a fearful dog's behavior, and do so in such a way that we get a classical conditioning side effect. We'll look at both of these approaches below. Since they both involve using food, there are some tips on using treats below. But the research on fear has some important lessons for our lives with dogs that apply outside specific training setups, so we'll start with those.

What to consider when choosing treats for training

Your dog's preferences. Pick something they like. Every dog has their own preferences. While almost all dogs love cheese, for example, there are a few who don't.

The type of training. For counterconditioning, it works best to use really special treats (see page 13, "Treats of various kinds," for examples, and below for the explanation of why). In operant conditioning, use small treats when doing lots of repetition and special treats when doing harder training, or when you have more distractions. For example, if you're at home in a room with few distractions and doing lots of repetition, you need lots of relatively small treats because you'll be giving a lot of them. On the other hand, if you're practicing recall outside, where there are distractions, use special treats so your dog finds it worthwhile to run to you.

Variety. Your dog may get bored if you keep on using the same treats, so change them up from time to time.

The delivery method. Often, you'll give individual treats, but sometimes you want your dog to get continuous treats, or you want those treats to last longer. For example, if you are using treats as management to distract your dog while you do up their harness or another dog goes by, consider a lick mat covered with peanut butter or a treat tube (available from the pet store, or make one at home by putting food paste in a squeeze tube). Freezing a lickable treat can make it last longer, if needed.

Your dog's dietary needs. Look for treats associated with your dog's special diet, if needed. Alternatively, use the canned version of their special food or an ingredient in that food (for example, cooked chicken, if chicken is an ingredient in the prescription diet). Ask your vet if you're not sure. The Clinical Nutrition Service at Cummings School of Veterinary Medicine has some useful suggestions on their website for dogs on special diets.[3]

IMPORTANT LESSONS FROM THE SCIENCE OF FEAR

RECENT DEVELOPMENTS in the science of fear give us valuable information about living or working with a fearful dog: fears can come back, positive experiences (especially first ones) can help prevent fears, and counterconditioning is an effective technique.

Fear renewal

Research on fear conditioning shows that the original fear memory does not go away. Instead of being deleted like a file from your computer hard drive, it is inhibited in some way.[4] In counterconditioning, this means the fear memory is at risk of fear renewal and essentially coming back. Renewal can often happen when the context has changed. For example, suppose the scary thing happens at the park, and training using counterconditioning happens at home. It's possible that even though the training works at home, the fear may renew once you get to the park. To prevent a relapse of the fear, it's a good idea to do your training in different contexts and to continue to do occasional "maintenance training" after you've finished the training proper. Training in different contexts helps with new learning so that the context itself does not become a predictor of the cs-us pairing. And, of course, it's best to prevent the fear from occurring in the first place.

Positive first experiences (and multiple experiences)

We also know that learning to like something through counter-conditioning takes longer than conditioning something for the first time. This means it's a great idea to make the most of any firsts that your dog has.[5] We especially like to give puppies lots of fantastic first experiences, but even an adult dog may still have a number of firsts in their life. For example, a dog who has previously lived in a deprived environment and who has never seen the outside world—such as a dog adopted after some cruelty-and-neglect cases, or from a laboratory or breeding facility—will have many firsts. Be ready with the treats to ensure any first time for your dog is a positive experience. When something is already familiar, it is harder to learn new things about it.[6] The technical term for this is *latent inhibition*. In practice, what it means is that if your dog has already had lots of good experiences with a particular stimulus, and something bad happens once in the presence of that stimulus, the dog is less likely to become fearful of it. The fact that the dog is already familiar with it and has positive feelings about it makes it harder for one bad experience to make them afraid.

Counterconditioning works best

Some of what we know about counterconditioning comes from research on people. The approaches taken to help people with fears and phobias include extinction exposure and counterconditioning.

Extinction exposure involves a person experiencing the thing they are afraid of in a safe environment until the fear is extinguished. Counterconditioning involves associating the thing they are afraid of with something they like (known as an appetitive stimulus), which in experimental research is often chocolate or money.

Extinction exposure and counterconditioning both involve learning something new: that the thing is no longer to be feared after all. We know that exposure (desensitization) approaches rely on a process of extinction. In other words, the fear is assumed to be extinguished. We suspect that counterconditioning uses the same mechanism, so we don't know if counterconditioning is really a distinct process from extinction. But a range of studies of both people and lab animals suggest that, overall, counterconditioning works better than standard extinction.[7]

Of course, people can be consulted on how to approach the therapy and may play an active role in it; talking can help explain things to people and reach agreement on the way forward. This is not possible with dogs, and we typically use desensitization and counterconditioning together (although there are some exceptions).

LEARNING TO LIKE SOMETHING: HOW TO DO COUNTERCONDITIONING

COUNTERCONDITIONING IS A TYPE of classical conditioning in which we are teaching the dog to like something they are already afraid of. When counterconditioning dogs, we are teaching them that the conditioned stimulus (CS) predicts the unconditioned stimulus (US). The CS is the thing that's considered scary. The US is something that the dog already likes—yummy snacks such as unanticipated steak or unexpected sardine.

When you're trying to teach your dog to like something they are currently scared of, it's important to make sure that your training includes a wonderful surprise whenever the scary thing appears.[8] There's a technical term for it: it's an *expectancy violation*. The aim is to create a big difference between what the dog is expecting (presumably, a terrifying experience) and what actually happens (a wonderful surprise) when they see the scary thing. The size of this difference, or expectancy violation, is important to the training. In practice, this means that you don't use regular treats and you definitely don't just use kibble. Instead, put some thought into what would be a wonderful surprise for your dog: maybe some Parmesan cheese or spray cheese or roast beef or sausage or chicken or sardine or . . . Pick something that your dog thinks is really special and keep it just for this training.

In fear conditioning, an unexpected or surprising outcome (the US) leads to better learning than an outcome that is expected. If something is initially paired with a large shock, more learning occurs in the first few trials than in later ones, when the shock is expected. In counterconditioning, that element of initial surprise—this time a positive one—will lead to more learning on the first few trials than on later ones. The size of the prediction error—the difference between what's expected and what actually happens—matters. That's why you need to be prepared with your cheddar cheese or Parmesan or roast beef.

Aim for a one-to-one relationship between the thing that you are conditioning (the scary thing) and the lovely treats. Every single time the scary thing happens, the dog should get those treats. Since the scary thing will sometimes happen without you expecting it, you should be prepared to give those treats at any time (ad-hoc counterconditioning). Put some thought into how you're going to prepare and store the treats. They need to be ready at hand, but at the same time you don't want your dog to see you preparing them (or reaching for them) right before the scary thing happens. You might need a bait bag or a plastic baggie to carry these delightful morsels with you on walks, and a treat jar or a designated spot in the fridge for training at home. Make sure you are always ready.

For counterconditioning to work well, you need to create a contingency, or an if-then relationship: the scary thing predicts a treat. There have been decades of debate about whether the important relationship in classical conditioning is one of contingency (one thing predicts another) or of contiguity (both things happen at the same time), and whether the animal (human or nonhuman) needs to be aware of the relationship or if it just happens automatically. Although some studies have found otherwise, there's plenty of evidence that awareness of the contingency is needed.[9]

Common mistakes: Compound stimuli and improper timing

Good technique when using counterconditioning is essential. You need to make it very clear to your dog that it's the thing they consider scary (CS) that is causing all the yummy snacks (US).

Compound stimuli: It's easy to accidentally do something that blocks or overshadows the scary stimulus (the CS). Let's say the CS is some nail clippers. In *blocking*, one stimulus already predicts a treat; for example, the rustle of a plastic baggie predicts cheese. When they are presented together as a compound stimulus, the rustle of the baggie blocks learning about the nail clippers. There is no surprise, because the dog already knows that the rustle predicts cheese.

In *overshadowing*, two stimuli are presented together with no prior training (both novel stimuli). If one stimulus is stronger, it will overshadow the other. Suppose that just as you present the nail clippers to the dog, a kitchen timer starts to beep. The beep is probably a more salient stimulus, and so it will overshadow learning about the nail clippers.

In terms of your technique, what this means is that you want to avoid compound stimuli; present the nail clippers (CS) on their own. As well, don't reach for the cheese (US) until after you have presented the nail clippers.

Improper timing: As the trainer, you know about the contingency between the scary thing and the treats, because you're the one creating it. But for counterconditioning to work, it's your dog who needs to be aware of that contingency. If you reach for the treats because you can see another dog coming, but your dog hasn't yet spotted that other dog, that's too early. You can end up with a situation where, when you reach for treats, your dog starts looking around to see where something scary is. So pay close attention to your dog and make sure they have seen the other dog (or whatever it is that you are working on) *before* you start to dole out the treats.

Out in the real world, this timing can sometimes be tricky. You may be able to tell from looking at your dog's eyes and their direction of sight, or you may notice a subtle change in behavior that tells you they've seen the CS, whatever the scary thing is. If you're working on setups indoors, you are controlling when the CS appears in front of the dog, so you should have a clear idea of when the dog spots it. You can make the contingency extra clear by waiting for a beat between showing the thing and starting to reach for the treats.

For any CS with duration, like presenting the nail clippers or a stranger standing at a distance, you can use Jean Donaldson's "open bar–closed bar" technique. The way this works is that once the CS happens (the thing that's considered scary by the dog), the bar is open and there's a party, and you start to feed lots of yummy snacks like unforeseen salmon (the US). Once the CS stops, the bar is closed and the party is over, and you stop giving the US. I especially like this framing for two reasons. First, it encourages you to get your technique right, because you have to think of the timing: the CS starts and then the party (US) starts; the CS stops and then the US stops. Second, this framing of the bar being open and you throwing a party for the dog encourages you to use the ultimate snacks as the US, and to be generous in giving those treats. This approach gives you that element of wonderful surprise that will help make the conditioning work.

One finding that really struck me from some research about dogs who are afraid of noises is that ad-hoc counterconditioning worked well.[10] I think that's in part because it introduces some variability to the training. Of course, you never deliberately introduce things that are scarier than your dog can handle at any one time, but you should be prepared to respond appropriately if that situation happens by chance. Always have treats on your person or somewhere you can get to quickly when needed. And do not linger—get out of the situation by putting distance between you and the trigger whenever possible, and then give your dog plenty of treats. To make variability part of your training, use different stimuli instead of exposing the dog to the same stimulus over and over. If you're doing setups with a friend's dog, for example, find more than one friend with a friendly dog who can help. Over time, you can do the same work with your dog, but with different dogs acting as the stimulus dog.

Tips for counterconditioning

- Prepare any treats well in advance, so that treat prep doesn't block learning.
- Wear your bait bag when you're training and at other times when you aren't.
- Use treats your dog really likes so there's a nice element of surprise when the scary thing predicts lovely treats.
- Be careful to present the conditioned stimulus (the scary thing) on its own—without anything else—so that you don't have any compound stimuli.
- Be careful not to reach for treats until after the cs has happened.
- If presenting a thing (say, nail clippers) and then following it with treats (say, cheese), also present other things that you aren't conditioning, like a kitchen spoon or a clock, and do not follow with treats. Doing this makes it really clear that only the nail clippers predict cheese.
- Remember that you are aiming for a one-to-one relationship in which the cs means treats every single time.
- Watch your dog's body language closely. Don't move to a more difficult level in training until you are certain your dog is happy (and expecting treats) at the current level.
- If something unexpected happens (like a dog appearing too close for your reactive dog), make the situation less scary by moving away and giving plenty of treats. Offer the treats even if your dog isn't wanting to take them.
- If things go wrong, see it as a learning experience for you. Think about what you could do next time to make the situation better.

How to use desensitization

Desensitization is the process of very gradually getting a dog used to something. It's the opposite of sensitization, when repeated exposure to a stimulus can cause the dog to sensitize and get more and more worried by it. Sensitization can happen accidentally if you get desensitization wrong, or it can happen if a stimulus occurs that the dog is a bit worried about and you don't do anything.

Desensitization involves thinking about the different aspects of the scary thing and coming up with a hierarchy of them. For example, all loud noises may cause alarm to a dog, or just the kind that sound like thunder or are accompanied by clouds or heavy rain. For a dog who is reactive to other dogs, dogs that are moving may be more scary than those that are still, and big dogs or dogs of a certain color may be more alarming. If you've been paying attention to your dog, you can probably predict that certain aspects of the stimulus are more concerning than others. This will help you begin to work out a hierarchy that you can use in training.

Start with the easiest version and gradually work up to the harder versions. If you're working on a sound sensitivity, for example, you might play your dog a recording, perhaps starting with the sound of fireworks on the lowest possible volume, from a room adjacent to the one where your dog is. Only *very* gradually would you increase the volume on the dial. Or, if you're working on dogs, and bearing in mind your dog's particular preferences, you could ask a friend with a small, well-behaved dog to stand still at a very large distance. Desensitization is typically combined with counterconditioning, except for separation-related issues and sometimes with sound sensitivities.

Whenever you're using desensitization, pay close attention to your dog's body language to ensure that they are "under threshold" and completely happy with the situation. For example, if they start to react to the sounds you are playing them, it's not desensitization. Turn the volume down right away or stop the sound altogether.

Working from a plan

Following a plan is an important way to structure your training. In desensitization and counterconditioning, we start with a very low version of the scary stimulus, at a level that isn't scary. This least-scary-to-most-scary approach ensures that fearful dogs are always working on the least scary exposures (the previous least-scary ones having become perfectly normal and fine); there is never a point at which the dog is deliberately put in a situation where they are scared.

To develop a plan, think about different aspects of the scary stimulus. For example, suppose your dog is afraid of the stairs in your home. It is a straight set of stairs from one floor to another, without a landing in the middle, and they will not go up and down them.

Start by thinking about other flights of stairs in your house or any steps in your neighborhood. Maybe a local park has a small, wide set of steps between one area and another, and a dog-friendly business has two steps at the entrance. Next, taking account of things your dog may be affected by, draw up a hierarchy of steps and stairs: how high they are, whether they are open or enclosed, whether they are solid or have openings between the steps, whether the treads are opaque or see-through (which might make them "harder," as your dog can see the drop), and so on. Now you can build a plan that starts with the easiest steps for your dog and gradually builds up to the harder ones. Eventually, you'll be able to get your dog to try the stairs in your home again.

No matter what fear you're working with, the general principle of breaking things down into easy stages of a plan is always the same. If you're working with a dog trainer, they will do this work for you.

In real life, some experiences will be outside the hierarchy that you chose to work on. For example, however careful you are to help a reactive dog feel safe, at some time another dog will spontaneously run right up to you. And however carefully you work on training to a sound sensitivity by using recordings, you can't stop your neighbors from setting off fireworks. Real life will introduce variability to your training regimen without you doing anything about it. This is where ad-hoc counterconditioning comes in and you throw a party for your dog. And, if possible, get your dog away from the scary thing.

"The one thing I wish people knew about fearful dogs is, time is your friend. In an age when nearly every question can be answered, item received, movie watched, and picture shared almost instantly, it's no wonder the patience it takes to see results when working with a fearful dog is thin. Helping a dog feel comfortable in a situation that scares them is best done with slow, deliberate exposure that never puts the dog in the position of feeling overwhelmed.

Whether it's our desire to help our dog feel better, or to just get that nail trim off our to-do list, we look for shortcuts. However, pushing harder and faster than the dog is ready for may result in their becoming so flooded by the frightening situation, they give up trying to protect their safety. We think they are fine and calm, but it is much more likely they are simply enduring the offense and holding it together. This can result in a dog living in fear, trusting their human less, and having to escalate their defenses when the feeling becomes too much.

Time and patience for the process are our allies in teaching dogs that we can be trusted to keep them safe, respect their communication, and allow them to enjoy the world without the threat of fear."

—EILEEN HOLST-GRUBBE, CTC, manager of education and training at Richmond SPCA, Virginia

LEARNING TO DO SOMETHING: OPERANT CONDITIONING

IN ADDITION TO LEARNING by association, dogs learn from consequences. This is operant conditioning. We've already gone over the reasons not to use aversive types of operant conditioning in Chapter 3, but positive reinforcement is a great way to train your dog. When you teach your dog to do something and then give them a reward, thus increasing the likelihood of them doing that behavior again, you're using positive reinforcement. It's a type of operant conditioning that is kind and humane. There are some tips on life skills to teach your fearful dog in the table below. You can also use positive reinforcement to teach your dog to do a behavior as a way of helping them cope with a situation they find difficult. For fear that is less severe, you have a choice of whether to use counterconditioning or operant conditioning (see below).

When using positive reinforcement, pick treats that will be a nice reward for your dog when they do what you are asking. (You can also use play in some circumstances, but generally treats work best.) See the table on page 13 for suggestions for treats. Give the treat as fast as possible once the dog has done the behavior; this helps them know that it's the behavior that earns them a treat. If you are too slow, they may also have done various other behaviors

Useful skills to teach your dog

To eat treats when you're there, and to follow a treat that you throw.	Most dogs can do this—but for a fearful dog, it's something they have to learn, as they may initially be too scared to eat in your presence, and may be scared if you throw a treat.
To sit on cue, with a short duration, so that they don't pop out of the sit right away.	In other words, a short sit-stay, but you'll probably just call it "sit." This skill can be a really helpful way to stop your dog from doing something—ask them to do a sit instead.
To come when called (recall).	This skill takes a lot of practice in different situations (see the section on running dogs in Chapter 6 for some safety tips).
To go to bed or go to crate.	(If you're using one.) Sending your dog to their bed in another room or to their crate can be helpful in keeping them apart from visitors to your home. With some fearful dogs, you may need to put them in a crate to safely get them to the vet. Note that if you are sending your dog somewhere, it should not be to their safe space, which they must always have a choice to go to or from.
To do a nose touch to your hand, or similar behavior.	This skill can be a good way to move a fearful dog around or to distract them from something that's going on. It's also just a fun activity to build confidence and your bond with your dog.
To walk on-leash without pulling you along, and/or to wear a harness to reduce pulling.	Remember that walks are for your dog, so they should have choices on walks and opportunities to sniff.
To leave it and drop it.	To help keep them safe by preventing them from picking things up on walks and to help prevent resource guarding.
To greet someone nicely.	Some people don't mind being jumped on, but a lot of people do. So train your dog to keep all four paws on the ground when meeting someone, or to sit if you prefer.

in the interim, like jumping up, spinning in a circle, sniffing at the floor, and so on.

You can use a clicker if you like. A clicker makes a click noise to mark the moment when the dog is doing the behavior you want. Some people love to use them, while others find them an extra complication. For behaviors that have some kind of duration, they aren't necessary, but for some training it is very useful to use a clicker or a marker word (like "Yes"). The click or marker word can be a bridge between the instant the dog does the behavior and you producing the treat. (Note that you don't use a clicker in classical conditioning, because there's no behavior to mark.)

You can also use training simply to build your dog's confidence and your relationship with them. Getting treats for doing things will provide a nice classical conditioning side effect that makes them feel good about you and the situation. If your dog is fearful or anxious, it's especially important to structure the training to make it easy for them to earn those treats. A fearful dog may be too afraid to take treats from your hand, but you can throw the treats to them.

Erica Beckwith, owner of A Matter of Manners Behavior and Training in Santa Fe, New Mexico, explains how to break training down into achievable steps: "If your dog is extremely fearful, don't start by asking your dog to come across the room to touch your hand (hand target), for example. You may need to start with tossing five treats for your dog simply looking at your hand while remaining in their safe place. You need to break tricks down into the smallest steps for our fearful friends, work in whatever environment they find safest, and you need to pay very well for these behaviors.

"In fact, my goal is to remove as much of the pressure as possible and teach that dog that great things happen when they interact with the environment in any small way or offer any new behaviors. For example, I may place a mat down, sit across the room, and toss treats when the dog interacts with the mat in any way (looking at it, taking a step towards it, getting onto the mat, sitting on the mat, and so on). The dog learns to go to the mat and eventually maybe lie down on it, and I didn't encroach on his personal space at all. The dog learns that it's safe to try new things with me around as well."

How to teach new behaviors: Using luring, shaping, and capturing

Luring means getting the dog to follow a food lure. It's a common way to teach new behaviors, including tricks, but some dogs may be unsure about it, so you may need to teach them how to follow a lure first. Beckwith suggests starting "with a slight head turn or luring their head slightly up or slightly down. Make this movement so simple and easy that they will happily follow the movement, and feed liberally! When your dog is reliably following the food lure to move their head, then you can add one or two steps. Avoid jumping from your fearful dog turning their head to something like following the lure across the room or luring into a full spin trick. That's asking too much too soon."

Once your dog has the hang of being lured to do the behavior, you can lure them without the food in your hand (have it nearby so you can immediately feed them when they've done it). If this is too hard, have an in-between stage where the food is in your hand but harder to get at, such as under your thumb. Then the movement of your hand becomes the hand signal to do the behavior. When your dog knows this, start to say the cue (whether it's "Sit" or "Touch" or whatever) just before you do the hand signal. Soon your dog will begin doing the behavior on the cue, before you've done the hand signal, which is known as "jumping the prompt."

When they are jumping the prompt reliably, you can fade the hand signal out and just use the cue.

Shaping means reinforcing small approximations of a behavior and gradually building up to the behavior you want. For example, to teach your dog to lie down on a mat with shaping, you may start with any movement close to the mat (or even looking at the mat). Gradually move to putting one paw and then four paws on the mat, and then start to look for anything that involves the dog getting lower, until they lie down on the mat. Use a clicker so that you can mark the exact moment your dog is doing the thing you will reinforce them for. If your dog is afraid of the loud clicker, use the click of a ballpoint pen, which is typically much softer, or your voice (for example, the word "Yes").

Beckwith explains how she uses shaping to teach tricks, and even to let her dog decide what the trick should be: "One of my favorite games is to put any object down on the floor (do not use a scary object) and mark/reinforce any little interaction my dog has with the object. If I put a pen down, my dog may initially look at the pen. I mark and toss a treat right away. After a couple of repetitions, they may come over and sniff it. A little while later, they may start nosing or pawing at it. At some point, I pick a behavior my dog has repeated several times and run with it. They may create a 'jump over the pen' trick, or 'pick up the pen and bring it to mom' trick. Many of my dogs' best tricks are ones they have either created or added their own personal flair to."

Some dogs may feel too scared to offer any behavior, so make sure to click and treat often and keep the training at a level that is easy for your dog.

Capturing relies on waiting for the dog to do a behavior that you want, then clicking and treating. If your dog has a really cute behavior that you'd like them to do more, this is a great way to put it on cue. "If you have a dog who sneezes quite often, mark every sneeze with a clicker or 'Yes!' and give a treat," says Beck-with. "Your dog will start offering more sneezes (mark and treat), and then you can put it on cue when you can tell when your dog is about to sneeze (you'll pick up on a tell). Maybe you say 'Ah-choo!' or whatever cue you want to use, and eventually, *bam!*, you have a sneeze on cue. How impressive!"

Whether you are working on tricks or on training important behaviors such as recall, pay attention to your dog and make sure they have many, many opportunities to earn treats. They should always have the choice of whether or not to train with us, and the aim is for that training to be fun. Beckwith says, "We need to move slowly, keep it simple, speak softly, and let our fearful dog call the shots. If they are not able to perform the training step you are asking, that likely means it's too hard, you are asking for too much. Lower your criteria and up the amount of reinforcement. If your dog is leaving the training area when you try to train, that means it's too scary or too much pressure. Work at whatever level your dog not only can handle, but also finds fun. When in doubt, toss treats away! Let your dog chase the treats and decide if they want to come back and interact/train/play, or not."

It's okay to spoil your dog

Although people have sometimes recommended protocols where dogs with behavior issues are asked to do something to earn every treat or interaction with you, I don't recommend them. These protocols have various names; a common one is "nothing in life is free" (NILIF). The proliferation of these programs led Kathy Sdao to write her book *Plenty in Life Is Free*, which argues they may damage the relationship between the dog and their guard-ian. NILIF programs instruct you to ignore the dog at times when they actually need your support. As well, I think these programs confuse people. When you think about counterconditioning, you are not asking the dog to do anything—and you have to give the treats in order to create a CER (conditioned emotional response), whatever behavior your dog is doing.

Although you can use operant conditioning to help build confidence in your dog, don't make this the only way they can get treats and pats from you. Remember, it's perfectly okay to give your dog treats for no reason, and the research on pet caregiving mentioned in Chapter 3 emphasizes that you need to be responsive to your dog's needs. Feel free to spoil your dog.

Working from a plan

Your training will be more efficient if you work from a plan. Think about the final behavior you want from your dog, and be really specific. That's your end goal. Then think about what your dog can already do. To make a plan, create gradual steps that will get you from what your dog can do now to what you would like them to do.

I like to use Jean Donaldson's push-drop-stick rules to move up and down in a plan. These rules are designed to help make sure that your dog stays engaged in the training, because they are earning treats 80 to 90 percent of the time. We do this by working in sets of five. If your dog gets four or five goes correct in a set, it's time to push on to the next stage of your plan. If they get three correct, repeat the stage you're on. And if they only get one or two correct, go back to the previous stage. It's normal to have to go backwards in a plan sometimes, so don't worry if this happens. As you'll see below, when working with a fearful dog, we can choose to work in sets of ten instead and use very conservative criteria.

Getting a classical conditioning side effect

Some people feel more comfortable using positive reinforcement instead of counterconditioning, often because they've had a lot more practice at it. If you want to use positive reinforcement to work on something the dog is afraid of, keep a few things in mind.

If you want to teach your dog to do a new behavior at a time when they may be scared, think carefully about what you'd like them to do. Let's imagine you're working with a reactive dog and you want to use positive reinforcement to teach the dog to behave differently in the presence of other dogs, and also to teach them that other dogs are not to be feared after all. The behavior you want needs to be nice and easy. Options include getting them to sit while other dogs go by, or to give a nose touch to your hand, look at you, or sniff the ground. Getting your dog to lie down could be more difficult, as they may feel more vulnerable in that position. Let's imagine you've picked a nose touch to the hand, which your dog already knows. You're going to ask for this behavior and then reward it with a treat whenever you see another dog—well, actually, whenever your dog sees another dog.

Dog trainers like to say that "Pavlov is always on your shoulder." This is referring to the positive conditioned emotional response (CER) you can get by using positive reinforcement—those positive experiences are affecting how the dog feels about you and the training situation. (It can work the other way, of course, if you're using aversive methods.) Jean Donaldson says that if we're working with a fearful dog using operant conditioning, we need to think about "what's going on in the classical side of the ledger." That means we want to ensure that there's a positive CER. "What we want is a dog to enjoy it, not just to do the actions," she says.

To make it work as counterconditioning as well, "we want to have conservative criteria," says Donaldson, "because we want the CER side effect, and our side effect is the CS to US one-to-one ratio that we're looking for. And we'd push to the next stage in the plan on things like ten-for-tens rather than four-for-fives." In other words, we wouldn't move to the next stage in the plan until the dog has got things right ten times out of ten.

To make sure there's a counterconditioning side effect, you need to ensure the dog does the nose touch and gets a treat every single time—that preserves the one-to-one ratio for counterconditioning. This is another reason to pick an easy behavior; if the dog is distracted by the other dog and unable to do the nose touch, it will disrupt your one-to-one ratio, and that's not good for your training. The training will also benefit from an element of positive surprise, so instead of using your regular training treats, use something the dog really loves, like cheese or steak or chicken. You still need to make sure that the dog is at a distance from other dogs where they feel comfortable and safe. If you walk your dog right up to another dog (or let another dog come too close), they may be too upset to do the behavior. However, if you have these things in place—great treats, a one-to-one ratio, a safe distance from any triggers—then a nice positive emotional response will develop as a side effect of the positive reinforcement training. However, if the dog is very fearful, it makes more sense to do something directly about the dog's fears and use counterconditioning instead.

RELAXATION TRAINING FOR DOGS

TRAINING A FEARFUL DOG to relax is not a widely used approach, but sometimes veterinarians, veterinary behaviorists, or other professionals recommend it. There isn't a lot of research on relaxation training for dogs, but one study found that 69.3 percent of people who use it for fear of fireworks said that it helps, which is promising.[11] In another study that looked at treatments for dogs with aggression, relaxation training was reported by dog guardians to significantly reduce the likelihood of aggression, and it was also found to be beneficial for fear.[12] However, these studies didn't collect any detail on which training protocol people had followed. A number of different approaches to training relaxation are available, including protocols from veterinary behaviorists Dr. Karen Overall and Dr. Kelly Ballantyne.

One approach to relaxation training is to use capturing (see previous section) at those moments when the dog is lying down and relaxed, or for individual behaviors that are part of being relaxed, such as taking a deep breath. You mark the moment and reward it with a treat. Another approach is to basically train the dog to lie down on a mat or towel and then shape their behavior until they are lying down, relaxed, on their side. Or you could simply train them to lie down on a mat and continue to reward them for lying down on it, aiming to get a classically conditioned side effect (a CER) from this operant training.

Another set of approaches is based on classical conditioning and may involve petting or massaging the dog while they happen to be lying down on a mat, so as to induce a feeling of relaxation that will in future be associated with being on or near the mat. We don't have any research comparing different training protocols for relaxation, so if it's something you want to try, pick the approach that most appeals to you—or the one that is recommended by your trainer or veterinarian.

Bear in mind that the best way to help your dog relax is to make sure that their needs are met, which includes having an environment where they feel safe. Sometimes people are very concerned that they want their dog to be "calm," but actually they mean that they want their dog not to show any behaviors. A familiar, predictable environment will help. But it's important to look at things from the dog's perspective, and if they do feel stressed, it's not something to punish them for.

"My wish for fearful dogs is to do away with euphemisms that we humans use to describe their fearful behaviors. I often hear well-meaning guardians who love their dogs describe fearful behaviors using watered-down language.

'She gets a little reserved with new people.'

'He's just shy around strangers.'

'She can be a little protective of our family.'

Don't let the words *reserved, shy,* and *protective* fool you. These dogs are fearful around unfamiliar people. Some of them might be mildly afraid. Others might be downright terrified. A dog who isn't trembling, tail-tucking, growling, or biting might still be very, very afraid.

The language we use matters. We don't do our dogs any favors by downplaying their bona fide fears. Sugar-coating our language only delays helping our dogs. Let's start by saying out loud what is actually happening. Fear is happening. Period. Now let's get to work helping our fearful dogs."

—OLEG SOBOL, JD, CPDT-KA, CTC, owner of KinDog Behavior and Training

EXERCISE AND ENRICHMENT

. . . .

AS PEPPER SETTLED IN, he began to formulate ideas and plans. One day, I came home to find him on the kitchen counter. That was a surprise—he was too small to jump up there. But our house is open-plan with a family room adjacent to the kitchen. He must have jumped on the settee, scrambled up the back of it, and from there clambered onto the kitchen counter. We could no longer leave food out, assuming that our little dog couldn't reach it.

Another time, we had gone to bed, turned the light out, and settled down to sleep. I heard Pepper get out of his bed, pad towards the door, which we had left open for the cats, and go down the hallway. I got up to investigate and found him eating the cat litter from the box. Not the cat's pee or poop, but the litter itself, which is made of corn. I admired his naughtiness, the way he had waited until he thought we were asleep. In a way, Pepper was providing his own enrichment.

I felt that this showed he now felt comfortable in our home. Pepper sneaking out of bed and eating the cat litter didn't make him a bad dog—after all, it's normal for a dog to want food (even if they define *food* differently than us). But if I didn't take action to prevent these behaviors from happening again, they would be my fault. Management like this is simply part of the job of being a responsible dog guardian. It is up to me to make sure that things that Pepper isn't supposed to eat aren't left where he could get them.

Exercise and enrichment are essential for good welfare, and our job involves making the environment interesting and providing opportunities for our dog to engage in normal canine behaviors. But if a dog is fearful, they may not be able to take advantage of those opportunities. It can take an adult dog several months to settle in, and you may not see their full personality or normal behaviors during that time. They often need to settle in before they are able to take advantage of these enrichment opportunities. And as they settle in, they may also start to do some things we'd prefer them not to. In this chapter, we'll look at the idea of naughtiness first, and then at providing enrichment to fearful dogs in ways that keep them feeling safe.

NAUGHTINESS CAN BE GOOD

SOMETIMES IT'S REALLY FUN and adorable when a dog is naughty. Maria Karunungan, PhD, owner and head trainer at Fetch the Leash in Vermont, takes pleasure in this kind of behavior at times. "I think nobody wants a dog that's just a robot," she says. "A good reason you get an animal for a companion is because there's an element of unpredictability. I think that people inherently are not necessarily looking for the expected, the traditional way. They find the unexpected to be refreshing and charming and adorable. You know, if you were to predict everything that your companion would do, you might as well get a plastic toy and sit it down next to you."

Some kinds of naughtiness make the dog difficult to live with, and that's when we need to do something about it. Some kinds of naughtiness are the dog doing normal dog behaviors, and if the way they do them isn't acceptable to us, it's up to us to find a way that is acceptable (for example, by giving them chew toys or a place where they can dig). And some kinds of naughty are fine to allow, like having fun shredding their toys. If it's not causing any harm, it's okay to let them do it. Karunungan says, "There's a lot of things that I think we should let them do because that's what they want to do."

Karunungan gave me an example of a time when one of her dogs was naughty and, as I thought with Pepper, she thought it was a sign of growing confidence. "I had a roommate who was roasting some chicken for her own dogs, and I came home and found a letter that she had written in her left hand that was apparently from my own fearful dog. It was to the effect of 'I ate Auntie Sarah's chicken.' And basically it was like he stole the chicken off the counter. He ate two entire chicken breasts that she was going to cut up as treats for her own dog. She was a little bit annoyed and I made it up to her. But we both knew that it was a sign of him being competent enough to investigate his environment and find something tasty that he wanted and eat it. In fact, I framed the little note that she wrote."

Providing a range of toys, including balls, ropes, stuffed toys, squeaky toys, and chew toys, helps your dog engage in normal canine activities. Leila Kullar has found that many of the anxious dogs that she fosters like to chew. "I give them tons of chew sticks, bones, rubber toys, etcetera, to chew on, which they love," she says. However, she often finds that some of them still like to chew on things like the baseboards or her shoes. "Yes, I get frustrated, but I understand that this chewing comes from anxiety, and objects are just objects that can be replaced. So I hold my breath and let them go through that chewing stage. Many of the dogs chew on personal items. Maybe they are taking in our scent somehow while chewing on the things we love, or maybe they just want to drive us mad. They all eventually grow out of that stage."

Chew toys satisfy your dog's need to chew on things with options you're happy with. Puppies like to explore the world with their mouths, so have lots of chew toys for puppies. If your dog chews something you don't want them to, you can offer a chew toy as a safe swap item. Over time, they will learn that they are okay to chew on the chew toys and will lose interest in chewing other kinds of items.

In addition to providing toys, there are plenty of ways to provide enrichment opportunities for your dog. Just as some dogs need to settle in before you see their full personality, they may need time before they feel like taking walks or engaging in other activities. But even fearful dogs need exercise and enrichment.

MEETING YOUR DOG'S NEEDS FOR EXERCISE AND ENRICHMENT

HAVING POSITIVE EXPERIENCES is an important component of good animal welfare. The challenge is to find ways to do this that keep your dog feeling safe. The good news is that despite the potential difficulties, there's a lot you can do to ensure fearful dogs have good experiences. These activities are often great fun for you too, and help improve your bond with your dog. But since dog walks are what everyone thinks of first, let's start there.

When the daily walk is a struggle

If taking your dog for walks is difficult because they react to people, dogs, or things you meet on those walks, it helps to think of ways to do the walk without putting your dog in situations they find hard. That might mean:

- walking early in the morning or late at night, when not many people or dogs are about

- choosing places to walk where dogs are required to be on-leash (and where people usually follow that rule)

- borrowing a friend's fenced yard or renting a space like a tennis court or other fenced area where your dog can safely run free

- keeping walks shorter to reduce the likelihood of coming across something difficult

- seeing each walk as a training trip and going into walks prepared to do counterconditioning as and when it's needed

- suspending walks and finding other activities to do instead

When walking with a fearful dog, scan the environment so that you see what's coming before your dog does. Be ready to move away and give treats as necessary. Think about how you can use the environment to help. A parked car or a low wall can make a barrier so that your dog doesn't see another dog, or maybe you have friends and neighbors who will let you nip onto their driveway for a moment as another dog goes past. Whenever your dog spots something they consider troublesome, be ready to give lots of treats (see Chapter 5) and to move away.

Other people can be troublesome too, especially those who insist their dog is friendly or who try to give unwanted advice.

You don't owe other people an explanation; put your dog first. The world would be a better place for fearful dogs if people were respectful and kept themselves and their dogs at a safe distance and the dog on-leash in places where this is required.

It is okay to skip the walks, at least for a while, to give your dog relief from scary situations. If the walks are a regular struggle, this can be a relief for both of you. Other times, it can be a shock to realize that the dog we've got—the one we wanted to take on long hikes through the forest, to swim in the sea at busy beaches, to walk on the crowded seawall with us—is not actually able to do those things. Then it feels like a big loss to realize that life with the dog is not going to go as planned. Whether you feel a sense of relief or sadness that there may be days (stretching to however long...) when you don't walk your dog, it's a good idea to acknowledge those feelings.

The risk of running

Whenever you bring home a new dog, or have a dog who is fearful, it's important to be very aware of the risk of them running away. Consider a GPS tracker on the dog's collar, and take steps to prevent escapes from the home or on walks.

When entering and leaving the house, a double-entry approach reduces the risk of the dog escaping through an open door. For example, if you enter/exit your home via a garage, ensure that the garage door is always completely closed before you open the door to the house. That way, even if the dog manages to escape as you go into the house, they will only get into the garage. If you don't have a garage, you may be able to use pet gates or exercise pens to make an extra barrier by the door.

Keep the dog on-leash when outside and hold the leash securely (put a knot in it to help, if you like). If you're walking a dog who is a flight risk, you might want to have two leashes. For example, you can attach one to a collar and one to a harness, so that you have two points of contact (and maybe even one person to hold each of those leashes). Only adults should walk the dog; children or teens should not, because the dog is at a greater risk than usual of running away. Only relax this rule once you are sure the dog has settled in and knows where home is. It's helpful to walk them around your neighborhood so that, if they do get lost, they might at least know their way home.

If you have a yard, check the fencing carefully to ensure that a dog can't dig or jump their way out. Think about who comes in and out of the gate and if it is ever likely to be left open. Don't rely on an electronic fencing system for two reasons: the first is that (as explained in Chapter 3) you should never apply electric shocks to any dog, and especially not one with issues; and the second is that dogs are twice as likely to escape from an electronic fence than from a physical fence.[1] If your dog is afraid of loud noises like fireworks or thunder, make sure they are inside when these events are likely; it's very common for dogs to escape from yards (or leashes) when there are loud noises like this.

Other precautions to take include having a rule that if someone is at the door, the dog is put on-leash (and someone is holding that leash) before the door is opened. Put a note on the inside of the door to remind all members of the family to check that the dog is secure before they open the door. And you could put a note on the outside that says "Dog in training" or something similar to explain that when the doorbell rings, it will be a moment before you can open the door, as you have to secure your dog first.

Teaching your dog to come when called is a priority for any dog guardian, but it's especially important for those with fearful dogs. Because recall is such an important behavior, you need to use amazing treats, something that will hopefully trump chasing a squirrel (a happy running) or running away from a noise (a terror run). But don't put that to the test. To start with, practice in a room in the house where your dog is already comfortable, and with your dog right next to you. For your recall cue, pick a new word that doesn't have any existing associations, and that you'll be happy to call out in public. "Come," "Here," and "Come here" are obvious options. If you've tried to teach a recall before, it's best to start fresh with a completely new word like "Yoohoo," "Pup pup," or "*Cheeeeeese.*" It's a word that you'll only use when you have amazing treats like sardines or cheese to give your dog.

Prepare your treat in advance and stash it in the fridge. Wait until your dog is not expecting it and they happen to be close to you, say your recall cue "*Cheeeeese,*" run to the fridge to get the reward, and give it to your dog. They don't have to follow you to the fridge; what you're doing is creating an association between the recall cue and the treat. The word "*Cheeeeese*" in our example is the cs that predicts cubes of mature cheddar cheese (us). Only once you've got that association will you start to add in the behavior of the dog coming to you (that is, make it operant conditioning). Build up very gradually, with very small distances indoors. Also make sure that you always give the cue before there is any suggestion of treats.

Eventually, you'll feel ready to take this training outside. Start in a securely fenced area with few or no distractions. It takes a lot of practice to build up from recall as an everyday behavior in easy situations to the almost Olympic-level stage of recalling from squirrels and other living things. A long line can be helpful as you practice, because it can give your dog more freedom while you still have a hold of them, or a way to get hold of them if you let go. Be careful, though, because it's easy to burn your hands with a long line; always wear gloves. This is also something you can practice with a dog trainer.

ENRICHMENT ACTIVITIES FOR YOU AND YOUR
FEARFUL DOG: SCENT GAMES, DOG SPORTS, AND MORE

MANY ENRICHMENT ACTIVITIES can be done at home, so that your fearful dog does not have to leave the house. And others that involve going places can still be suitable for dogs who don't want to meet other dogs or people.

Scent games are a great way to provide enrichment for fearful and reactive dogs. To play scent games at home:

- Try snuffle mats and treat scatters, and hiding treats around your house.

- Put treats in a muffin tin and put tennis balls on top, then let your dog move the balls to get at the treats.

- Fill a cardboard box with shredded paper and hide treats in the box for your dog to find.

- Buy Kong chew toys, or food-puzzle toys such as those by Nina Ottosson, which come in graded levels and require your dog to manipulate them to get at treats.

Change up the fillings in the food toys to keep the games fun. Try tuna, treats, kibble, cottage cheese, yogurt, meat or fish paste, bacon, pumpkin puree, applesauce, peanut butter... basically, any kind of food that your dog likes can go in a Kong. To cut down on preparation time, fill a set of Kongs and keep them in the freezer so that you've always got one ready to pull out. Start with delicious treats that will easily fall out of the toys before you start putting purees inside or making layered parfaits—this is especially important with fearful dogs because you don't want them to get discouraged.

Scent-work classes can work well for reactive dogs because only one dog is in the arena at a time. That means your dog does

not have to meet other dogs during the class, and people are usually very considerate about moving dogs to and from the arena
to give reactive dogs plenty of space. Ask the trainer in advance
if you're not sure. Pick a class in which the dog is given the
chance to follow their nose, instead of taking directions from
you, because choice and control are especially important for fearful dogs. A six-week nose-work class has been found to increase
optimism in dogs.[2]

Other dog sports, such as agility, freestyle (dog dancing), and
rally obedience, may seem out of reach if you have a fearful dog,
but they're not necessarily, according to Ayoka Bubar. Bubar is
a dog sports enthusiast and trainer in central Canada who takes
part in multiple dog sports with her Rottweilers. She tells me that
sometimes people don't realize their dog is fearful until they try to
take a sports class or compete. But if you already know your dog
is fearful, she recommends giving dog sports a try anyway. "Most
sports, especially if people are using positive reinforcement in
their training, help build the bond between the dog and handler,
and that's always helpful when we're talking about fear."

Of course, some sports may not be suitable for your dog. For
example, agility has a fast pace, and each run may take only thirty
seconds, meaning there are dogs and handlers lined up to wait
for their turn, which may make some dogs uncomfortable. "The
sports that lend themselves to more fearful dogs are sports that
are a little slower in the pace," Bubar says. "Freestyle tends to be
a little bit slower because the routines are a little bit longer. Then
some other sports are in a dog park, or it's out in public but generally not with other dogs, like scent work. I think scent work and
tracking are invaluable for fearful dogs. There's something about
using noses that is so helpful."

Herding is another sport that could work for fearful dogs because
it's "not inside. Big, loud buildings can be hard on fearful dogs."

In barn hunt, dogs compete individually to find rats in a tunnel made of hay bales, so this sport may also suit some dogs. (Pick a class that uses scent, rather than live rodents, for better animal welfare.) In Treibball (sometimes known as urban herding), dogs move big inflatable balls around, and again, dogs and their handlers compete individually, so it is suitable for reactive dogs.

These days, virtual classes provide opportunities to take part in dog sports from home. Bubar explains the benefits: "You don't need to expose your dog to all the people and dogs and scary things and scary buildings. Virtual options offer a lot, and it's cheaper because you don't have to pay for the travel." You follow classes online and you may need someone to take a video of you, but that person can be another member of your household, which is much easier for a fearful dog. And for competitions, Bubar says, you only send in qualifying performances, so that makes it cheaper too—you don't have to travel to a trial only to have a nonqualifying performance.

Dog sports give you and your dog the opportunity to work towards titles, if you like. A title shows your dog's accomplishment and means you will get a certificate and ribbon, and maybe some letters to go after your dog's name. Perhaps the most well-known title is Canine Good Citizen from the American Kennel Club.

If you're interested in trying sports, Bubar recommends taking a trick class first, because you don't need equipment and many tricks can be the first steps of a sport such as rally or agility.

Trick training

Erica Beckwith teaches trick classes in person and online. She tells me that tricks are especially great for fearful dogs. "When we keep tricks simple, non-invasive, and highly reinforcing, we can build a fearful dog's confidence through fun and success," she says. "A huge benefit is the bond it creates or strengthens between the guardian and the fearful dog." Beckwith adds that "because people see trick training as less serious, that allows them to loosen up and work more in partnership with their dogs (which can always be the case, by the way, even when dealing with serious issues). Guardians let their dogs be more creative when they aren't as stringent about what the dogs 'should' be doing."

Beckwith enjoys letting her dogs be creative when working on tricks. "That's right," she says, "dogs can be creative and often come up with the most interesting tricks when they are given the chance to. How empowering for fearful or anxious dogs! And the biggest benefit is helping our fearful dogs learn that offering and trying out new behaviors is safe, reinforcing, and fun!"

Beckwith's favorite tricks for beginners are "hand targeting (dog's nose touches our hand), or any kind of nose targeting, paws-up (two paws on an object), up-up (all four paws on an object), and around-me (the dog walks in a circle around you). They are easy to teach and easy to learn and can ease a fearful dog into training games. Paws-up and up-up become exciting ways for fearful dogs to explore new environments; playing around by jumping up on rocks or benches and getting good treats can help make these new places less scary!"

Of course, she emphasizes that we should not ask dogs to do things they find scary, so bear this in mind in a new environment. If the dog doesn't do a behavior they know, that can be a sign that a situation is too overwhelming for them.

Beckwith explains how much her late dog Ruckus, who came from a hoarding situation and was very fearful, benefited from trick training. "Ruckus was so scared of everything new—new places, people, dogs, sounds, everything. When I first got her, I didn't realize fearful dogs could even be trained, and I definitely did not know how much fearful dogs can love trick training. Turns out, Ruckus was a trick dog superstar! The more we trained, the more she blossomed, and the more her sassy side came out. She could not get enough sit-pretty, waving, piano playing, jumping over her brothers, up-up on rocks, and her favorite trick, grimace (show teeth/wrinkle nose on cue). I would use tricks to help her shake off the nerves while waiting at the vet. She would throw out all her tricks with a hundred percent exuberance, and that made the vet a more fun place to visit."

Trick training helped Ruckus feel better around strange new objects, because she got delicious treats when interacting with them. Beckwith recalls: "Giving her a bell to ring meant it was fun to put her paw on a weird, loud object, instead of that being a threatening item. She learned to spin, twirl, close doors, wave into the camera (although she taught herself that one), jump, crawl, play dead, roll over, cross her paws, take a bow, say her prayers, fetch tissues—there was almost nothing this tiny, fearful dog could not do. Over our eleven years together, she became a confident, sassy, spicy lady who loved tricks and showing off, and all of that made learning other new behaviors (even the more

Ruckus demonstrates up-up (all four paws on an object). *ERICA BECKWITH*

'important' ones!) much easier for her (it's all tricks to our dogs!), and created a very special relationship between us."

Jessica Ring of My Fantastic Friend in Weaverville, North Carolina, told me she loves teaching dogs to target with their nose, because it is such a versatile skill and because you can use it to ask your dog to move around, such as to the scales at the vet. Dogs can be taught to target your hand with their nose (the most common), but also to target a target stick (a stick with a ball on the end that you can get from pet stores), sticky notes on the wall, or any other object. "Nose targeting can be used as the first step in other training plans," she says, "whether it's for fun tricks or for something practical, like teaching your dog to be comfortable with a harness, or helping a hand-shy dog learn that hands aren't scary. If you're looking for ways to provide physical exercise indoors, you can set up an object for your dog to target that is across the room, so they run back to you for a treat after targeting. Or they can ping-pong between people, nose targeting each person and getting a treat. My dogs love nose targeting, as it's a fun and familiar game they play in a variety of contexts—and yummy treats are always involved!"

UNDERSTANDING INDIVIDUAL DIFFERENCES IN EXERCISE AND ENRICHMENT NEEDS

SOME DOGS HAVE GREATER NEEDS for exercise and enrichment than others. In particular, any dog from a "working" line or of a breed that was designed to have a job is going to need more exercise and enrichment. This includes Border Collies, Australian Shepherds, Belgian Malinois, German Shepherds, Blue Heelers, and many others.

Emily Priestley of Wild at Heart Dog Training specializes in herding dogs. I asked her what tends to surprise people about these breeds once they have brought one home. "I think a lot of people, unless they've experienced it, probably don't expect the level of exercise and enrichment that the dogs will have," she says. "Normally, those dogs are going to outlast us when it comes to exercise. Simple walks often just aren't enough. So, if we're looking at the average senior Pit Bull that just wants to go for a nice, ambulant walk, and that's good for him in a day, the Border Collie, especially the adolescent young Border Collie, is going to need a lot. And then there's a lot of enrichment that comes along as well. Sometimes, for these dogs, just walking them or exercising them isn't enough. They also need to be able to exercise their brain."

If they don't get enough exercise and enrichment, they may become frustrated, and that can play a role in fear and anxiety. "I see a lot of dogs who are right off the farm from working lines, who have never been off-leash," she says, "never had the opportunity to stretch their legs and run." Priestley says that high-intensity exercise is great for them once they are old enough. She says that although she hears people worry that providing opportunities for exercise will make the dog need more of it, "it's simply not true; they will still need a rest, just like Olympians do."

This type of dog especially benefits if you can find a safe space for them to run around every day, and they also do very well in sports like scent work and trick training. With herding dogs, Priestley says, "I do a lot of teaching herding directional cues off of stock and using a toy instead, to give them an approximation of what they were bred to do. These toys include flirt poles, jolly balls, any of these herding-type toys."

While some enrichment activities may be just for the dog, a lot of them are fun for both you and the dog. Taking time for you both to have fun is especially beneficial when you have a fearful dog, because it takes you out of dealing with the problems and helps you remember why you love your dog. So it's worth thinking about what you enjoy too.

I asked Jessica Ring about her tips to help someone have fun with a fearful dog. "Take a break from all the practical tasks you're likely working on with your dog to make time for fun activities," she said. "Online trick classes are great for dogs who are more comfortable in the safety of their own home. Tricks can be modified (or skipped entirely) to keep your dog feeling safe. Have fun searching out a variety of food puzzle toys, chews, and scent games for your pup to try. Take slow, sniffy walks in quiet places where you can both decompress. Go at your dog's pace and stick to what feels safe to them. A good understanding of body language is key. Find joy in the little things!"

Exercise and enrichment are good for the dog—and they can also be good for us.

"One thing I wish people knew about fearful dogs is that, similar to people, dogs sometimes react to perceived threats or danger with aggression—a 'fight' response. Though these dogs look scarier than those that resort to flight or freeze responses, the message is the same: 'I am scared, please give me space.' These dogs are often labeled difficult, headstrong, in need of leadership and a firm hand. These beliefs can lead to the use of methods that may stop the reaction but increase the root fear; the dogs learn that the world is indeed a scary place. But if we recognize this response for what it is—a plea for safety— we can meet this request with empathy and patience. These dogs aren't broken, and they can be taught that the world is safe with cookies and kindness, just like all of the others."

—ALLIE KIRBY, CTC, CSAP-BC, FFCP-Trainer, owner of Sky's the Limit Animal Training and Behavior

UNDERSTANDING THE ROLE OF MEDICATIONS

· · · · · · · · · · · · · · · · ·

WHEN I WAS A STUDENT at the Academy for Dog Trainers, one of the assignments involved training your dog for a vet exam, including looking at the ears, teeth, and tail, and giving your dog a pill. For most people, this assignment is a breeze. Teaching a puppy these skills is easy and helps set them up for vet visits for life. But I wanted to do it with Bodger, who hated going to the vet and hated to be handled. I thought this assignment was a great opportunity for him to get used to being handled and for me to practice this training on a dog who really needed to go slowly.

The ears part and the tail part were slow but okay. But touching Bodger's snout was not a good idea. A couple of times I made a mistake, resulting in him growling and snapping at me. It was good news that he gave warnings, but I felt like a lousy trainer, and I felt terrible for upsetting Bodger like this. I worried that my clumsiness would damage our relationship, and I almost felt like giving up, but I knew the end result—a more handleable dog—would be really good for him. Kind feedback from Academy staff helped me spot where I was getting my order of events wrong and moving for the treat before reaching for Bodger (oops). In the end, what made the difference was Jean Donaldson writing me a training plan just for Bodger. It was a plan that moved in the tiniest of increments, and it made all the difference. Finally, we reached the stage where I could open Bodger's mouth and pop in a piece of cheese. If ever there was a lesson in going at the dog's pace, this was it.

A few years later, Bodger became ill. He ended up needing immediate surgery at the emergency vet and was ultimately diagnosed with hemangiosarcoma. Then we had a decision to make about chemotherapy, which can't cure this awful disease, but only buy a little more time. We decided to try it, hoping that the side effects wouldn't be too bad. Chemo for animals is not as harsh as chemo for humans, and it aims to preserve a good quality of life.

But nausea is a potential side effect, and soon after the first treatment, Bodger had it. Nothing would get him to eat. He could smell the food and he looked interested, but when he went to eat it, he would suddenly look sad and walk away. We were prescribed anti-nausea meds, but how to get them into him when he wouldn't eat a thing? The only option was to pill him, like we had practiced all those years earlier. I couldn't even follow up the pill with something tasty, because as far as he was concerned, nothing was tasty. We hadn't practiced the training after finishing that assignment, but with butter on the pill to help it slide down, and my husband and I working together, we were able to get the pill in him without anyone being bitten. I was so grateful to Donaldson for that plan, which, so many years later, saved the day.

After seeing Bodger so sad after the first dose of chemo, and knowing that its effects were limited anyway, we called a halt to it. Bodger recovered from the treatment and we had four lovely months in which he was just like his old self. Then he suddenly went downhill, and we had to say goodbye. I remain eternally grateful to all the vets and vet techs who helped us with Bodger through that time, and of course to Donaldson for her guidance on that training.

If you have a puppy, it helps to train them to accept being pilled and having their teeth looked at. With most puppies, you can simply open their mouth and then give them a lovely reward. With an adult dog, you have to train them, and with adult dogs who are not very handleable, that training might be very slow, just as with Bodger.

WHEN TO SEE A VET OR VETERINARY BEHAVIORIST

ANY TIME YOU SEE a sudden change in your dog's behavior, whether they're doing something they didn't used to do, or no longer doing something they used to do often, it's important to see your veterinarian. That includes a sudden change in which your dog becomes fearful or anxious.

Your veterinarian will let you know if they think you will benefit from seeing a veterinary behaviorist (VB). A veterinary behaviorist has completed a veterinary degree and done considerable extra training and examinations that give them a thorough understanding of the interplay between physical and emotional wellness in pets. Unfortunately, there are only about a hundred veterinary behaviorists in North America, so you may have to wait for an appointment. You may also need to travel if there isn't a VB near you; in some cases, they may do a vet-to-vet consult that you will likely not be present for, but that will help your vet with the case.

THE ROLE OF PSYCHOTROPIC MEDICATIONS

IF YOUR VETERINARIAN THINKS that pain or other medical issues are contributing to your pet's behavior issues, they will investigate, a process that may include a trial of a painkiller and/or referrals to specialists. They can also prescribe psychotropic medications when they think they will help. Psychotropic drugs, such as anti-depressants, anti-anxiety meds, and mood stabilizers, have an effect on the brain and central nervous system that affects moods and/or behavior. Some of these drugs are short-lasting (to help with a short-lived fear-inducing event, for example, such as a night of fireworks or a trip to the vet), while others are long-lasting. In some cases, your dog may need these medications for the rest of their life, and in other cases, only for a shorter time.

When a stressor is frequent or unavoidable, your veterinarian or veterinary behaviorist may recommend long-term medications. Medications can help when the dog's quality of life is being affected by fear or anxiety, and when this response is affecting the bond with their person. Medications are often used alongside a behavior and training plan and can help to reduce levels of fear, anxiety, and stress so that behavior modification is more effective. Pharmaceuticals are tested extensively before being used. Some are intended specifically for use with animals, but veterinarians also draw on medications that are designed and tested for people.

If you're not sure why your vet is prescribing a medication, talk to them about it. Sometimes it can take a little while to know if a medication is working or not, and they can give you an indication of how long that is likely to be. For some meds, it can be five to eight weeks.[1] Sometimes the first medication that's tried doesn't work as well as hoped. In that case, your dog may need a different dose, or another medication either on its own or in combination with the first one. When changing medications, sometimes a period of no meds is needed to prevent interactions as the first med "washes out" of the system. This means that the process of starting your dog on medication can take time. It can feel frustrating, but it's part of finding the right medication for your dog. Work with your vet and describe the response you see as well as you can, to help them help you.

People sometimes worry that psychotropic medication will change their pet's personality. It's a common misconception, according to Dr. Claudia Richter of Pacific Veterinary Behavior Consulting. "The way I explain it to people is that, yes, there are some side effects potentially initially; maybe the dog is going to be a little bit sedated. That's perfectly normal, but it shouldn't be excessive and it shouldn't last past the first one or two weeks. And if it does, just communicate that, because that's not what I would want for my pet either, and it's definitely not my goal for you."

As she explains to clients, "the anxiety is floating up on the top and just drowning your dog's personality, and my goal is to turn that around. We're probably not going to get rid of the anxiety completely, or not in every case. But maybe we can get his or her personality to float up to the top and suppress the anxiety, and then you can really see that personality shine."

Dr. Richter adds that, once the medications are successful, most people tell her they wish they had tried this route sooner.

Understanding commonly used psychoactive medications

Many hormones and brain proteins play important roles in activating the stress system (see Chapter 2). Different classes of drug target different aspects of this system. The main groups are described below, but you should discuss specific questions about medications and your dog with your veterinarian.

Selective serotonin reuptake inhibitors (SSRIS) block the reuptake of serotonin in the brain to make sure that more of it is available. Serotonin is involved in many bodily functions, but importantly it helps regulate mood. The most commonly known SSRI is fluoxetine; a chewable version for dogs is available under the brand name Reconcile. Other SSRIS include paroxetine, sertraline, and fluvoxamine.

Tricyclic antidepressants (TCAS) block the reuptake of serotonin and noradrenaline. Different TCAS have different modes of action. The most common is clomipramine (sold under several brand names, including Clomicalm).

Monoamine oxidase inhibitors (MAOIS) inhibit an enzyme called monoamine oxidase, which is involved in removing serotonin, norepinephrine, and dopamine. Blocking this enzyme makes more of these chemicals available. Selegiline is an MAOI used with pets.

Azapirones are a class of drugs that affect a serotonin receptor (5-HT1A). Buspirone is the type of azapirone used with pets.

Benzodiazepines are a class of drugs that work by helping the amino acid GABA bind to GABA receptors, which inhibits other nerve cells. GABA is involved in slowing down messages in the brain, preparing for sleep, and controlling appetite. Benzodiazepines include alprazolam, midazolam, and gabapentin.

Alpha-2 adrenergic receptor agonists work to reduce the release of noradrenaline. Sileo and clonidine fall into this class of drugs.

Imepitoin and trazodone are other options that your vet may want to use.

Anti-anxiety medication is not a last resort, so speak to your vet sooner rather than later about whether it is suitable for your dog.

If your vet prescribes medication for fear and anxiety, or any other issues, it helps to have a way to get meds into your dog. Although it's relatively easy with some dogs, it's a challenge with other dogs. Below, you'll see some ideas for giving meds to dogs. You can also train them, like I trained Bodger.

Giving meds to your dog

- Put the meds in food and give them at mealtimes (check later that they've been eaten).
- Put the meds in Pill Pockets, Pill Assists, Hide & Treats, or similar capsules.
- Put the meds inside empty chicken-flavored gel capsules.
- Put the meds inside a tasty food such as a spoonful of peanut butter or a slice of cheese or beef.
- Put the meds in a pill paste that's designed to hide the taste.
- Give several pieces of unadulterated food before and after giving the food with the meds. A quick delivery can help.
- Put the meds in delicious food on a plate with other nice foods. Give your dog space while they eat from the plate (then check later that the meds have been eaten).
- Mix the meds into a pâté (a watered-down cat-food pâté works well) and use a syringe to give them orally.
- Put butter on the meds.
- Train your dog to accept meds.
- Ask a compounding pharmacy to help make the meds pet-friendly by, for example, putting them in a flavored liquid or treat. Some pharmacies specialize in medication compounding for pets, but any compounding pharmacy should be able to help.
- Always check with your vet about the timing of medications and meals.

NUTRITIONAL AND OTHER COMPLEMENTARY APPROACHES

PEOPLE SOMETIMES WONDER if a special diet or nutritional supplement might help their dog. Of course, it's important that whatever food your dog is on, it's a "complete and balanced" food (look for this wording on the label). Some prescription foods and supplements are designed to help reduce stress or reduce the frequency of stress-related upset stomachs. Pet stores also sell a range of nutritional supplements and complementary approaches that do not require a prescription. It's thought that some nutritional substances have an effect by making more of the precursors of brain chemicals and hormones available. These dietary substances include tryptophan, phenylalanine, L-theanine, omega-3s, tyrosine, and a diet that is low in protein.[2] So there's a plausible reason why they might work, and a number of studies that have looked at their efficacy. Better-quality evidence would be helpful, and for some substances there's little research.

I asked Dr. Richter about nutraceuticals, and she told me that for her client pool, made up of people who have already tried behavior modification and likely also failed a first-line treatment, nutraceuticals aren't as appropriate. "Giving a nutraceutical to the type of patient that I see is like giving a guy that just fell off his bike and broke his leg an ibuprofen. That doesn't mean ibuprofen is a bad drug, and once his leg is healed and is only painful when it's cold, that ibuprofen is going to work really well."

She says there are times when she uses nutritional supplements and probiotics as a supportive treatment. And she says they have a place in general practice, "especially for what I would consider a normal or nonfearful dog that is going through a mildly stressful period, like a new baby arriving in the house."

Another example she gives is of a new puppy from a responsible breeder coming into the home, because being taken from their mom and going to a new place is stressful for them.

If you want to know whether a particular diet would be appropriate for your pet, speak to your veterinarian. And if you're giving nutritional supplements to your pet, let your vet know, as some may interfere with medications that your vet prescribes.

Dietary supplements

The effects of a dietary supplement containing fish hydrolysate were tested on Beagles to see if the pills affected the dogs' fear response to a recording of a thunderstorm.[3] The supplement was derived from cod and mackerel, and is thought to affect the HPA axis. It reduced anxiety compared with a placebo. Another study tested L-theanine supplements on pet dogs who were anxious in thunderstorms.[4] L-theanine is an amino acid found naturally in green and black tea and in some mushrooms. Dog guardians reported an improvement in their dog's behavior during storms, and that it took less time after the storm for their dog to return to normal. However, there was no control, so a placebo effect can't be ruled out. All participants were also given standardized advice on such practices as using blackout drapes, playing white noise, and not punishing the dog, which could also be responsible for the results.

A double-blind randomized controlled trial looked at the effects of a supplement that included fish hydrolysate and melon juice on dogs in a mildly stressful situation.[5] When dogs had the supplement, they showed signs of reduced stress, such as being more comfortable in approaching an unknown person and whining less. People who had given the supplement also reported a reduction in their dog's stress, but so did some of the people who had given the placebo, showing the importance of a placebo condition. Overall, it seems that the supplement was helpful. A large questionnaire study found that dog guardians said that dietary changes or nutritional supplements were helpful for generalized anxiety and fears of inanimate objects.[6] And in a study of dogs who engage in tail chasing behavior, those dogs who had nutritional supplements did less of it.[7]

Dog-appeasing pheromones (DAP)

Canine pheromones are chemical signals detected by the dog's vomeronasal organ. Dogs register the pheromones of other dogs, and this may influence their behavior. Adaptil is a synthetic version of the dog-appeasing pheromone that bitches produce when nursing their puppies, and it is believed to have a calming effect. It is available in different forms, including as a spray, on a collar, and in a diffuser. Another version of Adaptil, called ThunderEase, is available as a diffuser designed to help with fear of loud noises, separation-related issues, barking, and chewing.

A 2010 review reported that although one study found DAPs were effective in decreasing fear and anxiety in puppies, other studies did not, and there are issues with the design of the studies.[8] A study that tested DAP spray on dogs in a stressful environment, an animal shelter, found that they barked just as frequently, albeit slightly less loudly, when exposed to the spray. However, it's possible that in highly stressful environments DAP might work better when used with other stress-relieving measures.[9] A small study of a DAP diffuser found no effects on dogs when they were separated from their guardian during a test at a laboratory.[10] On the other hand, a study that gave adopters of shelter dogs a DAP diffuser when they took their new dog home found improvements in dogs' behavior that are in line with reduced stress.[11] A double-blind study, in which nursing bitches were exposed to either a DAP diffuser or a placebo, found that breeders reported improvements in maternal behavior in response to the DAP.[12] There's also some evidence that an Adaptil diffuser improves the relationship between a dog and cat in a multi-pet home (as does the feline version, Feliway Friends).[13] So, although we need more research on how pheromones can help dogs, and in particular some randomized controlled trials, they may be worth a try.

Pulsed electromagnetic field therapy (PEMF)

In dogs, pulsed electromagnetic field therapy was originally used to reduce pain, swelling, and arthritis. To test whether PEMF helps dogs with separation anxiety, scientists recruited healthy dogs with moderate or severe separation anxiety for a six-week randomized controlled trial. Based on video data, PEMF seemed to make a difference. However, questionnaires completed by the dogs' guardians showed none of them perceived any difference in their dogs' behavior. More research is needed.

Pressure vests

A pressure vest provides pressure to the dog's body. One study found that when dogs were left alone for fifteen minutes in a kennel, they had a lower increase in their heart rate if they wore a pressure vest properly, compared with dogs who wore one improperly (that is, too loosely) or didn't wear one, but there were few behavioral differences.[14] A complication in this study is that some of the dogs were on anti-anxiety medication, which makes interpreting the results difficult. Another study tested whether a pressure vest made a difference around loud noises and found that dogs who wore the vest were more likely to stay near their guardian during the gaps between noises.[15] Again, the study showed no clear benefits, although the scientists say that a pressure vest perhaps helps with recovery after fireworks or other loud noises. Finally, in a survey that asked people what helped calm their dog's fear of loud noises, 44 percent of those who had used a pressure vest with their dog said that it worked.[16]

Cannabis products

Cannabidiol (CBD) is a nonpsychoactive substance derived from *Cannabis sativa* plants (including hemp). We know little about its ability to affect behavior. Two studies have found that it has no effect on reducing anxiety in dogs.[17] In one of those studies, shelter dogs were given either CBD oil or an olive oil placebo for forty-five days, and there was no effect on aggressive behavior or stress. A third study, which was placebo-controlled, looked at dogs in two types of stressful events (separation from the guardian and travel in a car) and found some beneficial effects from a single dose of CBD oil prior to the stressful event.[18] A review of CBD studies for a range of conditions in dogs found wide variability in both the kind of dose and the way it is delivered (for example, in gel capsules, tablets, and nasal spray). So, at present, the evidence that CBD oil has beneficial effects for fearful and anxious dogs is poor.

It's important to note that these studies looked specifically at CBD products for veterinary use, which should not be confused with marijuana. The American Veterinary Medical Association warns that some dogs have become very ill or even died as a result of consuming cannabis, especially in the form of edibles.[19] The association also points out that the legal status of CBD products is changing. Some companies are being fined for selling them in the US, and the US Food and Drug Administration says it is not clear how such products can meet safety standards for nutritional supplements for people or for animal food.

Complementary therapies are not a substitute for doing the real work of training, management, and keeping your dog feeling safe. If you decide to try any of these therapies, always let your vet know, in case there are any contraindications or potential negative interactions with the medications your dog is on.

"There are two reasons I don't wait to start medication for my fearful patients. The first is probably the most familiar to most of us. Medications that reduce anxiety can actually improve the effectiveness of the training, just like they help humans find more success in therapy. If we can bring a dog's baseline anxiety level down a few notches, it should be easier to find a foothold to start training, and the training should be able to move a little faster.

The second reason is even more important from a welfare standpoint. Fear, like pain, is an extremely uncomfortable sensation and should be addressed as such. When a dog comes in with a broken leg, we don't wait for the surgery to be over (or for the bone to heal!) to start pain medication. We give them appropriate pain control first to reduce their suffering, then take X-rays and plan surgery. Similarly, anxiety medications for a fearful dog should not be a last resort. They should be considered a first-line intervention *to reduce suffering* while an appropriate behavior modification plan is being designed and implemented."

—**DR. RACHEL SZUMEL**, small-animal veterinarian, South Lake Tahoe, California

PART
2

HOW TO MANAGE YOUR DOG'S SPECIFIC FEARS

SOCIAL WALLFLOWERS AND BASHFUL BEASTIES:

WHEN YOUR DOG FEARS PEOPLE OR OTHER DOGS

MY LITTLE DOG Pepper is a darling when it comes to meeting new people. Whenever someone comes to visit, he rushes to them with his tail wagging to greet them and sniff their ankles (the only bit he can easily reach), even if he's never met them before. Out on the street, it feels like he wishes everyone would stop to admire him and say hello. He looks hopeful if someone walks towards us and seems sad if they just walk on by without paying attention to him. I feel lucky to have such a friendly, sociable dog. Not all dogs are like this. Some are nervous when meeting new people, but warm up once they know someone or if their guardian is around, while others are afraid of anyone except for a handful of special people.

Of course, the same is the case with dogs' interactions with other dogs. For many of us, the dream is a dog who is prosocial with all other dogs and is not bothered in the least if another dog snarks at them, who recovers quickly from doggy arguments and is always happy to meet another dog, but this doesn't always happen. Some dogs are friends with a few other dogs that they know well but not so keen on meeting new dogs, and some dogs are very picky about the dogs they like to spend time with. Whether we're talking about fear of other dogs or fear of other people, these are social fears.

Dogs should have a choice in interactions. Many people assume that all dogs will be friendly to all people, but they don't have to be. As a dog guardian, it's our responsibility to protect our dogs from situations they don't like. It would help dogs if more people understood that it's important to ask the dog before saying hello. Children are taught to ask before petting someone else's dog, but a good dog guardian will take into account whether or not the dog consents. Use the dog's body language as a guide.

WALLFLOWERS AND SHRINKING VIOLETS WITH PEOPLE

DOGS DIFFERENTIATE between people they know and people they don't, so it can happen that the dog is aggressive to family members, or aggressive to strangers, but not necessarily both.[1] And aggression towards other dogs seems to be a separate thing from being afraid of people. So, if your dog lunges and barks at other dogs when on-leash, it doesn't necessarily mean they will be aggressive to people (but be careful when they are roused up, because a redirected bite is possible in those situations).

Get a good dog trainer to coach you through what to do whenever there is a risk of a bite (or the situation is simply difficult). If you think your dog might be aggressive to people or dogs, and especially if they have already bitten, muzzle training helps keep everyone safe.

Management is important to help keep people away from the dog. For example, if your dog is afraid of people visiting the home, set a house rule that the dog is shut away (in another room or in a crate) before the door is opened to let someone in. It may sound easy, but remembering to do this every single time, and making sure that every single member of your household follows the rule, can be rather hard. If you leave your dog in your yard, you need to make sure that the yard is fenced, that no one leaves the gate open and accidentally lets the dog out, and that your dog is not in the yard if delivery people or other people are likely to come into it.

Use training to help your dog feel more comfortable around people

One way to deal with fear of people is to use desensitization and counterconditioning (see Chapter 5). For the desensitization part, you're trying to make the person as unscary as possible to your dog. Distance is always a great thing to manipulate; it's likely that the farther away the person is, the less scary they will seem. As well, ensuring that the person is not facing or looking at (or walking towards) the dog can be very helpful. Staring can make dogs uncomfortable. The counterconditioning part is where you give the dog yummy treats while the person is around.

When looking for people to help you by meeting your dog in a safe way, choose with care. Sometimes it feels like people who say they are good with dogs really mean that they expect dogs to be good with them. Pick someone who will listen to your directions and follow them, who is patient and won't mind doing multiple trials of the same thing, and who is sympathetic to your dog. If you're going to ask them to ignore your dog and stay at a certain distance, for example, pick someone who will do that, instead of someone who might come right up to your dog and try to pet them (setting back your training). Over time, you will need many different people so that your dog can generalize from the training, but to start with, pick one trusted person.

Make sure you are the one giving your dog treats, at least at first. If you ask the person helping you to deliver the treats, your dog has to choose between getting a delicious treat and approaching someone they think is scary. Avoid that situation completely by giving the treats yourself, and make sure you give them generously and quickly. Later in the training, when your dog feels less anxious around people, you may well ask the person meeting your dog to help by tossing treats to your dog. Be sure they do not aim directly at your dog, who might feel like they're having stuff thrown at them; instead, have them aim just off to the side, so that your dog will feel safe eating the treats and doesn't have to approach the person to get them. But this is already another step forward in training.

Another thing to bear in mind is that you need to work in gradual steps. The first time your dog meets a new person is going to be the hardest for the dog. As you work through multiple trials with the same person, the dog will get "warmed up" to the situation and the person. When you haven't met this person for a few days, go slowly. Don't start right at the point where you left off before; instead, go back a stage or two to make it easy for your dog to get warmed up again. You will likely get through those easier stages more quickly than before and be able to make progress from there.

Ask new people to respect your dog's fear

Outside training setups, you will probably have to ask people to behave differently around your fearful dog, at least for a while. For example, even if it's safe for people and comfortable for your dog to be in the same room, you may need to ask people not to look at the dog (and especially not to stare), and not to interact with the dog, because the dog might find that scary. Asking people to do this can feel very difficult, since people who love dogs of course want to interact with the dog. Detailed instructions can help.

"Enlist their assistance ahead of time," Jessica Ring says. "Tell them what to do, rather than just what not to do. An example might be to have your friends or family play games on their phone in a chair that's facing away and at a distance from the dog. This keeps them busy, so they aren't staring at or reaching for the dog, which some dogs find very scary. Let your friends and family know when they are doing something well. Be specific so that they're more likely to keep doing it! 'Thank you so much for texting when you got here instead of ringing the doorbell. That was so helpful to us.'"

But, of course, it's sometimes better for your dog not to meet the person, and so you can set up a safe space for them and keep them away (see Chapter 3).

If you can't speak to everyone your dog might meet, you can use signage to help. For example, if the sound of the doorbell sets your dog off, put a note by the door asking family and friends to send you a text message instead of ringing the doorbell. If you're expecting deliveries, post a sign asking for your package to be left by the door without ringing the bell. Some people find it helpful to have a sign that says "Dog in Training," explaining that, if people ring the bell, it may take a moment for you to answer because you are working with your dog.

Always give your dog a choice. Dog trainer Bonnie Hartney's dog, Dixie, has mostly got over her fear of other people, but Hartney still always gives her the choice of whether or not to meet them. "If Dixie doesn't want to meet somebody, she won't go forward and we just don't," she says. "But the majority of people now, she will want to go forward and meet them. And she's pulling us to every neighbor down the street when she sees them, because she's so excited!"

The holidays and other gatherings

The holidays and other social occasions can be challenging times for any dog, as new people come into our home, along with new objects (like trees and decorations) that they are not used to. For fearful dogs, it can be especially difficult. The list below gives some tips on how to help a fearful dog cope at these times.

- Try to keep your dog's routine the same as usual.

- Set up a safe space for your dog—a room with a barrier, so that your guests can't go in.

- Take your dog for a walk or do some fun enrichment activities before the festivities or visits get started.

- Put your dog in the safe space before guests arrive.

- Keep candles, tinsel, Christmas trees, decorations, and other hazards out of the reach of your pet.

- If people are staying for a long time or overnight, plan to get your dog outside for pee breaks without them meeting any guests. For example, ask guests to stay in a room while you take out and bring back the dog .

- Visit your dog in their safe space from time to time, and give them treats. They can tell there are other people in the home.

- Some guests, who will follow your instructions, may help. with training. Do this training at a time when things are quite relaxed for your dog. Open the door, wait for your dog to see the guest, throw lots of nice treats, then shut the door again.

- Take special care to keep a reactive (or bouncy) dog away from small children, seniors, and anyone who is a bit unsteady.

- If there are likely to be fireworks in the neighborhood, make sure you've toileted your dog before the pyrotechnics start.

Fear of people, whether they are familiar or not, is one social fear. Another social fear is that of other dogs. Although these fears are different in certain ways, some of the same ideas apply—from protecting your dog from exposure to the people or dogs they are afraid of to finding ways for that exposure to happen, when appropriate.

BASHFUL BEASTIES: WHEN YOUR DOG FEARS OTHER DOGS

HAVING A DOG who doesn't like other dogs can feel embarrassing. It feels tricky when someone walks past with their beautifully behaved dog and yours is going off at the end of the leash and you're holding on tight to make sure they don't get near the other dog. Reactivity is also an issue where size matters: many people seem happy to let their little dog bark and growl at other dogs and just laugh it off—but if you have a big dog doing this, it feels much more serious. Even little dogs benefit from help with reactivity, however, and ignoring it won't help resolve the issue. Some dogs may seem fine with certain types of dogs but reactive to others.

This situation can sometimes reflect past experiences, such as having been attacked or growled at by a particular type of dog.

The thing to remember is that your dog is not trying to embarrass you: they are upset. And most likely, they are upset because they are frightened of other dogs (though not necessarily—see below). You will need to keep your dog at a safe distance from other dogs. Remember that safe distance is from the dog's perspective—a distance at which they are not reacting and seem to be quite happy and comfortable. For mild reactivity, this distance may be the other side of the street, but for some dogs it may be a football field away. Sometimes a dog may be okay with other dogs who are relaxed and friendly, so long as they don't have to meet, but may be very reactive to other dogs who are stressed. Pay attention to your dog's triggers so that you can help your dog to avoid them.

Safety is important, no matter why your dog is reactive. In those moments when your dog is "going off"—barking and growling and lunging at another dog—you may be at risk of a redirected bite. For example, if your dog is at the window, reacting to another dog going by in the street, and you reach for their collar to move them away from the window, there is a risk that they will turn their head round and bite you. It's because they are very amped-up, and since they can't get at the trigger but are full of excitement, they might lash out at the nearest thing. If your dog has ever bitten another dog, muzzle train them before walking them in public, because you can't risk them biting another dog again.

Walking your dog on a front-clip harness will give you more control and is better than using a collar, because if they pull on the leash, a collar may be too tight on their neck (and may also be aversive, thus making things worse). Most dogs will accept a front-clip harness quite readily, although it's always a good idea to give lots of treats when you're putting new equipment on your dog. Some fearful dogs will need training to be happy wearing it. An alternative is a head halter, which slips around the snout and gives you a close point of contact. It doesn't hurt your dog, but you have to train them to wear it; otherwise, they will try to get it off. Some people find a head halter more useful, especially with big dogs, but it's not a substitute for taking steps to make the environment feel safe by avoiding other dogs while you do the training.

Use training to help your dog feel more comfortable around other dogs

Counterconditioning involves giving your dog yummy treats whenever they spot another dog. If you want to use operant counterconditioning with a dog who is afraid of other dogs, a behavior such as "sit" (off to the side, at a distance from passing dogs), a nose touch to the hand, or "leave it" can be a good choice. Remember to practice the behavior in easy situations first, and be generous with treats. If you need to use management in a pinch, a treat scatter will sometimes distract your dog while another dog goes by, or a treat held to the nose (lickable treats work especially well for this) will distract your dog as you get them past another dog.

What if your dog really likes other dogs? A dog who barks or lunges at other dogs on-leash isn't necessarily afraid of other dogs. Some dogs are friendly to other dogs but frustrated that they can't get to them to greet them or play. Ask yourself what your dog is like when they meet other dogs off-leash. If they are friendly, then perhaps the reactivity is due to frustration. In this case, try to give your dog more opportunities to meet and play with other dogs. If a dog is friendly with other dogs, it's a shame to deprive them of canine companionship. Once you've satisfied your dog's social needs, they will find it easier to pass other dogs on-leash; they won't be desperate to meet other canines, because you'll have given them those opportunities.

Introduce a dog who is afraid to other dogs gradually, using a structured approach. Maybe you have friends with prosocial and relaxed dogs who could meet up with you for playdates in a fenced yard. You, as the dog's guardian, will probably feel happier meeting up with dogs who are known quantities to begin with, and then, as you see your dog enjoying hanging out with other dogs, you can choose whether to try a local dog park, starting at a quiet time. Hire a dog trainer who can help supervise the play and maybe even recruit some volunteers and their dogs to play with your dog.

Everyone has an opinion on dog parks: people love them or hate them. Dog parks have an important place in a world where there are few places for dogs to run freely off-leash. For the dogs who love them, they're a wonderful place to run around, sniff a lot, and play, or simply hang out with other dogs. Being able to run freely is so different from a leash walk and is something dogs do with such joy and abandon. But dog parks are only for dogs who like them. If your dog is not keen on the dog park, don't take them. If you decide to go, approach with your dog's safety and well-being in mind.

Orlando dog trainer Tim Steele of Behavior Matters Academy told me: "I like dog parks because the many dogs who enjoy going get the chance to socialize, stretch, sniff, and engage in normal play behaviors, including chasing, being chased, and wrestling. Obviously, my appreciation for dog parks comes with a ton of caveats: not all dog parks are the same, and not all dogs are good candidates for going to the dog park. And even good dog parks can have a less desirable mix of dogs and humans, so I never barge into dog parks without taking a good look around for a few minutes first. Yes, injuries could happen, and dog fights can happen too.

But on any given morning, there are thousands of dogs playing happily with their friends in parks they visit frequently. I think that's a very good thing."

Steele has successfully used the dog park with many reactive dogs. "Mostly, that means that we stay a safe distance away so the reactive dog can see the other dogs without being upset. With time, and careful application of desensitization and counterconditioning procedures, we can move closer and closer until the dog simply isn't responding to other dogs in dramatic ways and genuinely looks content with their presence (based on their body language and behavior, of course—we can't really know what a dog is thinking, but knowledgeable dog trainers can make some assumptions based on their outward appearance).

"I've had a few cases where I deduced that a reactive dog was acting in 'crazy ways' while out on leashed walks because they were craving the opportunity to get together, greet, hang out, or play with other dogs. Careful introductions at dog parks with known dogs had remarkable effects. Once their desire to be with other dogs was satiated, the undesirable behaviors simply faded away. There was no reason to be frustrated about not being able to meet another dog walking by if they'd just played with ten others at the dog park."

Young puppies shouldn't go to dog parks, because of the risk of disease and the risk of a bad experience. But Steele has also used empty dog parks as a safe space for "sufficiently vaccinated puppies, to give them a safe place to sniff, exercise off-leash, and practice basic training in new situations which are a bit more distracting. Empty and fenced dog parks are a splendid place to practice things like recall and stay, because they offer more space than many yards do. Of course, going to a dog park situated next to a busy street or next to a school with children shouting and running might be too distracting. So careful planning is still required. Later, I add one or two known, safe dogs to the mix, and then work our way up to more and more dogs once the puppy has had sufficient padding with great experiences. It's easy to instill fear in dogs, especially puppies. So this needs to be done with real caution. I encourage people to go with their qualified trainer the first couple of times, instead of going alone."

He adds: "There's little that's more heartwarming to me than a confident young dog engaging happily with other dogs doing normal doggie things."

It helps if everyone knows good dog-park etiquette. Most have a requirement that your dog is up-to-date on vaccinations and wears a flat collar with tags to show their dog license and identification. Before you go, teach your dog to come when called so that you can get them back if needed or when you want to leave. Take a good look at the park as you approach, and if there are too many dogs in the park, too many dogs at the entrance, or anything else you're not happy about, wait before going in. If there's a puppy and your dog doesn't like puppies, don't go in (or leave if a puppy arrives). Once in the park, take your dog's leash off right away; mixing on- and off-leash dogs can make the leashed dog feel nervous, as the other dogs have freedom to move but they don't. Keep an eye on your dog and stay close to them while you're there, so that you can intervene if necessary; keep your phone in your pocket. And, of course, clean up after your dog.

"Call dogs away from the gate where dogs are coming in," says Steele. "If there are going to be fights in a dog park, I notice that they often happen when dogs are rushed by a big group as they first enter the park. Allowing dogs to come in and look around a bit seems to lower the likelihood of problems."

But fights at dog parks seem to be extremely rare.

Steele has some other tips too. "Please don't bring your lunch to eat inside the dog park and then expect that dogs will leave you and your food alone. Not only are you likely to get jumped on and harassed, some dogs may have problems with resource guarding, and the presence of your meal could trigger arguments with other dogs or even with you. On the other hand, I never enter a dog park without dog treats, and I don't have problems—though I sometimes do get jumped on and followed around a bit. So be careful if you decide to carry treats."

Pay close attention to your dog's body language, vocalizations, likes, and dislikes

It's easy to mistake dog play for a fight if you don't know what to look for; after all, physical contact, bared teeth, and growling can happen in both play and fighting, since dogs in play "borrow" action patterns from other activities. But play looks different. For one thing, you'll see a beautiful sign called the play bow, with the front legs down to the ground, on the elbows, and the rear end up in the air. Although scientists aren't a hundred percent certain whether this signal aims to start play or to continue it (or perhaps both), or to say "I'm just playing," it's a play signal that's found in other canids too, like coyotes and wolves.[2] Other signs to look for include play face (a lovely open-mouthed, happy look), a bounciness in the step, and role reversals—in other words, not just one dog always chasing another, but the two switching roles and maybe switching activities from chase to wrestling and so on. Dr. Carolyn Walsh has researched dog parks, and says "these sorts of reciprocal behaviors are indicators that both dogs are invested in continuing the interaction, so it is probably rewarding to them, and is probably going well."

Play growls can sound a little different than a growl that means "Back off"; some studies (but not all) find a higher pitch. A play growl also seems to be shorter than a growl in an aggressive context.[3] Dogs can interpret these growls, and they respond differently when played recordings of "play" versus "guarding" growls.[4] Growls also give information about body size—and it turns out that a play growl makes it seem like the dog is larger than they really are, which is thought to be another play signal.[5]

Heidi and Cody playing. *JEAN BALLARD*

Bodger playing with a stick. *BAD MONKEY PHOTOGRAPHY*

Walsh found that some dogs seem to really like dog parks and others don't so much. "In our dog park data," she told me, "age is certainly a factor, with younger dogs being more 'social' and willing to engage in certain types of play with other dogs, while older dogs appear less interested in this. In my opinion, these opportunities for young dogs, in particular, are important for the development of good social behaviors; however, care needs to be taken that young dogs are not getting negative experiences, which can probably create fear or reactivity in some dogs (but not all)."

And dogs seem to make friends. "In some of our data, we see dogs preferentially playing with some dogs in the dog park. One factor related to this seems to be familiarity, i.e., dogs that regularly go to the park and get to 'know' each other. These inter- actions seem to be the least stressful for dogs, based on behaviors and some of our salivary hormone assessments. So we could extrapolate that the opportunity to interact with a few known 'friends' with whom interactions are positive, versus many unfa- miliar dogs, might be one of the best ways to socialize dogs with other dogs. This can happen in some dog parks, but it can happen on walks and in other places."

Ultimately, it's important to pay close attention to your dog and to what they like and don't like. If you're worried about play tipping over into fighting, Dr. Walsh says, it's important to look for the more "subtle," early signs of something going amiss. "Warning signs that things are not going well would be if the inter- action is mostly one-sided (i.e., one dog is 'pestering' the other, with the other trying to disengage), and if either dog shows signs of stress—particularly changes in posture. We found that dogs who 'hunched' their backs, which can be associated with tucking their tail, had higher levels of stress hormones in the dog park, so they're probably not having a good time there.

"In a more global sense, I'd encourage guardians to see if their dog seems okay to them after a few minutes of the interaction . . . and if they don't, then reconsider letting the interaction continue, or maybe change it in some way (e.g., by leaving the dog park or, if it is a one-on-one interaction with a friend's dog, taking the dogs for a walk together instead of letting them romp together off-leash)."

Fear of other dogs and of other people are both social fears. That means there are some aspects of the training that are the same.

A COMMON APPROACH: AVOIDING TRIGGERS AND USING STEP-BY-STEP TRAINING

A GENERAL RULE for fearful dogs is to avoid their triggers as much as possible. As part of fulfilling your responsibility to keep them safe, you need to make sure they keep their distance from other people or other dogs (whichever they are afraid of). Pay attention to your dog's body language so that you know if they are under threshold (happy and relaxed) or over it. Some dogs can go from one to the other very quickly, but you want to stay under threshold at all times. That applies whether you decide to work with an approach based on desensitization and counterconditioning or on operant conditioning. For desensitization and counterconditioning, consider how to structure your training in easy steps that your dog will be able to manage. For operant counterconditioning, you'll still want to break your training into manageable steps to get the side effect of a positive CER.

When developing your training plan, consider the three Ds: distance, duration, and distractions. *Distance* is the most obvious way to break your training down into manageable steps, as it's generally easier for your dog if scary things are farther away. As your dog becomes more confident around new people and other dogs, you gradually move closer. You can also play with *duration*, as shorter durations around the scary thing are probably easier for your dog to manage (but remember the open bar–closed bar technique described in Chapter 5). Again, as your dog becomes more confident, you stay around the new people or other dogs for longer. Remember that it makes a difference what the other dog or person is doing. If they are engrossed in something else and paying no attention to your dog, that's easier and less scary for your dog. If they are looking at your dog and approaching, that's harder and much scarier. Bear these things in mind when working with your dog. (A dog trainer will take all of this into account for you.) The other D of dog training is *distractions*. You want fewer distractions when training, in part because you don't want a compound stimulus, but also because you don't want other scary things around. The presence of many scary things is known as trigger stacking, and it makes things harder for your dog.

"One thing I always counsel expecting parents and families with babies about is to learn their dog's subtle body language. It's important for a safe home environment that they understand what their dog looks like when completely relaxed and happy, and also know what their dog looks like when feeling anxious or fearful. Understanding their dog's comfort levels can ease a lot of parental anxiety around integrating their dog and baby.

For instance, baby equipment—which typically moves and makes noise—may be frightening for an otherwise happy-go-lucky dog. We introduce the family dog to baby gear slowly, always pairing the items with fabulous treats, starting with a level of comfort the dog can handle.

Similarly, a dog who seemed to ignore an infant may start to show subtle signs of fear or discomfort as the baby becomes more vocal and mobile. Parents, grandparents, and extended family members with dogs need to know their own dog's subtle body language, which can include yawns, lip licks, flattened or twitching ears, sudden grooming, small body shifts, and whale eyes (showing the whites). That way, they can develop a strategy to keep the child safe and dog feeling safe as well."

—**JANICE ZAZINSKI, CTC, CSAT, owner-operator and licensed Family Paws parent educator at Janice Z Dog Training**

9

THUMPS, BUMPS, AND BANGS:
WHEN YOUR DOG FEARS LOUD NOISES

. . . .

SOME YEARS AGO, when we still had both of our previous dogs, Ghost and Bodger, we went for a walk on a sunny afternoon. We ambled at dog pace, letting them sniff here and there and, in Ghost's case, listen for mice in the long, dry grass, cocking his head from side to side. We were partway up the hill on our way home when we heard a distant rumble of thunder. It was still bright sunshine, and the storm was way off on the other side of the valley. Even so, we decided to pick up the pace. Just two minutes later, big drops of rain began to fall, slowly at first, but quickly becoming heavy. The storm had jumped many kilometers all at once. We were hurrying now—not easy, as Ghost's health issues meant he was slow. I was already soaked to the skin when I felt the hairs on the back of my neck prickle and stand up. Just as we approached the top of the hill, there was a blinding flash of light and simultaneously one of the loudest noises I've ever heard.

Time seemed to slow right down. I was aware of light in the sky, approaching fast, and then a finger of blue stretched out to touch the transformer at the top of the hydro pole just meters away. In front of me, Bodger levitated several feet in the air and then landed on the road again. His coat was dripping, and he was pulling hard on the leash, desperate to get home. Behind me, my husband was doing what you're supposed to do when you sense that a storm is so close—get down to the ground. Ghost was standing still, staring at me. Even he looked startled.

"We have to get home," I said.

And then we set off, not at a full run, because Ghost couldn't manage it, but moving as fast as we could towards home. The road was running with water. I held on to Bodger's leash for dear life because I didn't want him to escape in the middle of a storm. Holding Bodger back, splashing through what was now a stream, encouraging Ghost to move faster, I was afraid of another bolt of lightning. The last two hundred meters felt like ten kilometers. Finally, we were home—safe, scared, and sodden.

The next few times I left the house on foot, it felt like the sky could no longer be trusted and might smite me at any moment. Bodger seemed to feel the same, only worse. Over the next few days, he was reluctant to go outside in the dark. It took patience and many, many pieces of deli meats to get him to go out and pee at night. For weeks after, if it was even slightly cloudy, he was not interested in a walk. I can't say I blame him. Being almost hit by lightning was one of the most terrifying moments of my life.

RECOGNIZING A FEAR OF LOUD NOISES

FEAR OF LOUD NOISES is the most common fear in pet dogs, affecting between a quarter and half of dogs, depending on the study.[1] The sounds of thunder, fireworks, and gunshots are upsetting for many dogs, but any loud sound—even routine domestic noises like the vacuum cleaner—can upset some dogs. In one study, 25 percent of dog guardians said their dog was afraid of loud noises. But in follow-up interviews with a subset of the participants, it turned out that half of the dogs were afraid of loud noises. The most common responses to noises were trembling or shaking (43%), barking (38%), and seeking out people (35%). Perhaps surprisingly, some people who said their dogs trembled when there were fireworks, or sought out people in response to a sudden noise, nonetheless said their dog was not afraid of loud noises. This suggests that some people don't recognize the signs of their dog's fear, which is a problem because it means they don't do anything about it. In fact, less than a third of dog guardians had sought advice for their dog's fears. Unfortunately, fear of loud noises does not go away on its own.

A study of over 13,700 pet dogs in Finland puts the prevalence of sound sensitivities at 32 percent, and fear of fireworks in particular at 26 percent.[2] The scientists suggest that genetics are one factor, and that breeders could help by not breeding from animals with known fears and anxieties. At the same time, they stress the importance of socialization. Positive early experiences can go a long way towards helping dogs cope with loud noises. This is also the finding of a study that has similar ballpark figures of 20.5 percent of dogs afraid of fireworks and 30.9 percent afraid of storms.[3] Dogs who had been to a dog training class were less likely to be afraid of fireworks. However, it's not known if this is because people who take their dog to training class are more likely to be clued up on dog behavior, or if the classes included prevention exercises. Similarly, another study found that dogs who had been to puppy class were less likely to be afraid of noises; however, it also found that gradual exposure to sounds was one of the things least likely to be included in the puppy class curriculum.[4]

Taken together, these studies show that if your dog is afraid of loud noises, you are definitely not alone. A number of approaches can help. The sooner these techniques are implemented, the easier it will be to make a difference, as every time the dog is subjected to the experience can make things worse. If your dog has spent many years cowering every time they hear fireworks, expect it to take some time to resolve the issue. When a fear of loud noises develops in an older dog, see your vet to rule out any medical issues (see Chapter 4).

One study looked for signs that might distinguish a dog simply being afraid of loud noises, from a dog being afraid of loud noises because they were in pain.[5] Later onset of the fear was one sign, as dogs in pain were typically four years older than the fearful dogs without pain. Another sign was that the fear quickly generalized, so that, for example, the dog also became afraid of the situation in which the loud noises had occurred, no longer wanted to go out in the car, or became afraid of other dogs. The dogs in the study were examined for musculoskeletal issues such as hip dysplasia. When the dog was in pain, they were prescribed painkillers, and the dog's guardian was given advice on how to manage the dog to avoid making the pain worse. An individual behavior-modification plan was given for all dogs, and all improved—with the exception of one dog deemed to be in pain whose owner declined pain meds.

Another reason to see your vet about fear of loud noises is that in many cases psychoactive medication can help. Your vet may prescribe long-term medication. Or, if an event known to include fireworks is approaching—a national holiday like the Fourth of July, Halloween, or Bonfire Night (Guy Fawkes)—they may pre-scribe short-term medication to help your dog get through (see Chapter 7). I asked Dr. Rachel Szumel, a small-animal veterinarian in South Lake Tahoe, California, when to consider seeing your vet about medications if your dog is afraid of loud noises.

"Now. Yesterday. Right away," she said. "Because we know that noise phobias are notoriously difficult to treat with behavioral modification alone. So, if they're showing any signs of fear, you should be talking to your veterinarian about medications that help lower their sensitivity to noise so that you can start the behavioral modification part of things. If the dog is over threshold, no amount of chicken is going to make them love thunderstorms. But if they are on [a medication like] Xanax, that chicken actually does make those thunderstorms a little bit better. You can get a lot further with medications onboard."

Dr. Szumel also stressed that there can be times when pain is a contributing factor in fear, and that's another reason to see your veterinarian.

TRAINING DOGS NOT TO FEAR NOISES

IT WAS A HOT AND HUMID EVENING after another sunny day. Bodger and I set out for a short walk. But we only got halfway up the drive when we heard two loud bangs from a neighbor's property. It sounded like bear bangers set off to make a black bear go away. But it didn't matter what it was. Bodger immediately turned to run home, and I, as the one holding the leash, had no choice but to be dragged along by him. He was a big, strong dog, and so scared that nothing would stop him. I would have liked to offer him a treat, but it wasn't an option until we got back in the house. Then I gave him some of his favorite treats and put his leash back in the drawer, hoping to try the walk again in half an hour or so.

The approach I was using was counterconditioning: teaching Bodger to associate the loud bang with something great (see Chapter 5). I carried his favorite sausage treats in my bait bag and reserved them for when there was a bang. Research on what helps dogs with fear of loud noises shows how important it is to do something, rather than to wait and see, because doing nothing is associated with the problem getting worse.[6] This research also shows that the approach I was taking with Bodger—known as ad-hoc counterconditioning, because I was responding to sounds as they happened to occur, rather than arranging for them to happen—can be very successful. In fact, 70.8 percent of people who used it said that it helped. This is good to know, because, traditionally, approaches to fear of loud noises have focused on desensitization, a gradual exposure training. Desensitization works too, but it relies on a controlled environment. In real life, it's easy to suddenly find yourself in a situation where loud noises are unexpected and unpredictable. In those situations, if you don't do counterconditioning, you are undermining the desensitization process you had so carefully planned.

According to this research, relaxation training and preventive exercises also help dogs with sound sensitivity. Overall, this study showed that both puppies and adult dogs benefited from some kind of training. And given that dogs who were or were not being trained were equally likely to be on medication for their fear of noises, the research suggests that training, not just medication, does benefit dogs.

In fact, less than half of the people in the study (43%) had done any training to either prevent or resolve their dog's fear of loud noises. But amongst people whose dogs were afraid of fireworks, 70 percent had sought help, commonly from a trainer, veterinarian, the internet, or a book. And most people said their dog recovered from the fright within half an hour or an hour, or even right away, although some dogs took several days.

If you want to do desensitization, be sure to set it up very carefully. There are plenty of apps, CDs, and YouTube videos designed to help with this kind of training. Expect it to work better for things like fireworks and the sound of a car backfiring than for thunder, which is accompanied by atmospheric changes that you can't re-create. Listen to the sounds on a headset first (so your dog can't hear them), so you know what to expect. Set the volume super, super low. The aim is to have the volume so low that your dog barely even notices it—a volume much lower than you'd expect. As well, you should be prepared to do counterconditioning to those super quiet noises. This means setting up your treats well in advance. Once you start to play the sound, you can run to the fridge or the dog's cookie jar to get the treats. The open bar–closed bar technique is great here: once the noises start happening, so do the treats, but once the noises stop, treats stop too.

While it may be tempting to do this training at the same time each day—say, 5 p.m., when you happen to be around and preparing dinner—it works better if it happens at random times. You don't want to associate a specific time of day with the noises. You want to make it really clear that the (now very quiet) noises predict the treats, and nothing else predicts the treats. Over time, you can very gradually increase the volume of the recording.

But unfortunately, while training helps, many people make mistakes. I've been guilty of these training mistakes too. If you notice even the slightest sign of stress from your dog while attempting desensitization, stop the noises right away. And still offer food to the dog, because even if the desensitization part went wrong, you still want to get the counterconditioning part right. It's very common for people to play the sounds too loud and accidentally terrify their dog.

A common mistake with counterconditioning is to get the order of events wrong (see Chapter 5). If you know that sounds are going to happen and you reach for your treat before they occur, your training is not going to work the way you intend it to. This situation is called "backwards conditioning," and dog trainer Kate LaSala of Rescued by Training sees it often with her clients.

"Instead of teaching that fireworks predict chicken, we're getting chicken predicts fireworks, because you're doing it backwards," she says. Another time she sees this happen is when people are using a pressure wrap, such as the ThunderShirt, with their dog, to help calm them by applying gentle, constant pressure. "As humans, we have the benefit of knowing it's the Fourth of July or it's New Year's Eve. I know at 10 o'clock people are going to start shooting off fireworks. So we anticipate that this is going to happen and we prepare and say, 'Oh, I'd better put the ThunderShirt on the dog because I know they're about to shoot off fireworks.' That can actually backfire, because then the ThunderShirt becomes a tip-off to the dog that fireworks are about to happen, and the shirt itself can become panic-inducing for the dog."

Like Dr. Szumel, LaSala stresses the importance of seeing a vet in case your dog is in pain, or in case medication is recommended. One of the times when clients especially struggle, she says, is when the dog is too anxious to take food. "If you have a dog who's really over threshold and they just are so anxious and over threshold that they won't even consider taking food, it's really difficult to make progress in training, because they've got bigger fish to fry. They're just so panicked. The world is exploding around them, and the last thing they want to think about is your chicken and cheese. So getting that anxiety down to a manageable level where they don't think the world is ending around them is not just the most humane thing to do, it's the best thing to do for training."

One thing is certain: as with so many other fears and anxieties, seeking help from a professional is a sensible idea.

COPING IN THE SHORT TERM

IN SOME SUMMERS, many bears ambled through the neighborhood where we live, and therefore many bear bangers were set off to frighten them away. This wasn't good for Bodger's nerves, but it did provide lots of training opportunities. It became a recurring theme on sultry summer nights. Bodger and I would set out on a walk. Sometimes we would get halfway down the street, sometimes we would not even leave the driveway. Then we'd hear a loud bang. Bodger would turn to run and I'd follow, offering treats that he would not eat till we got safely indoors. But there was progress, of sorts; he was not running quite so fast, and I no longer felt like he was going to pull me over. It was encouraging, and showed the training was working even though it was only ad-hoc, whenever loud noises occurred.

After a while, something interesting happened. He would hear the bang, I would grab some treats from my bait bag, and he would eat them hurriedly. Then we'd run home.

Training takes time, maybe months or longer. What I was doing in those moments was training, along with giving Bodger a choice— the choice to run home, where he felt safer. So what can you do if there isn't time, and you know that a bout of fireworks is just hours or days away—say, that the Fourth of July or Bonfire Night is coming up fast, or that there's a thunderstorm in the weather forecast? One thing is to make sure you know that your dog can't escape. It's not unusual for dogs left in the yard to be so terrified of thunder or fireworks that they find a way out and run away in a complete panic (even though they've never escaped before). So keep them safe by keeping them indoors. And, as always, make sure your dog has both a microchip (that can't be removed) and a collar tag, so that if they do get loose and are found, the finder can identify your dog and call you directly. Also plan ahead by taking your dog out to toilet well ahead of the start of any loud noises.

Make sure your dog has somewhere safe to hide during the noisy event. In a thunderstorm, that's not in the bathroom next to a pipe, even though that may be where they would like to pick because it's the smallest space. Remember that lightning can transmit through the ground, and that if it strikes the house, the electrical current can travel along the plumbing. It's the same reason that you shouldn't take a shower during a thunderstorm. The hiding place should be in a room with the drapes closed to block out the light from fireworks or lightning, or in a basement, which will block some of the noise too. If your dog happens to be crate-trained, their crate might make a good safe space, and you can use blankets to block out the light.

Masking the sound is another good idea, but it can be hard to do a good job of this. Simply turning the TV on does not work so well, according to dog writer Eileen Anderson, who also happens to have a background in acoustics.[7] She recommends using something with a low frequency for acoustic masking, because those low frequencies will help drown out the low rumbles. She says the best options are to use a fan or to play random noise (especially something called brown noise) through your speakers; running the dishwasher or washing machine, or putting a pair of sneakers in the dryer, are other good options. The masking noise needs to have some low frequencies to do the best job. At other times—for example, when you want to mask the sound of workers in your house—you can use an audiobook. But it's important to know that the masking sound isn't something your dog is afraid of, so pick something they know and like. In other words, only play loud rock music if you know already that your dog is okay with it!

And remember that it's fine to comfort your dog if that's what they'd like. Some dogs will be too terrified to take food or to want comfort, but if they will take treats, that's great, and if they seem to want to be petted, then you should pet them.

ON SOME OF THE LAST summer evenings before Bodger was taken ill, we made real progress with his fear of loud noises. When we heard a bear banger, he'd turn as if to head home, then stop and look at me expectantly. "I'll have my treats, please," he was saying. And so I gave him some of his favorite sausage treats. Then we didn't even have to run home. We could walk, slowly. Sometimes he would even change his mind and we could turn and head back out again. He trusted me that he had the choice to go home, and he was no longer so terrified of the loud bangs. We'd gone from what felt like a near-death experience with thunder to seeing bear bangers as a signal for a snack. Counterconditioning may take time, but it works.

"For us, with dogs, it's often love at first sight. But not all dogs immediately love us back. Fearful dogs need patience, time, and empathy as they encounter new things and people in the world.

I wish that people would prioritize relationship-building over training. This means ensuring your dog feels safe. Put this need over your needs to cuddle, walk, or show the dog off to your friends. Help the dog create positive associations with you. These associations are more important than learning to sit or fetch. Show the dog that your presence predicts something wonderful: lots of treats, a game or toy, anything you are sure the dog loves. Be lavish with treats and toys and fun. Be patient as the dog learns to associate you with good stuff, and eventually is happy to see you coming. Use this time to reflect on your dog's needs and commit to meeting those needs. A great relationship with you is your dog's gateway to the rest of the world."

—ELISSA ORLANDO, MPA, CTC, dog trainer at Dog Educated

NEEDLES AND THERMOMETERS:

WHEN YOUR DOG FEARS THE VET

....

MY TABBY CAT, Harley, had an experience that sometimes applies to dogs too. He is 15 years old, and he is blind and has diabetes, high blood pressure, and heart failure (all controlled with medication). When he goes to the vet, a lot of tests are done to check up on these different conditions. Our vet and his team are incredible, and they are very kind to Harley. But even though he is a tolerant, handleable cat who is happy about his twice-daily insulin injections and heart pills, he doesn't like all the stuff that happens at the vet. One time, he was so stressed that the vet techs called off the tests because they decided it wasn't fair on him. I'm grateful to them for making that call. We made an appointment for another time and gave him some meds the night before and morning of. The medication makes the visit much easier for Harley, and the vet is able to do the tests that are needed.

How Harley felt about those tests is an experience that many dogs have too. Even if tests aren't involved, simply being in a vet's office, with new people and different smells and slippery floors, is enough to make many dogs feel stressed. Luckily, these days there's a lot we can do.

BEING TOUCHED, AND OTHER THINGS DOGS FEAR AT THE VET

SHOWING SIGNS OF FEAR, anxiety, and stress at the vet is very common, even if people don't always recognize the signs. In the past, if a dog was shut down and largely immobile at the veterinarian, it was seen as a good thing. These days, we recognize shutting down as fear-related stress and we know that it's important to prioritize dogs' emotional health, as well as their physical health. Fears that may manifest at the vet include:

- social fears of unknown people (and of other pets in the waiting room)

- physical fears, such as sensitivity to being touched, especially on the elbow, tummy, and chest[1]

- fear of the exam table and other objects (the clinic itself seems to be stressful, given that dogs are more likely to eat a treat outside than inside a vet clinic)[2]

- for some dogs, fear of being separated from their guardian when they are taken to the back of the clinic for tests

If a dog is fearful or anxious at the vet, their guardian may be less likely to take them there in future. In turn, the dog isn't getting veterinary care in a timely fashion. As well, if a dog is fearful at the vet, they are more likely to be aggressive, so the risk of a bite is increased for vet staff or the guardian. More than half of dogs are fearful to some degree at the vet, so it's important to take fear of the vet seriously.[3]

The risk factors for a dog to show signs of fear, anxiety, and stress while at the vet include the dog's breed group and size, where the dog came from, their previous experiences at the vet, and the guardian's choice of training method.[4] Toy breeds, hounds, and mixed breeds are more likely to be fearful at the vet. Dogs obtained from a pet store or a friend are most likely to be fearful, while those obtained from breeders are least likely. It's worth noting that forcing dogs to face something they are afraid of at the vet (flooding) is associated with increased aggression. One survey found that dog guardians who noticed their dog's behavior change following an experience at the vet were more likely to say that their dog had found the experience stressful.[5] This finding suggests that if you notice a change in your dog, it's a good idea to do something about it.

Your choice of veterinary practice and any cooperative care or husbandry training that you do can make a difference to your dog's vet visits.

CHOOSING THE RIGHT VETERINARIAN FOR YOU AND YOUR DOG

WORKING WITH A VETERINARIAN that you and your dog trust can make a big difference to your visit. If you already have a vet that you love, that's great. (Make sure you let them know, because it's hard work being a vet!) If you're looking for a new vet, several certifications tell you the vet works hard to keep stress to a minimum for their patients.

Preventing and alleviating stress, anxiety, and fear at the vet is important for your dog's health, and for the safety of everyone working with them. I recommend choosing a vet who follows low-stress practices like the ones below.

Fear Free

The biggest certification program is Fear Free. The Fear Free movement was started by Dr. Marty Becker in 2016, after he heard a talk by Dr. Karen Overall about the effects of fear. He realized that the way vets were working with pets caused fear, anxiety, and stress that was bad for their emotional well-being. Dr. Becker's daughter Mikkel Becker is the lead animal trainer at Fear Free. She told me: "Fear Free is about protecting both the emotional well-being and the physical well-being of the pets. In the past, a lot of care was about providing physical care, but sometimes it could come at the expense of the emotional well-being. When we were mainly focused on providing physical care, and sometimes ignoring or even causing detrimental impact to a pet's emotional well-being, there were some really big problems. Not only was that care more difficult and dangerous to do in that moment, but it actually increased the difficulty of doing it long-term. So the next time the pet would come back to the vet, they had a negative experience.

"What happens is the next time, and the next time after that, the pet gets harder and harder to handle, because a lot of times they go out of that frozen 'fear' mode and progress into 'fight' mode, because that's really the only way to get that care to stop."

Fear Free aims to prevent the stress that causes pets to get to that level of fear and aggression. "For a lot of pets, it's really a humane issue and a welfare issue," Becker says. "Why would we put this pet through something that's so distressing when we have so many options to help them feel more comfortable and relaxed?"

The Fear Free movement was the start of a big change in veterinary medicine. Becker explains that the Fear Free approach "teaches pets to voluntarily cooperate in their care and to feel happy and relaxed throughout." And when the pet feels more comfortable, the guardian will also find the vet visit less stressful.

Now, not only can individual veterinarians become Fear Free Certified, but so can veterinary practices, and there are courses for Fear Free vet techs, trainers, groomers, petsitters, and people who work in pet boarding and day care. Over ninety-five thousand people have taken the Fear Free Certified Professional course, so it's likely there will be someone near you. You can find a Fear Free Certified vet or practice via the Fear Free website.

Low Stress Handling

Low Stress Handling is another excellent course. This course is based on a set of ten principles originally developed by the late Dr. Sophia Yin, and teaches how to read body language, handling techniques, and desensitization and counterconditioning. It starts with creating a comfortable environment and aims to minimize restraint and support your pet so that they feel safe. The courses and certification are available for veterinary professionals, shelter workers, pet professionals, students, and pet guardians. You can find a directory of Low Stress Handling Certified facilities and pet professionals on the CattleDog Publishing website.

Other options

The Karen Pryor Academy has a course on Better Veterinary Visits that was designed with Fear Free. It's suitable for veterinarians, vet techs, trainers, and pet guardians, and you don't need to have done any training before. And Dr. Sally Foote is a veterinarian who runs training on animal behavior for vet staff, pet professionals, and dog guardians. Her training on low-stress veterinary care can be done in person or online. Finally, dog trainer Laura Monaco Torelli has an online course, Ready . . . Set . . . for Groomer and Vet, which is available via the dog-ibox website. This course is suitable for anyone who works at a vet clinic, and also for trainers and pet guardians.

PREPARE FOR YOUR VISIT

ONCE YOU HAVE CHOSEN the right vet, think about how to make the experience of going to the clinic easier and less stressful for your dog. Remember that they may need to go in a carrier or crate, travel by car, and enter a space with unfamiliar people and other dogs. The more you can do to make those positive experiences, the less anxious your dog will be. And if your dog is already fearful of these experiences, you may need to go step-by-step to prepare them. If they've had a negative experience before, even something as seemingly unrelated as the car turning a certain way that is associated with going to the vet can make your dog start to tremble. (You'll recognize this predictive relationship as classical conditioning.) And those past experiences affect how the pet will behave at the vet in future.

If your dog is afraid at the vet, start by planning a happy visit (aka a victory visit) so they can familiarize themselves with the people and the place in a relaxed and positive way. Arrange a time with the clinic when you and your dog can visit. Let the dog explore the waiting room and the exam room and meet the vet and other people who work there. Go at your dog's pace, take some of their favorite treats, and be generous with how many you give. The idea is that only pleasant things will happen to your dog, to help them learn that the vet is a good place to be.

Book appointments at a quiet time of day—often a weekday morning—as it will be easier for your dog if the clinic is not busy.

You can also ask the receptionist if it is okay to wait in the car with your dog until it is time for them to go straight into the exam room. This means that they don't have to cope with the waiting room and the other people and animals who are there.

Take treats to the appointment and ask your vet if it is okay to give them. There may be times when it's not possible—for example, because of tests that need to be done—but most of the time it will be okay. If your dog is uncomfortable on the exam table, see if the vet can examine them where they are comfortable—for example, in a lap, on a couch, or on a nonslip mat. Sometimes your dog may need to wear a muzzle to keep everyone safe, and if you've done muzzle training at home, that will make it easier for your dog. These days, vets sometimes decide that if your dog is getting stressed, they will either skip nonessential parts of the visit or ask you to come back another time (as happened with Harley). They may also prescribe a short-acting medication to give before the next visit to make it easier for the exam to be done.

People sometimes tell me they feel embarrassed about being asked to give their pet an anti-anxiety medication or to come back another time. But looking after your pet's emotional well-being is something to be proud of. Trust your vet and their team to make the best decision for your pet. If you've not come across this kind of care before, it can be a surprise, but taking pets' emotional health into account makes a big difference to them.

A strong bond between you and your dog can help them feel more secure at the vet too. Given that people are attachment figures for their dogs, you would expect that the dog guardian's presence during the vet exam would be helpful and reduce the dog's stress level. One study that gave dogs a mock vet exam found that dogs showed fewer signs of fear when their guardian was present and able to pet and/or speak to them, compared with when the guardian stood at a small distance and ignored them.[6]

In another study, if people said they felt emotionally close to their dog, their dog was more likely to take a treat at the vet clinic and to play either inside or outside.[7] Moreover, if, in the veterinarian's opinion, the guardian had a close relationship with the dog or was less worried about the costs of care, the dog was less likely to be stressed. Another study randomly assigned dogs to a seven-minute mock vet exam either with or without the guardian present.[8] The dogs displayed fewer signs of fear when the guardian was there, as shown by them making less noise, having a lower armpit temperature, and, in female dogs, having a lower heart rate. These findings suggest that it is better for dogs if the guardian is present during a routine exam. If your pet needs tests, ask your vet if you can stay with your dog, but understand that it's up to your vet. Sometimes having a guardian present is just not possible—for example, for safety reasons.

If you're having trouble getting your dog to cooperate at the vet, consider some training. These days, husbandry training, also known as cooperative care, is becoming a thing.

HUSBANDRY TRAINING

IF YOU HAVE A DOG who doesn't like to be handled, training can help. If you think your dog may bite or be difficult to train, hire someone to help. If you don't think that's a risk and want to try on your own, use lots of good treats and follow a plan. In addition to the courses mentioned above (several of which are open to pet guardians), a full set of training plans is available from the Husbandry Project at the Academy for Dog Trainers, which you can find on their website. In addition to basic plans that will help with ordinary vet visits, the plans include training for procedures such as blood draws and X-rays. These plans have been thoroughly tested on a range of dogs with input from veterinarians, so they are easy to work through and suitable for all dogs. If you want to muzzle train your dog, you'll find a great plan here.

Kristi Benson, staff member at the Academy, led the project through its development, and she told me about the range of plans available. "The stationing behaviors are mostly having the dogs in a loose stand, and then also having the dogs lie fully on their side in lateral recumbency. And there is also a sit for procedures. Then we have things like getting the dog to be comfortable and enjoy veterinary contexts and staff, enjoy veterinary implements. So we have the foundation plans, which are essentially stays, and then we have the emotional component, and the procedures. Once the dog is comfortable, we get them into position in one of the stays, and then get them comfortable having a vaccination or a range-of-motion exam. At the end, the dog is comfortable going to the vet."

She explained that most of these training plans are designed to be done at home, and some can be done on walks, but some are done at the vet's office. You would need your vet's permission to do this training at the clinic, but it is the best way to get the dog comfortable with those procedures at the vet.

Ruckus does a trick at the vet to help her feel more comfortable. *ERICA BECKWITH*

Dixie takes part in a training session at the vet. *BONNIE HARTNEY*

"Veterinary visits can be very scary for dogs and very stressful for us too. We can help to make vet visits better for all of us. Find out if there are any Fear Free or Low Stress Handling veterinary practices in your area. Call and speak to the staff about your dogs' particular needs to make sure you're a good fit. Ask if you can bring your dog to the clinic for happy visits, to get a lot of yummy snacks and become comfortable in that environment.

If your dog is one of many who feel more comfortable with their guardians present, request to stay with your dog throughout the visit, even during procedures like blood draws. Ask if you can wait in the car until an exam room is ready for your dog, so you can skip the stressful waiting area and head straight to the exam room. Work with your veterinarian to prioritize the procedures for that visit, skipping any that can wait if your dog is stressed. Discuss with your veterinarian whether pre-visit pharmaceuticals might be beneficial. Teach your dog to be comfortable with veterinary procedures ahead of time. You know your dog better than anyone, so observe your dog's body language closely, and communicate with your veterinary team about your dog's needs and comfort level."

—**JESSICA RING**, CTC, **My Fantastic Friend**

"DON'T LEAVE ME!": WHEN YOUR DOG IS AFRAID OF BEING ALONE

....

RECENTLY, I CAME HOME after spending the night away for the first time since we got Pepper. As I opened the door, I was expecting Pepper to greet me even more exuberantly than usual. Instead, my tabby cat, Harley, was right there, apparently waiting to see if he could sneak out of the house. There was no sign of Pepper. I called him, but nothing happened. And then I saw that the door we close to separate the dog and cats when we're out was ajar—opened, no doubt, by Harley, who is an expert door opener. I went to look for Pepper on the other side of the house, but he was not near the cat food as I thought he'd be. A little sound of frustration drew me to the top of the basement stairs, and there, at the bottom, was Pepper, apparently stuck. After some encouragement from me, he ran up the stairs—and finally I got my greeting, as Pepper wiggled his tail and leaped excitedly in the air.

No hard-and-fast rule exists for how long a dog can be left home alone. That time will vary depending on the dog, but, in general, four hours is a good estimate. Some dogs cannot be left alone at all without being very upset, which is a serious welfare issue for them and a very difficult situation for their guardians. Some dogs will bark or cry incessantly, pee or poop, destroy furniture or doors, and show other signs of being very upset. Separation-related issues are a common problem in pet dogs, with estimates ranging from 5 percent to 55 percent.[1] The fact that these issues occur while the dog's guardian is out makes it difficult to know for sure.

Because separation-related behaviors only occur when no one is at home, you may be unaware that your dog is distressed until a neighbor comments about excessive barking or whining. If you want to check what your dog is like while you're out, set up a camera to see what they do when you leave. Hopefully, they will be relaxed, but if you see behavioral signs that they are distressed, show your vet the video and discuss it with them. Only a veterinarian can diagnose separation anxiety, as it is a medical diagnosis.

BOREDOM OR FEAR: IS IT REALLY A SEPARATION-RELATED ISSUE?

TO BE CONSIDERED a separation-related behavior, other issues must be ruled out. For example:

- If the dog is peeing or pooping in the house while you're out, they may simply not be fully house-trained. In that case, you need to house-train them.

- If the dog is playing with your shoes, chewing things, or digging at the carpet, they may be bored or frustrated. Dogs
  that are not getting much exercise and enrichment and don't
  have anything to do all day will find ways to keep themselves
  occupied. The solution is more physical exercise and activities
  to keep their brain engaged. Consider asking a family member
  or friend to walk the dog, or hire a dog walker.

- If the dog is barking all day, they could just be doing what
  many dogs are bred to do: watchdog barking. Closing the
  blinds or drapes or applying window film to the lower part
  of a window may stop your dog from seeing all the exciting
  things going on outside. Leaving a radio on may also help to
  disguise some sounds. Whatever you do, don't try a bark-
  activated collar (see Chapter 3).

Separation-related behaviors are a sign that the dog is experiencing negative emotions such as anxiety, frustration, or panic.
Dogs with separation-related behaviors become anxious when
they see that you are getting ready to go out, and they go into a
full-blown panic when you are gone. Because of this, the common
advice to leave a food puzzle toy while you're out won't help; they
will only eat it when you get back home.

Signs of separation anxiety include destroying doorframes, walls,
carpets, and other things close to the door where you left, and whining or making other noises, often for more than fifteen minutes.
These are thought to be signs of the dog trying to get nearer to you.

Other signs of separation-related behaviors will only be appar-
ent if you have video to record your dog during your absence.
Watch for panting, salivating, trembling, hiding, pacing, grooming, and/or raising a front leg. Their ears may also be back and
their tail down.[2] You will recognize these from Chapter 2 as signs
of a negative emotional state.

In severe cases of separation anxiety, dogs may injure them-selves, try to escape (sometimes even by jumping through a window), become severely depressed, and experience diarrhea and vomiting. Crucially, these behaviors only happen in your absence.

If your vet diagnoses separation anxiety, they may talk with you about medications to help your dog as you work through a training plan.[3] In some cases, they may suggest a referral to a vet-erinary behaviorist. Medications are typically used with separation issues, and some trainers who specialize in separation anxiety will only work with dog guardians if they have seen their vet and got their dog on meds.

Your dog's separation-related behaviors can affect you too. You may feel anxious and guilty about leaving your dog. You may become frustrated about having to clean up toileting messes in the house and deal with damage to doorframes or carpets. Your neighbors can be affected by hearing barking or whining for long periods of time. Be sure to take care of your own emotional health and check in with your neighbors.

UNDERSTANDING THE CAUSES OF SEPARATION ANXIETY

WE DON'T KNOW exactly what causes separation-related behav-iors. Although a number of risk factors have been suggested, much of the research is contradictory. Some things that are not linked include letting your dog sleep on the bed, the dog's breed or tem-perament, their age, the guardian's gender, how many people are in the household, and whether there are other dogs in the household.[4] In some studies, it seems to be more common in dogs acquired from rescues, but in other studies, that's not the case.

Changes in circumstances are linked to separation anxiety. Shifting work schedules, moving houses, having a baby, and longer commute times may not always be within your control, but they affect your dog too, so take care when changing their routine.[5] Being left alone for long periods of time and, conversely, hardly ever being left alone have both been linked with separation-related issues.[6] The COVID-19 pandemic and its associated lockdowns and social isolation gave researchers a new opportunity to look at how changes in time spent alone affect dogs.

Most dogs (though not all) probably enjoyed having their people at home more during the pandemic. There was concern that as people returned to the office when the lockdowns were lifted, many dogs would be upset. In a survey of dog guardians in the UK, almost 80 percent said their dog's routine had changed during the first lockdown in March and April of 2020, when people were not allowed to leave home except for essential reasons, and 58 percent did not leave their dog alone at home for more than five minutes during this period.[7] When scientists compared the dogs' separation-related behaviors during this first lockdown with behaviors in a period of the same length in October 2020, when restrictions were minimal, they found an increase in reports of separation-related behaviors in October.[8] As you might expect, before lockdown, all of the dogs in this study were left home alone for more than five minutes at least once a week. Almost half (46.5%) were left for at least five minutes on five to seven days of the week, and during the lockdown that number fell to 8.7 percent. Of the dogs who did not have any signs of separation-related behaviors before the lockdown, around 10 percent did by October. While age was a factor, so was the amount of change in how long dogs were left alone.

The dogs whose home-alone time decreased the most during the pandemic were the most at risk of having new separation-related issues. Interestingly, of the dogs who had signs of separation-related behaviors before the lockdown, just over half (55.7%) no longer did in October. This could be in part because dogs were still not being left home alone in October for as long as they had been before the lockdown. This finding also shows that separation-related issues can be resolved, though the study did not collect data on what, if anything, people had done to try to resolve them.

Some research suggests that different types of separation anxiety may result from different causes. For example, dogs who see other people and/or dogs go by may become frustrated by the barrier (the window) that prevents them from interacting, and as a result they may come to find their guardian's absence unpleasant. One study found fifty-four different signs of separation-related behaviors that cluster into seven distinct groups.[9] In turn, the scientists grouped these signs into four different types of separation-related behavior. It's to be hoped that future research along these lines will lead to advances in treatment.

It used to be thought that some dogs got separation anxiety because they were too attached to their guardian, but it turns out that a dog who follows you around the house is not more likely to have separation-related issues. They may just be demonstrating the desire to be close to you that goes along with a normal attachment. And contrary to older advice, it's fine to greet your dog on departures and arrivals.

One small study looked at how dogs without separation issues behaved during a three-minute absence, depending on whether their guardian had petted them or ignored them beforehand.[10] This short absence was not stressful for the dogs, but they were calmer when they had been petted beforehand, as shown by a lower heart rate and by them lying down or sniffing the ground for a longer time (short sniffing, in contrast, was seen as a stress signal). Another study with newly adopted shelter dogs found that what the scientists called "high arousal" departures and arrivals (involving petting the dog, playing with them, and talking to them) were not connected with any increase in separation-related behaviors.[11]

One study suggests that when dog guardians have an avoidant attachment style (which means that they tend to ignore their dogs' attempts to get attention or affection from them), their dogs have an insecure attachment and are more likely to show separation-related behaviors.[12] This finding would be in line with research on children and separation anxiety. More research is needed to get a fuller understanding of whether there are links between attachment and separation-related issues in dogs.

PREVENTING SEPARATION ISSUES

IF YOUR DOG is distressed when alone, you might wonder if some canine companionship could help. Unfortunately, although having two dogs can be a lovely experience, getting another dog is not the solution, because it typically does not resolve the separation-related issues in your original dog. Perhaps the easiest way to think of this anxiety is that another dog is not a substitute for you, and it's your company that your anxious dog is missing while you are out. Also, there is a risk that the new dog will develop separation issues too, which will increase the work you have to do to resolve the issue.

Following good practice seems to help with prevention. One study found that when new adopters of dogs were given guidance on how to prevent separation-related issues, it led to fewer issues than when adopters received no such guidance. This was true even though many of the adopters only partly followed the advice.[13] The guidance given in the study included exercising the dog before departures, never punishing the dog, even if they had made a mess, and following a desensitization and counterconditioning program to get the dog used to the guardians going out.

First, some tips for dogs who don't have separation-related issues. With puppies, it's recommended to leave them for short periods to help them get used to being apart from you. Similarly, with newly adopted rescue dogs, it can be tempting to want to spend every moment at home with them for the first few days, but that's not likely how life will continue. So it's a good idea to go out and leave them for short periods. With newly adopted dogs, until you know they are house-trained, take them out for a pee break before you go out, and leave them in a dog-proof room where they can't come to any harm and also can't harm your stuff.

USING DESENSITIZATION TRAINING FOR SEPARATION ANXIETY

TRAINING DOGS to get used to being alone is based on desensitization, or gradual exposure to longer and longer absences, starting with whatever the dog is comfortable with. For separation anxiety, desensitization is typically used without counterconditioning and alongside medication prescribed by your veterinarian or veterinary behaviorist.

To ensure the dog remains under threshold, don't be away from them for any longer than they can cope with. For some dogs, that means never being left alone. Although this may sound like an extreme way to live your life, remember that it's only temporary as you work on their separation anxiety.

The general principle is to start with very short absences and gradually build up to longer ones. For some dogs, this might mean simply closing the door and then stepping right back in again. Only once the dog is happy with that first, brief absence can you start to think of increasing the time. Any increases must be very gradual. Don't keep increasing every time; some shorter durations should always be in the mix to help the dog feel comfortable.

Having cameras set up means that you can keep an eye on your dog the whole time you are out, so you can see for yourself if they are happy (and you can rush home if they're not).

It's likely that you won't be able to start with absences right away, because your dog can already predict when you are going to go out. Maybe the way you refill their water bowl, pick up your phone and purse, put shoes and a jacket on, and so on, are clues that you're about to leave. In this case, they are tip-offs for an unpleasant event of being left alone. The fact that your dog can spot these signs is classical conditioning at work. And that means you need to start your desensitization here.

Unfortunately, separation-related issues can be difficult to resolve, and it's hard to put a timeline on how long it will take. "There are so many factors to consider," veterinary behaviorist Dr. Claudia Richter says. "Are there concurrent medical disorders? We find out more and more that probably over 50 percent of animals with behavioral disorders have an underlying medical disorder that, in some way at least, contributes to the behavioral disorder. So I consider that. I consider how long this has been present for. How old was the dog when it first started? Why did it first start? Is this an animal that came from a shelter? Has this dog experienced the loss of a loved one or caregiver in the past? Is the dog maybe 12 to 13 years old and this is a sudden problem and has to do with cognitive decline? I think that for all of these dogs, the prognosis is going to be different.

"And then, on top of that, I have to look at the investment the family is able to make, and I'm not talking about financial investment. I'm talking about time and commitment from a perspective that may be an initial four to six weeks in which you can't leave this dog alone. Is that possible for you? How many times are you going to be able to practice leaving your dog home alone? Things like that."

She says that, after seeing how the dog responds over the first three to six months, she can give her clients a better idea of how things are likely to progress. There can be a lot of trial and error in finding the best way to treat the patient, and it takes commitment from the dog's guardians.

Because separation-related issues take time to resolve, it's a good idea to work with a trainer and a veterinarian and/or veterinary behaviorist. Some trainers don't enjoy separation-anxiety cases and won't take them, but some trainers specialize in them. There are two qualifications to look out for: CSAT and SA Pro. A CSAT is a Certified Separation Anxiety Trainer who has qualified via Malena DeMartini's school, whereas a CSAP-BC (Certified Separation Anxiety Pro Behavior Consultant) has qualified through Julie Naismith's school. Both are excellent choices. These trainers often work online, which makes it easier to find someone, because they don't have to live near you. They will meet with you virtually and arrange a training plan designed for you and your dog. They will also help you find assistance from others, so that you can go out if you need to.

It takes a village: Finding people to help

Once you've made the decision that you won't leave your dog alone for any longer than they can handle, there is the practical issue of figuring out how to make this work. Perhaps you can work at home some of the time, or, if your dog is friendly to people, maybe you can take them to work. A doggy day care can be an obvious choice, if there is a good one near you and you can afford it. Dogs that are friendly and sociable with other dogs are well suited to day care.

Finding a petsitter is another option. Friends, family, and neighbors may also be able to help, especially someone who is home a lot and loves dogs but can't have one of their own. They might love the opportunity to spend time with a dog without the costs or restrictions of owning one. Your vet clinic may be able to suggest someone. Or, if you live near a college or university, perhaps a student would like to earn some money by keeping your dog company. If you're working with a dog trainer, they may help you think of people to ask, or ask around on your behalf.

Separation-related issues can occur alongside other behavior issues, especially fear and noise sensitivities. Another behavior issue that dog guardians often find difficult to deal with is resource guarding, though here the solution is quite different.

"Some of the most common signs of separation anxiety, like vocalization, destructive behavior, house-training accidents, or issues with crate training, are often met with blaming the dog. I wish it were more widely understood that these dogs are not doing these things out of spite. These dogs are not mad that they've been left alone or doing things to get back at their owners. These dogs are scared. These dogs are having a panic attack. So, rather than looking for an indestructible crate or bark collar, we must address the fear these dogs are experiencing when left alone. We do this by following a systematic desensitization protocol. The unwanted behavior no longer occurs once we address the panic and the dog feels safe. Ensuring fearful dogs feel safe should always be our number one priority."

—SAUNDRA CLOW, CTC, CSAT, Alpine Dogs

"GRRR, KEEP AWAY FROM MY STUFF!":
WHEN YOUR DOG IS AFRAID OF LOSING THEIR THINGS

....

N MY HOUSE, the cats and dog get their evening meal before my husband and I sit down to eat. Pepper eats in the kitchen, while the cats eat in another room with their bowls or food puzzle toys separated so that everyone can eat in peace and no one tries to steal anyone else's food. Later, Pepper settles under the kitchen table while we eat, hoping perhaps for a fallen morsel, or at least keeping us company (he is very good at companionship). Sometimes the cats join us too. Harley is not interested in our food, but Melina watches to see what we're eating. Usually, it's of no interest to cats: bean stew or lentil curry, say. But maybe we've grated cheese on the bean stew, or it's one of those rare occasions when we are eating chicken or fish. Then she's interested. I never feed Melina from my plate, but this rule is not followed by the other person at the table, who likes to keep her happy. He also eats faster than me, so there comes a point when I am the only one still eating. As Melina comes closer, I arrange my glass of water and the ketchup jar to block her line of approach. My arm is ready to hold her back if necessary. I'm watching her closely. Then I realize: I'm guarding my food.

Dogs do the same thing—they sometimes protect their food, treats, toys, beds, and even their favorite humans. Resource guarding usually happens with things that have high value to dogs, like favorite toys or marrow bones. So when Melina is eyeing my food, I can understand why a dog growls when someone approaches while they're eating. Guarding food and other resources may even make sense from an evolutionary perspective. If you imagine a world in which food is hard for your dog to find, they wouldn't want to lose it to another dog or a person coming up to take it. However, a growl as someone approaches could easily be a sign that the dog is scared of them or, for example, of being forced to get off the settee. So if you notice signs of resource guarding, consider whether that is the real cause of the behaviors, or whether there is something else going on.

RECOGNIZING SIGNS OF RESOURCE GUARDING

WHEN PEPPER CAME to live with us, I noticed that he went slightly stiff the first time I put his food bowl down on the kitchen floor. There was a brief freeze as I took my hand away, but the freeze was so short-lived that you could have blinked and missed it. "That's interesting," I thought, but I forgot to warn my husband. One evening, when I was busy doing something else, my husband fed Pepper in the kitchen. He told me later that he put the food bowl down on the floor, walked away from it—and was followed by Pepper, who then sat down and growled for a bit before going back to his food and eating it. Indeed, I saw this happen the next day. My husband put the food bowl down and walked back into the middle of the kitchen, followed by a growling Pepper.

It's easy to laugh when a little dog growls and acts all tough, and I'll admit that we did. But in a way it wasn't very fair of me, because from Pepper's point of view the situation was serious. I'm pretty sure he was genuinely upset that someone might take his food. Of course, *I* knew that no one in my house would take his food, and I knew what to do about Pepper's food guarding, so it didn't take me long to resolve this behavior. But as I said earlier, we still make sure the cats aren't around while Pepper is eating, just in case. Melina would definitely be tempted to try and get his food.

The signs of resource guarding can be very subtle. A freeze was the first thing I noticed that indicated Pepper was not happy about me being nearby while he was eating from his food bowl. In general, people find it quite hard to spot the signs of resource guarding. In fact, in one study, people who were shown videos by researchers found it easier to say that a particular sign was absent than to spot it when it was there.[1] People who had been to dog training classes or who knew more about dog behavior were more likely to spot signs of resource guarding, which is not surprising. That finding is also encouraging, because it shows that people can learn to recognize the clues.

The most commonly identified sign was biting or snapping. However, a lot of behaviors can indicate resource guarding. If people were more able to recognize these signs, they could intervene before things reached a point where the dog was close to biting. In the study, people were not so good at recognizing these more subtle signs. The following behaviors may indicate that a dog is guarding their food or other resources:

- Biting or snapping

- Taking the item away or moving their head or body away from someone who is trying to take it from them (avoidance)

- Eating faster than normal, often with their head down and maybe even stuck into the food bowl (rapid ingestion)

- Showing their teeth

- Freezing

- Staring

- Growling

Research has also identified some of the factors that are associated with resource guarding behavior. Generally, it's based in anxiety. But dogs can learn to guard resources because we train them to. Some people have been told—erroneously—that they should take food away from the dog. Sadly, taking food away from the dog is one of those ideas that comes from outdated dominance approaches to dog training.

You should not be taking food away from your dog, and doing so is risky because some dogs will bite in order to keep their food. Research shows this practice is associated with dogs guarding food more often and more seriously.[2] There is no point in taking food away to show that you are the boss—you are the one who provided the food, so you already have control over it. As your dog's guardian, you should ensure that they can eat in peace. In a busy household, that may mean using baby gates or dog crates to keep children and other pets away from your dog while they eat.

Research also shows some things that help. Resource guarding is less frequent and less severe if dog guardians sometimes drop extra bits of tasty food onto the dog's meal (see more about this approach below). Dogs are less likely to bite or snap to guard food or to show avoidance (one of the early signs of resource guarding) if they have been taught a drop behavior (see below). There are also some dog-related factors associated with an increased likelihood of resource guarding behaviors, such as whether the dog is more fearful or impulsive, and whether they are a mixed breed or a neutered male. These characteristics may not be modifiable, but what you teach your dog and what you do while they are eating are under your control.

Resource guarding can also occur between dogs who live in the same home. In this case, signs of avoidance and eating rapidly tend to happen at the same time, and if they are present, biting and snapping are less likely to occur.[3] This finding fits in with the idea of rapid eating and avoidance as behaviors that may indicate concerns around food, but they are milder than an aggressive display. Again, dogs who are fearful or impulsive are more likely to show signs of resource guarding in the presence of another dog. And teaching a dog to "drop it" (drop something) is linked to lower levels of resource guarding.

Resource guarding can be context-specific: just because it happens in one location does not necessarily mean that it will happen in another (although, of course, it may). Resource guarding is one of those things that animal shelters typically assess, and they also may get information about it when a dog is surrendered to them. But a dog who shows signs of resource guarding in a shelter will not necessarily guard food or other items when adopted into a new home. One study looked at every single dog that was identified as a resource guarder at a particular New York–area shelter.[4] Over a period of five years, 15 percent of the dogs were resource guarders, according to the shelter's assessment, although most cases were mild to moderate, not severe. The study found that dogs were more likely to be resource guarders if they were adult or senior, and if they were small or large (but not mid-sized). Spayed females were more likely to be guarders than entire females were, but neuter status in male dogs was not linked to the likelihood of guarding.

Most of the dogs in the study were adopted to new homes, and the researchers tracked what happened. Only the dogs who had been identified as severe resource guarders were more likely to be returned than average. With mild or moderate resource guarding, the adoption was just as likely to work out as it was for a dog who didn't show any signs of resource guarding. As well, dogs who were identified as severe resource guarders at this shelter typically took fourteen more days than average to be adopted, but mild or moderate resource guarding had no effect on time to adoption.[5] It's worth noting that a number of different tests are used by shelters to assess dog behavior, and the evidence base for them is limited, both in terms of the role of specific behaviors in predicting adoption success and human safety, and in terms of the overall assessments' ability to predict successful adoptions.[6]

TRAINING YOUR DOG NOT TO GUARD RESOURCES

RESOURCE GUARDING is the fear that someone will take your stuff, so training involves teaching your dog that if someone approaches them, their food or toy will not be taken away, but instead something wonderful will be added to it. In other words, the dog's food or toy won't be removed *and* they'll get delicious treats. The dog therefore learns that they don't need to fear if a person approaches; in fact, they love it, because it means they will get scrumptious snacks. You will recognize this training as counterconditioning. It's the best approach for changing guarding behavior against people (though management is also useful—and essential if there are children in the home). For guarding against other animals, management (by such means as feeding dogs in crates or in different rooms) is usually easiest, but training can be done too. Here are some tips.

Training for resource guarding is best done under the guidance of a reward-based dog trainer (see Chapter 14). A dog who is resource guarding may bite, and since signs of the dog being unhappy can be subtle, they are often missed by ordinary dog guardians. An experienced trainer will be good at reading the dog's body language and able to keep everyone safe and the dog feeling happy. An experienced trainer will do the training in incremental levels, starting with something that's very easy for the dog and safe for the trainer. Knowing when to move up and down in the plan, according to how things are going, can be tricky, so it's best to leave this training to the pros.

The training will always start with something that the dog basically doesn't care about. It could be a cup or a paperweight, or anything you have on hand that you know the dog is not interested in and has never guarded before. In dog trainer terminology, this is a "dummy object." The use of a dummy object allows you to teach the dog that when you approach, reach for the item, and take it away, it's nothing to worry about—in fact, it's something to love—because this means you will give them wonderful treats. Never start this training with anything that the dog has guarded before and cares about; you have to build up very, very carefully to things like bully sticks, favorite toys, and full bowls of food.

The general steps of a training plan involve starting when the dog has an empty food bowl or a less-preferred toy and simply dropping a very tasty treat a few feet away. The trainer will stay far enough away that the dog is quite comfortable with their presence. Over time, the trainer will move closer to the dog, watching the dog's body language carefully. If they notice any signs of worry, they will de-escalate the situation (probably by giving extra treats and moving back) and return to an easier step in the plan. As the dog gets more comfortable with the distance, the trainer will work through different stages of items or states of the food bowl—for example, by approaching when the dog has eaten and there is no food in the bowl, or when the dog has not eaten and there's a little food in the bowl. The trainer will always work from a very easy level (from the dog's perspective) to a very hard one, proceeding at the dog's pace, de-escalating as needed, and using only reward-based methods. Your trainer will likely do a lot of this training for you. If they involve you in the training, they will probably share only one or two steps of the plan at once, so that you can just concentrate on that step.

Lisa Skavienski takes a lot of resource guarding cases. She can tell when the client has previously been to a trainer who's used aversive methods like punishing the dog for growling or telling them off. In these cases, it will take longer to resolve the issue, because the dog has learned to withhold their natural warning signs. "It makes it very difficult to go through that process," she says. "Those signs and signals that a dog gives, we use that body language as a blueprint to navigate our training plan."

She explains that as you work with a dummy object in the beginning, you are looking for lovely, happy body language. "And when we see the dog suddenly get loose and wiggly and that happy, expectant look that they know something wonderful is about to happen on our reach and removal, then we can move up the list of things until we get to that guarded object."

She explains how she might start with a set of dummy objects, then move on to a toy bone, before eventually arriving at a marrow bone with some marrow still in it. "The only way we know whether the dog is comfortable or not is by that body. That's how we navigate. So if I have moved on from the stuffed toy that the dog loves but never guarded to an empty marrow bone, and when I try to move on to that step, the dog suddenly starts to stiffen a little, or maybe they'll put their nose in there and paws in front, with three points of contact [on the item] and look up, that's very clear information to me that the dog is not okay, that I need to back up. I need to go back to the item they were comfortable with."

If that body language is not there because the communication has been punished in the past, "we have a very serious risk, for starters," she says. "We're probably going to push too far in the plan. We're going to push too fast, and if the dog's not showing discomfort, if the dog's communication has been punished out, what we have is a dog that might bite when we get too close. So not only will we set the training plan back, but it puts people at risk."

This means not only that you have to progress more slowly through the training plan, but also that you may also have to start with things like teaching the dog to be happy when hands are near them or with some body handling, so that you know they don't find the proximity of a person (in the absence of anything they might guard) to be scary. You also need to take extra measures to protect people from bites. When a dog has previously been punished for growling or showing other signs of being upset, things can escalate quickly, because you no longer know when they're starting to be upset.

While the training is in progress, remember not to try to take items away from your dog, because of the risk of upsetting your dog, you getting bitten, and causing setbacks in the training. But there may be times when your dog gets something they shouldn't have, and you need a strategy for that.

TRAINING AND COPING WITH EMERGENCIES: "DROP IT," "LEAVE IT," TREAT SCATTERS, AND SWAPS

YOU NEVER KNOW what a dog might decide to guard. It could be something rotten and stinky that they found on a walk, or it could be one of their favorite toys. Lisa Skavienski told me that one of the commonly guarded things she hears about is a used hankie. Of course, whatever it is, it's not necessarily going to be something harmless. This means that it's a great idea to teach your dog "drop it," so they let go of something they have in their mouth, and "leave it," so they don't pick it up in the first place. If your dog already guards resources, hire a dog trainer to help with this.

"Drop it"

Before I became a dog trainer, I learned how to teach "drop it" from a video by the UK-based animal trainer Chirag Patel, and have since worked through this plan with countless dogs.

Have lots of small treats ready. Say "Drop it," wait one second, and scatter a generous portion of treats. Over time, when they hear this cue, the dog will look to the floor for the magic shower of treats (a classical conditioning relationship). Once the treats are happening, you can start to point out the pieces of food to the dog to help them get used to the idea that hands can be around their food and they still get the food. You can help them find the food more quickly. A later stage involves practice with random objects on the floor, objects that aren't important to the dog and that you can pick up and put right back down again. Eventually, you can pick up objects and keep them. Once the dog is trained, it's still a good idea to practice from time to time, including times when they don't have anything in their mouth and when they are not expecting a treat.

"Leave it"

To teach "leave it," you teach the behavior first, before you give it a cue. To start, you need two different types of treats: something really tasty, like chicken or beef, and something blah, like a bit of kibble or a boring dry treat. Hide the tasty treat behind your back. Put the boring treat on the ground and cover it with your hand. It's still food, so your dog will likely come and sniff your hand and maybe even paw at it. Just keep still and make sure they don't get the food. The instant they give up and look away, say "Yes" to mark the behavior (or use a clicker). Then give one of the tasty treats from your other hand. Do this several times in a row. Eventually, your dog will stop going to your hand when you put the boring treats down, and will instead look at the place where the tasty treats appear. Once this skill is reliable, you can move on to the next stage: leave the boring treat uncovered but have your hand ready to cover it, if needed. When the dog looks away, say "Yes" and reward them with a delicious treat from your other hand. Try to make sure the dog doesn't get the food they are supposed to leave. But if they do, don't worry; let them eat it and then move on to another trial. You can go back to a previous stage at any time.

Once your dog has got the hang of looking away instead of going for the boring treats that you put down, you can add the cue "Leave it." Just say it normally. Sometimes people feel they have to be stern or yell it at their dog, but then your dog might be scared. Put the boring food down, have your hand hovering, ready to cover it, say "Leave it," and wait for the dog to look away. Then mark it and give them a tasty treat from your other hand. You can gradually work through a range of different items. Remember that some items are harder to leave than others—a sardine is much harder to leave than a pebble, for example—so practice first with items that are likely to be easier. You can expect a lot of practice and repetition before your dog is ready to leave a sardine!

Treat scatters and swaps

If your dog picks something up off the ground on a walk (a bloated squirrel, say, or a discarded brown-paper bag that you don't know the contents of), you can try a treat scatter or a swap. For the scatter, use a food your dog loves and scatter it. For the swap, offer the dog a safe item, and when they take it, remove the item they have. The safe item can be anything you have on hand, such as a toy or treat you have with you or a stick you find on the ground. You can make the safe item more interesting by paying attention to it yourself and talking as if this is an exciting thing.

Sometimes dogs will chew on unusual items such as rocks, plaster, or plastic, whether they guard those items or not. This practice is known as pica, and it's one of several compulsive disorders.

"There is so much focus on obedience training and getting dogs to 'obey commands' that people misunderstand when a dog is barking, lunging, or growling because they're afraid, that they're not 'misbehaving' in a lack-of-obedience sense. The dog is communicating the only way they know how to. The dog doesn't just need more obedience training to 'fix' their fearful behavior, yet this is where aversive trainers seize the opportunity and promise quick fixes to unknowing owners.

Fear is not disobedience. To truly help fearful dogs, we first need to help manage their environment so they feel safe. Then we can work on training like conditioning positive associations and training alternate behaviors; but safety, predictability, and choice in a fearful dog's world should all be paramount to obedience."

—KATE LASALA, CTC, Rescued by Training

TURNING, TURNING:

WHEN YOUR DOG'S ANXIETY LEADS TO DYSFUNCTIONAL REPETITIVE BEHAVIORS

....

WHEN BODGER FIRST CAME to live with us, one of the many difficult behaviors he had was grabbing his tail in his mouth and turning in circles. It was sad to see the way that he would spin and spin. I hoped that as he spent more time with us in his new home, with plenty of exercise and enrichment, he would stop doing this. And that's what happened; over several months, the spinning just faded away.

RECOGNIZING REPETITIVE BEHAVIORS

COMMON DYSFUNCTIONAL REPETITIVE BEHAVIORS in dogs include spinning in circles, chasing their tail, overgrooming, chasing reflections or shadows, or snapping at nonexistent flies.

Unfortunately, dog guardians often see these repetitive behaviors as amusing or no problem unless the dog injures themselves or does them for a long period.[1] There are plenty of videos on social media in which people think these behaviors are "cute" or "funny," but they are actually a sign that you should see your veterinarian. The information in this chapter cannot help diagnose or treat these conditions—only your vet or veterinary behaviorist can do that. But it will help you understand them and know what to do while you wait for your appointment.

We are more used to thinking of repetitive behaviors in zoo animals, and we associate them with boredom due to an unstimulating environment that does not let the animals engage in species-typical behaviors. In pets, it seems that some kind of stress or conflict situation can often be the trigger for a repetitive behavior.[2]

Repetitive behaviors may continue to the extent that they cause injury, as with repeated sucking or licking of parts of the body. The dog is aware while they are doing the behavior, but it can be very difficult to stop them once they've started. And although these behaviors may begin in a particular circumstance, such as a particularly stressful time, they can generalize. This means the dog starts to perform the behavior in a wider and wider range of situations. For example, licking may begin as a response to feeling itchy, but continue as a compulsive behavior.

Dysfunctional repetitive behaviors may co-occur with other behavior issues, particularly aggression, separation-related issues, hyperactivity, or impulsivity.[3] This can make it harder to spot repetitive behaviors, because the other issue gets more attention.

The words *dysfunctional repetitive behaviors*, *stereotypy*, and *compulsive disorder* are often used interchangeably, and there is some debate as to the correct terminology to use.[4] There are some parallels with obsessive-compulsive disorder (OCD) in humans, a chronic condition that involves intrusive thoughts (the obsession),

as well as mental rituals and repetitive behaviors, such as clean-
ing or checking (the compulsion). These compulsive behaviors
are thought to be a way of dealing with the unwanted obsession,
and are repeated because they reduce the anxiety (negative reinforcement).[5] Although it may be possible to use, for example,
tail chasing in dogs as a model for human OCD, more research is
needed.[6] The term OCD is not used for pets. It is difficult to establish the obsession part of OCD in dogs, for obvious reasons, and
there isn't enough research on the motivation for the behavior or
the brain systems involved in dogs to draw a comparison.[7]

UNDERSTANDING THE CAUSES OF DYSFUNCTIONAL REPETITIVE BEHAVIORS

JUST AS WITH ZOO ANIMALS, a poor environment is implicated
for pet dogs with repetitive behaviors.[8] Aspects of the environment that can contribute include a lack of control and a lack of
predictability, such as unpredictable times of food and walks or
inconsistent interactions with humans in the home (for example, if the humans punish the dog sometimes and are friendly at
other times). Not having opportunities to engage in typical canine
behaviors may also be a contributing factor. This means that it's
important to assess whether your dog's needs are being met (see
below on what to do while you wait for help).

There's an association with temperament, as repetitive behaviors are more common in dogs who are aggressive, inattentive, or
impulsive.[9] In some cases, repetitive behaviors may be reinforced
by the dog guardian's behavior.[10] There's also a suggestion that
some repetitive behaviors, but not all, are a way of coping, though
we don't know if coping behavior is the cause or if, once started, it
turns out to reduce stress and hence is maintained.[11] For example,
a dog may begin to lick themselves in a particular circumstance

because their skin is itchy from an infection or because they are feeling stressed, and then continue licking more often and in a wider and wider range of situations, until they cause bald patches and irritated skin (acral lick dermatitis).

Genetic factors play a role, and certain types of compulsive behavior are more likely in certain breeds. For example, tail chasing is most common in German Shepherds and Australian Cattle Dogs, while spinning in circles is more common in English Bull Terriers and Staffordshire Bull Terriers.[12]

Medical issues can also cause repetitive behaviors. For example, when dogs eat items that aren't food, such as wood, plastic, or plaster—a condition known as pica—pain may be the cause.[13] Gastrointestinal disease and food intolerances may be implicated.[14] Perhaps surprisingly, fly snapping can also be caused by gastrointestinal disease.[15] Fly snapping and light-chasing may also be linked to issues with the eyes or some other painful conditions. Overgrooming or biting may be linked to pain or skin disease. The vet can also rule out medical issues that might look like compulsive disorders but aren't, such as seizures. Remember, if something about your dog seems odd or unusual or just not like other dogs, get it checked.

There are a couple of other things to note. First, laser light toys are generally not recommended for dogs, in case the dog develops an obsession with lights and shadows. And second, playing fetch with your dog is not an issue. Play is a normal behavior that is good for dogs, and fetch involves part of the predatory sequence. For the more active breeds like Border Collies, fetch is a great outlet (and they may want to keep playing for longer than you do!). Some dogs have been bred to be drivey like this, and it's how dogs keep on herding sheep or searching for scent or doing the other kinds of jobs that dogs do. So fetching is a fun and normal dog behavior.

WHAT TO DO WHILE YOU WAIT FOR HELP

IF YOU SUSPECT that your dog has some kind of compulsive dis-order, the first thing to do is to make an appointment with your veterinarian. In turn, the vet may need to order tests and/or refer you to a veterinary behaviorist. Make notes of what has happened, or even keep a diary in the run-up to the appointment, so that you don't forget anything that might be important to share with your veterinarian. For example, did anything change in your dog's environment? Your vet may want to know about the first time the behavior happened, as well as about the most recent time(s). If you have video of the behavior, show it to them (but don't do something to cause the behavior just so you can get it on video). You could also set up a camera to get video of any relevant events while you're not there. It's useful information to know whether it happens when you're not with the dog.

Think about what happens before the behavior, in case you can identify something that triggers it. If you do, avoid that trig-gering event. In a study of tail chasing behavior in four breeds of dogs, the most commonly identified triggers were boredom and stress, with excitement being another common trigger.[16] Unless the dog is injuring themselves, it's not recommended to physi-cally prevent them from doing the behavior; if they are injuring themselves, ask your vet what they recommend (for example, an Elizabethan collar or neck pillow to prevent licking).[17] You may want to keep your dog close to you so that you can offer them a chew toy, rope, or other toy as an alternate activity if they start (or seem to be about to start) the behavior.

While you wait for your appointment, think about the extent to which you are meeting your dog's needs and what you can do to reduce stress. Start with the basics. If you've been using aver-sive methods to train your dog, stop. Don't yell at your dog. Have regular walktimes and regular mealtimes. Stick to a routine with your dog as far as possible. Give them some control over their environment, and the choice of a safe space to go to. (If you want to know more about what dogs need, that's the topic of my first book, *Wag: The Science of Making Your Dog Happy*.)

Once you've got the basics, increased exercise and enrichment is a good idea. Do more fun activities with your dog. Food puzzle toys, chew toys, and scent games are all great ways to give your dog more enrichment. If possible, increase the length and/or frequency of walks and make sure that your dog gets time to sniff on those walks. These are all things that are good for any dog.

Once your appointment comes round, your veterinarian will help.

"We often paint a picture when we get a puppy or rescue. Romanticizing having a dog can get the best of us sometimes, when that picture doesn't fit reality. You may be filled with grief for the dog you thought you would have, or what you thought being a dog parent would be like. It can sometimes be like shopping online. You feel you have done all your research and read all the product reviews. But, sure enough, your product is delivered, and it's damaged, or not what you expected, or doesn't have any of the features they marketed. Every dog is so unique; even your neighbor on their fourth purebred Golden Retriever can attest to this. You may go through a moment of grief for what you thought your relationship would have been with your dog. But you may end up finding things you never thought a companionship relationship would bring you."

—NICOLE BARNETT, CTC, owner of We Work for Treats

PART
3

HOW AND WHERE TO GET HELP

14

GETTING HELP

W HEN YOU HAVE a fearful or reactive dog, you learn a lot of new skills: how to read your dog's body language so that you know if they are feeling comfortable or not; how to get the timing right when giving treats; which kinds of treats your dog likes best; which situations they feel nervous in; how to structure situations in ways that are easier for your dog; how to cope with setbacks (hopefully, with good humor); and so on. Maybe one of the hardest things to learn is how to navigate other people's comments and expectations.

COPING WITH A FEARFUL DOG: MANAGING CAREGIVER BURDEN

HAVING A FEARFUL DOG is tough and can affect relationships with other people. Dr. Claudia Richter said to me that, before taking on a dog who is known to be fearful, she recommends people "think really, really hard about what impact having a fearful dog in your house might have on your life, your family, your time, your money, and whether or not you can do that." She adds: "Whether it is with or without medication, it will require some sort of commitment on your side, and it isn't as easy as having this regular, happy-go-lucky puppy that loves everybody."

But, despite the difficulties, she also mentioned the bright side: "I have a fearful dog, and I am so, so happy that I adopted this dog. And I love to him to pieces, with all his little fears. We have adapted to what he can and cannot do, and when it comes to situations that we cannot avoid, there are pharmaceutical options for him that help make that situation a little bit better."

Because having a fearful dog can be challenging, it can affect the guardian a lot. *Caregiver burden* is the phrase that we use to describe the difficulty of caring for a person who is sick, and there's some evidence that people can have this when caring for a pet too. Caregiver burden involves negative emotions such as stress, anxiety, and depression, as well as impacts on finances and time. Some research that looked at the challenges of having a dog with a behavior issue found that a lot of planning was involved in caring for the pet, and there were also costs (for example, of behavior support and medication).[1] People described a range of negative emotions, including sadness, worry, and disappointment. In another study, a questionnaire was sent to people who were seeking help for their pet from a veterinary behavior practice.[2] About two-thirds (68.5%) of these people had caregiver burden.

Against this backdrop, it's important to take care of yourself. Recognize that you may need time to process some of the emotions you have about your dog and the situation. Your feelings may also be affected by the ways people have acted towards you in difficult situations in the past, and/or by any history of anxiety or trauma. Having other difficulties in your life may make it harder for you to cope with your dog's issues or to find the resources you need. But even if everything else in your life is perfect, having a fearful dog can still be hard. So take time for yourself and remember that you have to look after yourself to be resilient. Think about what self-care means to you and make time for the things that will help you. Getting help for your dog from behavior professionals is one thing that people say really helps.[3]

Enjoying the small moments can help. Working with a fearful dog is a slow process, especially in the beginning. It can help to keep a diary to track progress. Make a note of things that go well and celebrate them with a friend or family member (and, of course, with your dog). It's easy to miss progress when it happens in small increments. For example, when the distance a reactive dog needs to be from another dog in order to feel safe decreases gradually, it's easy to feel like you're not making progress—when actually that progress can be measured in meters or even tens of meters.

Dog trainer Bonnie Hartney likens celebrating these small steps to the way that we would celebrate every milestone with a new baby. "The first time the baby lifts their head off the floor, it's a celebration. And the first time the baby turns their head or is on their tummy, that's a celebration. I think if we could capture that feeling and tell people about that, that's really what it is like with a fearful dog. The first time they step out of the laundry room—wow! That's a celebration. And the first time you get the leash on—oh my goodness! That was a party for us."

There will also be setbacks along the way, as there were when I was training Bodger to let me touch his snout and accidentally made him snap at me, or when Hartney put the leash on Dixie and it turned out to be too soon. It helps to know that setbacks are a normal part of learning. Your dog isn't the only one learning: you are too. You're learning how to handle the situation and how to train them and what their triggers are and so on. It's inevitable that there will be moments or days when things feel like a step back. When people have a reactive dog who "goes off," they can feel stressed, guilty, nervous, frustrated, sad, heartbroken, and like they've let their dog down.[4] Many people say that treating the setback like a learning opportunity can help. Say to yourself, "Okay, so something went wrong, but what can I learn from it?" And remember that, since your dog has made progress before, they can make it again.[5]

SEEKING HELP FROM PROFESSIONALS

IT'S BETTER TO SEEK HELP with behavior issues sooner rather than later. It's understandable that you might want to wait and see how things go, or you might need time to save up to pay for help, but the thing about fear is that it typically does not go away on its own; it usually gets worse.

Any time there is a sudden change in your dog's behavior, it's important to schedule a vet visit in case there is a medical issue. Your veterinarian can also prescribe medication (see Chapter 7) and will likely have suggestions about dog trainers in your area. Your vet can refer you to a veterinary behaviorist, if needed.

Dog trainers can help with basic obedience, often in a class environment, but if you have a behavior issue with your dog, look for someone with appropriate expertise and experience who offers private training. Some dog trainers specialize in behavior issues, and even in particular behavior issues such as separation anxiety. Unfortunately, because dog training isn't regulated, you have to be careful where you go to seek help. People sometimes tell me about the first dog trainers they hired, the ones who made the problem worse. I am horrified by these stories of so-called trainers who have done things that have made the dog feel unsafe, sometimes deliberately provoking the dog to bite, or tying the dog up and forcing them into a situation where they are scared. These situations are often ones in which the dog is terrified and the person who is seeking help is at risk of a bite. The upshot is that the guardians now have a worse problem to solve, and they feel bad about themselves for hiring someone who did something that is basically malpractice.

Sometimes people also tell me these trainers have been very rude to them, blaming them for their dog's behavior and even yelling at them. This makes them feel unhappy about the whole dog training situation. On the other hand, trainers who are encouraging and supportive and have good counseling skills can help people enjoy training and feel motivated to continue. You'll recognize the role of classical conditioning in both of these scenarios.

There are some amazing dog training and behavior professionals who get the job done sensibly and safely in a friendly, supportive, and professional manner. When you're looking for a trainer, bear in mind the things I said about dog training methods earlier. Essentially, you're looking for someone who will use food to train your dog. Sometimes force trainers are easy to spot: they post rants against using food and they show photos of dogs in prong, shock, or choke collars on their social media accounts. But sometimes they are trickier to spot, because the language of dog training is nebulous.

A good trainer should have a clear statement about their methods. But it can be difficult to find out the methods a dog trainer uses, according to a study that looked at the top ten dog trainers' websites in ten different cities across the US (that is, a hundred dog trainers in total).[6] The scientists found that some phrases were associated with trainers who use force: *electronic collar*, *e-collar*, *pack leader*, and *Mother Nature*. So those words are warning signs. Force-free trainers referred to electronic collars as shock collars (and in a sentence that stated they don't use them). Force-free trainers also tended to use the word *science*. It pays to look very closely at dog trainers' websites, because some obfuscate the methods they use, and others give proprietary names to their training techniques that can make it hard to know exactly what they are doing. It really is "buyer beware" when it comes to choosing a dog trainer.

One way to look for a trainer is to start with a directory from a dog training organization that does not use force or fear; a membership organization such as the Pet Professional Guild; a credentialing organization such as the Pet Professional Accreditation Board; or a dog training school such as the Academy for Dog Trainers, DogNostics, Karen Pryor Academy, Pat Miller's Canine Behavior and Training Academy, and Victoria Stilwell Academy. You can also look at the education, certifications, and continuing education that dog trainers list on their website, to get a feel for the approach they take. In the UK, look for someone who is registered with the Animal Behaviour and Training Council (ABTC) as a clinical animal behaviorist or animal training instructor (dog trainer). A handy practitioner directory on the ABTC website can help you find someone near you. You may also consider members of organizations signed up to the UK Dog Behaviour and Training Charter. A list of practitioner organizations can be found on the charter website.

Some of the most common dog training and behavior certifications are shown in the table below. Each organization has their own rules and procedures for certification and for dealing with ethics violations. The Pet Professional Guild is the only international membership organization that is committed to using reward-based training, so you can trust their members to use these methods. The Pet Professional Accreditation Board says "there is no place for shock, choke, prong, pain, force, or fear in pet training and behavior practices," which means you can trust that trainers accredited by them will only use reward-based methods.[7]

Some organizations and certifications, including the International Association of Animal Behavior Consultants (IAABC) and

Certification Council for Professional Dog Trainers (CCPDT) certifications, are based on a principle called Least Intrusive, Minimally Aversive (LIMA). Although this approach prioritizes positive reinforcement, some trainers with these certifications may use aversive methods, while others do not. LIMA was developed within a framework of using aversives, and the use of "minimal" aversives (however that is defined) is not reward-based.[8] Indeed, the CCPDT position statement on electronic training collars states that "the CCPDT does not forbid the use of electronic collars that are used within the constraints of the Humane Hierarchy."[9] So some trainers with the CCPDT certification may use shock collars. Meanwhile, the IAABC states that "the use of shock in training and behavior is not considered a best practice . . . and is strongly discouraged," and requires its members to consult with their supervision team if they plan to use a shock collar.[10] The IAABC also says that "LIMA guidelines do not justify the use of aversive methods and tools," and CCPDT uses similar wording.[11] Always ask questions before hiring a dog trainer so that you know their position.

Common credentials in animal behavior and dog training

DACVB	Diplomate of the American College of Veterinary Behaviorists, a board-certified veterinary behaviorist. Certified by the American College of Veterinary Behaviorists.
CAAB	Certified Applied Animal Behaviorist. Has a PhD in animal behavior and five years of professional experience, or is a veterinarian (DVM or VMD) who has completed a behavior residency (two years) and has three further years of professional experience. Certified by the Animal Behavior Society.
ACAAB	Associate Certified Applied Animal Behaviorist. Has a master's degree in behavioral or biological science with a focus on animal behavior and two years of professional experience. Certified by the Animal Behavior Society.

PCBC-A	Professional Canine Behavior Consultant—Accredited. Certified by the Pet Professional Accreditation Board.
PCT-A	Professional Canine Trainer—Accredited. Certified by the Pet Professional Accreditation Board.
CDBC	Certified Dog Behavior Consultant. Certified by the International Association of Animal Behavior Consultants.
CABC	Certified Animal Behavior Consultant. Certified by the International Association of Animal Behavior Consultants.
CTT-A	Canine Training Technician—Accredited. Certified by the Pet Professional Accreditation Board.
CBCC-KA	Certified Behavior Consultant Canine-Knowledge Assessed. Certified by the Certification Council for Professional Dog Trainers.
CPDT-KSA	Certified Professional Dog Trainer—Knowledge and Skills Assessed. Certified by the Certification Council for Professional Dog Trainers.
CPDT-KA	Certified Professional Dog Trainer—Knowledge Assessed. Certified by the Certification Council for Professional Dog Trainers.
CTC	Certificate in Training and Counseling from the Academy for Dog Trainers.
KPA CTP	Karen Pryor Academy Certified Training Partner.
VSA CDT	Victoria Stilwell Academy Certified Dog Trainer.
PMCT	Pat Miller Certified Trainer.
DN-DBC	DogNostics Dog Behavior Consultant.
DN-DTC	DogNostics Dog Trainer Certified.
FFCP-Trainer	Fear Free Certified Professional Trainer.
CSAT	Certified Separation Anxiety Trainer. Certified by Malena DeMartini.
CSAP-BC	Certified Separation Anxiety Pro Behavior Consultant. Certified by Julie Naismith.

Since dog training is not regulated, you may find you've hired someone who is not taking the right approach. Dr. Richter advises: "If you did get help and you're not comfortable with what that person is telling you to do, stop—even if you paid money to get that help from that person. Don't ever do something to your dog that you wouldn't do to your child, because that's going to do more damage than good and you're going to end up paying way more money to help the dog, or you might lose the dog. One of the biggest mistakes is to get the wrong help."

The costs of training and behavior help

Finding a suitably qualified trainer or behaviorist will save you time and money in the long run. These are people who have invested significant time and money in their education, often spending years working towards qualifications, and who continue to engage in lifelong learning to make sure they are using the most up-to-date knowledge. Needless to say, this help does not come cheap. Some behavior issues take longer than others to resolve, so you may need to hire these professionals over a period of weeks or months. It's much better to pay for the right kind of behavior advice that will help resolve the problem than to spend money on other approaches that will not work or may even make things worse.

If you have pet insurance, check the policy to see if it will cover training for behavior issues—some policies do. (And if you're getting insurance for a new puppy, consider whether you want behavior training to be one of the things you are insured for.) If you recently adopted your puppy or dog from a shelter or humane society, reach out to them for advice.

Quality training and behavior advice are well worth paying for, and you may need to save up to pay for them. If you are looking for ways to lower the cost, some trainers will do an initial consult that sets you up to continue the training on your own, without additional help from them. Not all trainers do this, as a package that includes follow-up sessions typically leads to better results. (Private sessions are usually needed for behavior issues, but in rare cases it may be possible to team up with a friend whose dog has a similar issue.) Some trainers will occasionally barter behavior services for something that you can offer them; one way to find someone is through a local online group or mutual aid society.

Remember that good trainers have invested in their education and will bring a ton of expertise to your dog's behavior issue; they deserve to be well paid for this work. Since we often grow up with dogs, many people think they already know all about them. We tend to devalue the knowledge and skills involved in working with dogs, the extent to which science has changed our ideas of what is best for dogs, and the time and effort people put into getting an education in dog training and animal behavior. It's not fair to expect free advice from a dog trainer friend, any more than it would be fair of them to expect you to work for free.

CONSIDERING AND COMING TO TERMS WITH REHOMING AND EUTHANASIA

MAKING THE DECISION to rehome or euthanize your pet can be very hard. If only there were lots of homes out there for dogs with more serious behavior issues. Some dogs may thrive in a new home, especially, for example, if they don't get on well with kids and go to a home without them, or if they don't get on with another resident dog and go to a home where they are the only pet. In cases like these, a move is sometimes all it takes for the dog to live a happy life. But sometimes it is very difficult, if not impossible, to find the right home. Many people who are looking for a dog would understandably prefer to find one without behavior issues. If the dog has a history of biting, you must disclose that information to any potential adopter, otherwise you're exposing yourself to a potential lawsuit (and it wouldn't be good for your conscience either). Rehoming is also stressful for a dog, and stress can sometimes make behavior issues worse.

If you decide to rehome your dog, and they came from a responsible breeder, it's probably in the contract that you should return the dog to the breeder. If the breeder won't take them back, finding a breed rescue is probably the next best option. There are rescues for most breeds, and many of them will keep a dog in a foster home until a new home is found. A reputable shelter or rescue is another good option, because they will assess your dog and make sure they go to a home that is well suited to them. You may have to wait for a spot to come up, and they will interview you or have a form that asks you about your dog. Be honest in this interview; a fuller knowledge of your dog's behavior issues will help them find an appropriate home. It doesn't help to hide things, as that may lead to an inappropriate placement, and if the shelter's behavior team needs to work with the dog, it's best that they know.

In some circumstances, shelters and rescues will euthanize dogs if the dogs have certain kinds of behavior issues or turn out not to be adoptable. Ask about this before handing over your dog, so that you find somewhere with policies that you agree with. Expect to pay a fee or make a donation if surrendering a dog to a shelter, because they have a lot of costs associated with caring for pets, including spay/neuter surgeries, vaccinations, and microchipping, if they have not been done.

You may also be able to find a new home by asking friends and family, and in some cases this may even give you the option of still seeing the dog from time to time. There are no guarantees if you rehome a dog via a website or social media. For all you know, the person is just looking for a dog to sell, to breed, or to use for other purposes. That's why a shelter or rescue will give you more peace of mind.

If your dog's welfare is a serious concern, if they are responsible for serious bites, or if your family's quality of life is badly affected and rehoming doesn't seem like an option, then euthanasia may be on the table. If you've been working with a dog trainer or your vet, they may even raise the topic themselves. If something has just happened, don't rush into a decision; take your time to think about the options. Seek help if you haven't already (though ideally seek help long before you reach this point).

When a family is considering rehoming or euthanasia because of behavior issues, seeing a veterinary behaviorist can often result in successful resolution of the matter.[12] Risk factors for the dog being rehomed or euthanized include large size, aggression towards people, a history of bites, and the presence of teenagers in the home. Although management—such as muzzling a dog or keeping them behind gates or doors when other people are around—can be very helpful, it's not foolproof. If the risk of management failure is too high, such that a person or pet is at risk of a serious bite, then that's one situation in which euthanasia may be considered the best option.

If you are seriously considering euthanasia, you may want to see if you can find a kennel where the dog can stay for a week or two (if appropriate) while you think things over. Maybe you will feel relief that you are not having to deal with them anymore, or maybe you will miss them and want to try again to resolve the issue. Euthanasia is easier to arrange, and usually easier for people to deal with, when the pet is older or sick; it's much harder when the dog is younger.

Although it can be devastating to lose a dog to euthanasia, it may also come with peace of mind. If you do decide to rehome or euthanize your pet, take some time to grieve afterwards. These are difficult circumstances for everyone, and even if you know you did your best to help your dog, there are bound to be many feelings about what happened. You may also find some comfort in knowing that the dog is no longer suffering, and that you were with them until the end. If you need to, reach out and find support from a pet grief counselor, and lean on your family and friends at this difficult time.

LEARNING ABOUT AND WORKING WITH DOGS

THE MORE YOU KNOW about dog behavior, the better you'll be able to help your dog. Borrow books from your local library and look out for local or online talks and webinars where you can learn more about dog behavior and training from reliable sources. Read blogs such as my own, *Companion Animal Psychology* (and sign up for my newsletter while you're there). Other great online resources include blogs and social media from the American College of Veterinary Behaviorists, the American Veterinary Society of Animal Behavior, Dr. Patricia McConnell, Dr. Marc Bekoff and Dr. Jessica Pierce at *Psychology Today*, Fear Free Happy Homes, the Academy for Dog Trainers, Victoria Stilwell Academy, Karen Pryor Academy, the Fearful Dogs website and Facebook group run by Debbie Jacobs, and blogs and social media from organizations such as the British Columbia Society for the Prevention of Cruelty to Animals (BC SPCA), American Society for the Prevention of Cruelty to Animals (ASPCA), Dogs Trust, and Royal Society for the Prevention of Cruelty to Animals (RSPCA). Some of the individuals quoted in this book also have excellent blogs, including Kristi Benson, Kate LaSala, Jessica Ring, and Tim Steele.

Sometimes people are inspired by their fearful dog to learn more about dog behavior and, ultimately, to find a career involving dogs. Having a fearful dog gives you experience at setting up the environment to help a dog feel safe and to protect them from situations where they may feel scared or potentially bite. It gives you practice at choosing the right kinds of treats and at timing when those treats are delivered—not to mention reading a dog's body language, which can become second nature once you have enough experience.

Becoming a dog trainer, of course, requires many skills. One way to develop those skills and put what you already know into practice is to volunteer with a local animal shelter or rescue. There are many different kinds of volunteer positions. Fundraising, welcoming and training volunteers, dealing with social media, or helping with a local pet food bank may not involve direct contact with animals, but they are important activities without which many organizations might not exist. For those who prefer to be directly involved in animal care, many shelters and rescues have a dog walking program where volunteers take shelter dogs for walks throughout the day. Some places even allow dogs on longer outings. Help may also be needed for other animal care activities, including bathing and grooming dogs or driving them to and from appointments at the vet. Fosters take dogs into their home for short periods, often because the dogs have medical needs or do better when not in a kennel, and sometimes because a mom and a whole litter of puppies need a safe space for nursing and puppy-raising. Fosters make a huge difference to the animals they care for, and help make the dogs more adoptable. All of these roles are great ways for the right person to gain experience with dogs.

Be sure to check out any shelter or rescue before you get involved with it, to ensure that it uses modern dog training techniques and is not putting prong collars, shock collars, or other outdated tools on dogs. Indeed, there are few regulations for animal rescues. Before signing up with an organization, check that it has the kind of policies you would look for as a potential adopter of a dog—that is, that it will take animals back if something goes wrong with the placement. This will help you filter out some of the organizations that may be problematic.

Some animal welfare and behavior organizations have membership options for the general public, which can be for people who want to learn more, become involved with the organization, and/or make donations. For example, the Pet Professional Guild, BC SPCA, ASPCA, and the UK RSPCA all have some kind of membership option for pet guardians.

If you've really got the training bug, get your learning on. Most jurisdictions allow anyone to call themselves a dog trainer, but it is, of course, best to get formal instruction. In addition to reading books about dog training and behavior, and attending lectures, webinars, and conferences, studying with a dog training school can give you the knowledge and confidence to set up your dog training business. It's important to note, again, that any school should be committed to using only reward-based training methods; don't waste your money on anywhere that uses aversive approaches. Think about what kind of dog training appeals to you most, as this information will help you choose a school. For example, maybe the experience of having a fearful dog has made you want to help others with their fearful dogs, or perhaps it has left you with a strong desire to run puppy classes to help prevent fears from developing in the first place. Each school has its own focus, so look carefully at the curriculum. Dog training schools may be completely online, completely in-person, or a mix. Many have scholarships available, including some aimed specifically at shelter workers and volunteers and/or people from underrepresented groups.

There are, of course, other careers that involve working with dogs, and other ways to get an education that will help with a dog training career. For those wanting to study at university, options for undergraduate, master's, and PhD studies include animal behavior, psychology, biology, and zoology, with a strong component in animal behavior and welfare, or anthrozoology (the study of the human-animal bond). Working for animal welfare organizations offers a wide range of careers. Becoming a veterinarian or a vet tech (known as a vet nurse in the UK) is another option. And, of course, if you want to become a board-certified veterinary behaviorist, you have to first become a veterinarian. Veterinarians and vet techs with a particular interest in animal behavior are eligible to join the American Veterinary Society of Animal Behavior, and membership is free for students. Those with a relevant doctorate degree can become an affiliate member. (Full disclosure: I'm proud to call myself one of them.)

Another way to get involved in the field is to campaign for dogs' welfare. Consider writing to your local and national politicians to ask that something be done about puppy mills, or about the use of aversive training methods. Talk to family and friends or post information on social media to help educate people about dog behavior. Or simply share your own experiences of living with your fearful dog. But I have a plea to be careful not to spread misinformation, even to rage or complain about it: social media can make such posts spread like wildfire. Sadly, when we share erroneous information, all we are doing is making sure more people see it and giving it legitimacy. There's a whole science behind science communication that tells us it's important to focus on accurate, useful information, ideally with a story behind it. This is where sharing your own story—or your clients' stories—of doing the things that keep your dog feeling safe can really make a difference.

EQUITY, DIVERSITY, AND INCLUSION

DOG TRAINING AND ANIMAL BEHAVIOR have a reputation for being very white. If you don't see people who are like you working in those roles, it can sometimes be hard to imagine doing them yourself. While we need a lot more work to diversify the fields of animal behavior and animal welfare, social media can reveal people outside your immediate circles who are doing the work you imagine yourself doing, because there are some fantastic Black, Indigenous, and people of color dog trainers making a difference in the profession. Some groups are working for change too. The Animal Behavior Society has awards and programs, including the Charles H. Turner Award—named after one of the first African American animal behavior scientists—which supports undergraduate travel to the society's annual meeting.[13] Companions and Animals for Reform and Equity (CARE) is the first Black, Indigenous, and people of color animal welfare organization in the US, and is involved in research, policy, truth-telling, and other work. They provide scholarships to Black veterinary students at the historically black Tuskegee University. Souly Alliance is a US nonprofit that aims to increase diversity and inclusion in the field of animal welfare. Also in the US, the National Association for Black Veterinarians aims to "advocate, provide support, and cultivate an inclusive community for blacks in veterinary medicine."[14] The Black Veterinary Association of Canada aims to support diversity and inclusivity, and has bursaries for Black-identifying students who want to get into a vet med or vet tech program.

In the UK, Animal Aspirations aims to encourage students from diverse backgrounds to be interested in veterinary medicine. They have a wonderful social media presence and have teamed up with the Easter Bush Equality, Diversity, and Inclusion group to make a podcast series called *Vets in Diversity*. The British Veterinary Ethnicity and Diversity Society aims to bring more diversity and inclusivity. They have prepared training modules and are engaged in research on diversity and racism in the vet profession. Many dog training or pet professional organizations now have diversity, equity, and inclusion committees and/or diversity and inclusivity scholarships.

OF COURSE, there's no requirement to take up a career in dog training simply because you have a fearful dog. If you don't feel like changing careers or volunteering for a rescue, that's absolutely fine. I hope you will still feel proud of the knowledge and skills you've learned from your fearful furry friend.

"Munchie came into my life as a foster dog and soon to be a *foster-fail*. She wasn't the first but definitely the most fearful dog I've encountered. I expected she would require decompression time and eventually adjust to life in the city. Well, I was wrong.

A few months went by and nothing changed. I enlisted a trusted force-free trainer, who then recommended medical intervention. I didn't see this coming, but exhausted and sleep-deprived due to Munchie's ongoing restlessness, I acquiesced.

By doing so, I had to let go of a lifetime's worth of convictions that being medicated will only lead to addiction and a diluted version of one's self. Nevertheless, for Munchie's sake, I gave this a shot. Fast-forward a few months on medication and training, and Munchie walked down our busy street for the first time. The fear and anxiety were parting, allowing space for her beautiful personality to emerge.

Participating firsthand in Munchie's journey made me realize that medication doesn't have to be a last resort. It's a *kindness* that both you and your fearful dog deserve."

—**TAYEF FARRAR**, CTC, **director of operations at** NYC **Second Chance Rescue**

15

FEARFUL
FIDO NO MORE

· · · · · · · · · · · · · · · · ·

T'S AN UNREMARKABLE EVENING a few nights before Halloween, and Pepper is snoozing in the armchair, occasional little snores escaping from his peaceful body. There's a loud bang from a firework somewhere nearby. I look up from my book and across at Pepper. He's still sleeping. I think back to when we had Bodger, and all the nights I spent feeding him sausage treats or cheese for every bang of a firework, clap of thunder, or hoot of an owl. It was slow progress at first, but in the end it helped enormously. And Bodger was no less of a good dog because he found those noises frightening. He was an amazing dog. I think he would have approved of Pepper, of his relaxed nature and the way he's so nice to the cats. If Bodger were still with us, he would have enjoyed herding him together with the cats. It's definitely easier having a dog like Pepper who loves everyone and doesn't mind loud noises. Every dog is unique in their personality and what they bring to our life. With a fearful dog, it helps to remember and celebrate what you love about them and not just focus on the hard times.

LESSONS LEARNED

IT WAS ONE OF THOSE super bright days in August with tempera-tures in the low 30s (around 90°F), and it was ages since we'd had rain. I was walking up the driveway with Pepper, him mov-ing slowly on the grass, me on the gravel beside him. I had on my baseball cap and was looking down when I heard a sudden flap of wings that started nearby and seemed to be incoming. I ducked instinctively, and the flapping seemed right at my head; then the wingbeats became more normal and rhythmic and continued down the driveway. When I dared to raise my head, Pepper was looking up at me with big eyes, like "What on earth was that?!" What, indeed? I hadn't seen it coming, and the bird was already in the trees now, out of sight. It wasn't the bird that I'd heard in the moments before the flapping, which was a raven, a couple of hundred meters away in a tree. Perhaps I'd been flown at by the juvenile raven that, a few weeks earlier, I'd seen fly into the forest after its parents, followed by the *crunch-crunch-crack* of knocking on dry wood, a clumsy flight into the parched forest. The noises didn't sound good, but these were aerial crashes, not followed by the sounds of a bird plummeting to the ground, so the raven sur-vived. Maybe they had now learned to avoid trees and it was my turn to be flight practice.

The experience put me in mind of a time some years earlier, when we still had Bodger, who was terrified of barred owls. This was a fear we spent several years working on, mostly in the mid-dle of the night, when the owl came by and called "Who cooks for you, who cooks for you all?" As we were nearing the top of the driveway one time in the autumn, when Bodger was already sick, a barred owl flew at us from a tree in my neighbor's yard, apparently taking aim at my hat. We both saw it coming across the street towards us. Bodger leaped, barking, into the air, as high as the leash would allow him, and the owl did a U-turn, so slow that for a split second it seemed poised in midair, as if about to fall, before slowly flapping and gaining height and moving to another tree. Four times in the space of two weeks, that young owl flew at me, each time less awkward than the last, until the final time, when it swooped silently just over my head and continued on, elegant at last, into the trees behind our house.

Working with a fearful dog is kind of like the flight of that teenage owl. At first, it can feel clumsy and awkward, as if you'll never learn all the stuff you need to know and things might come crashing down at any time. Over time, it becomes a beautiful dance as you and your dog move through the environment, no longer troubled, a team. Knowing what to avoid, when to treat, how to spot the tiniest signs of anxiety, all become second nature. And in the end, your dog and you become a perfect pair, each molded to fit the other, attuned to what's needed and with enough relaxation to love, laugh, and just be together.

I like to think I've learned something from all the dogs I've worked with. Even in the cases when there wasn't a happy ending, I've come to terms with the fact that the dog is at peace (that doesn't mean I didn't wail at the time). And I've learned from my own dogs, because, after all, they're the ones I've spent the most time with. From Ghost, I learned how long it can take a sad, desperate dog to settle in and feel like he's really at home (six months, in his case). Bodger arrived as a whirlwind of hope and anxiety, and I learned how to prioritize his issues, to stay on track, and especially to check my training mechanics. Amongst the things Pepper has taught me is the importance of pain relief, because he's so much better when his pain is under control. I already knew the value of my vet, but all three of these dogs, and my cats, have shown it time and time again.

We lost Bodger too soon. By then, he was over his fear of owls (unless they were right overhead) and most of the other fears he'd had. He was a wonderful friend and soulmate; from this awkward creature who had joined our home, he became a perfect fit for us, and we for him. I think back to everyone who said we should return him to the shelter, and how, if we'd done so, we would have missed out on the most amazing dog. His lovely disposition wasn't obvious, back in those days. Progress came in fits and starts until, after a while, I realized everything had been much easier for him for quite some time.

And just now, we've lost Harley—our beautiful tabby cat who would start to purr as soon as I walked into the room. He was cuddly and easygoing, loved routine, and always wanted to keep warm. From time to time, we would lose Harley in the house and, after we had searched high and low for him, he would suddenly be sitting in the middle of the hall where we had first looked for him. It was as if he had teleported there. One of the other remarkable things about Harley was how readily he learned to accept the twice-daily medications that kept him going for so long.

There are no guarantees with behavior. No one can wave a magic wand and say how things will turn out. Plenty of approaches will make things worse, and the approaches that actually work can take time. If you have faith in the process and keep going, learning as you go, you'll be surprised how well things can turn out (but not always). Training, management, exercise, and enrichment are all important parts of the process to ensure that your dog feels safe and can improve their bond with you too. If you take up a dog sport together, you can even work towards a title (see Chapter 6). But helping a fearful dog to feel safe is a reward in itself.

This is what Bonnie Hartney says about how her dog, Dixie, turned out: "She's lovely. We're going to do her trick title. She's got all the tricks in place. She's honestly the best dog now. She really is. She's adorable and fun for everybody."

It's a big turnaround for the dog who, at first, would not come out of her hiding place.

SOCIETAL CHANGES THAT WOULD HELP DOGS

THE APPROACHES DETAILED in this book for helping anxious, fearful, and reactive dogs overcome their fears are, of necessity, individual ones. But it would be remiss of me not to mention the role that societal factors play in creating so many canine fears and anxieties in the first place. From puppy mills and poor breeding practices to lack of education and the use of outdated aversive training methods, the list is a long one. It often seems that because people love dogs, they assume that things are rosy in dog world, and they simply do not notice that many things are actually badly wrong. While, as individuals, we need to have our "buyer beware" hat on, there are changes at a societal level that would make a big difference to the lives of dogs.

Aversive training methods cause many issues. Many more people are using reward-based methods at least some of the time—99.7 percent, according to one UK study.[1] The trouble is that too many people still also use aversive methods like shake cans or prong collars some of the time. The fact that some dog training organizations still allow aversive approaches, despite the evidence, is a serious problem. I find it hard to understand why some organizations that say they care about dog welfare do not take stronger action on aversive dog training methods.

First, I want to give credit where it's due, and show some gratitude for those who make a difference by taking a stand. The American College of Veterinary Behaviorists' position statement advocates against the use of aversive methods, and the ACVB consistently provides up-to-date information to help pets with behavior issues. The American Veterinary Society of Animal Behavior's position statement on humane dog training makes a strong, evidence-based argument and is a model of clear communication. The BC Society for the Prevention of Cruelty to Animals' AnimalKind guidelines help people in British Columbia find a trainer who uses only kind, humane methods, and their review of the literature on dog training methods (which has been updated since first being published) is excellent.[2] The American Society for the Prevention of Cruelty to Animals developed a new program that's making a big difference to extremely fearful dogs at their Behavioral Rehabilitation Center.[3] The Canadian Association of Professional Dog Trainers updated their code of ethics in 2021 to prevent members from using aversives. Their "STOP list" includes shock collars, loud noises, anti-bark collars, prong collars, alpha rolls, hitting, and more. In the UK, a coalition of animal welfare organizations—including the Kennel Club, Dogs Trust, Royal Society for the Prevention of Cruelty to Animals, Battersea Dogs and Cats Home, British Veterinary Association, and Blue Cross—has campaigned hard for a ban on shock collars.[4] Also in the UK, the Animal Behaviour and Training Council is a registered charity that sets humane standards for animal behavior and training. Around the world, many individuals and organizations work tirelessly to teach people why it's so important to use reward-based methods (and to demonstrate that these methods work). There are many more than I can mention here, so I apologize if your organization is not included, but please know that I appreciate all that you do.

If only *all* organizations were professional and put animal welfare front and center. Given the mounting evidence against aversive training, it's past time for every organization of professional dog trainers to ban membership or certification to anyone who uses these methods. Not doing so gives legitimacy to those trainers and helps them find more clients. It makes it difficult for ordinary people to find a good dog trainer, because they can't rely on those certifications to mean the training will be humane. And it makes it difficult for dog guardians to find good sources of advice. Even articles in reputable newspapers and magazines sometimes include quotes from trainers who still, mysteriously, espouse pack theory, dominance, or other ideas that try to justify aversive methods. Again, the trainers who give these interviews can point to professional memberships and certifications to give themselves legitimacy, which no doubt makes it harder for journalists to weed out these ideas.

For fearful and anxious dogs, it's especially important to avoid aversive methods. As Jean Donaldson says: "Fear is kind of baked in to aversive methods. So for trainers to try and fix fear by putting the dog in essentially a double bind, and say, 'Yeah, you're afraid of that child and you're growling. If you growl, I'm going to cut off your air and hurt you and scare the pants off you, so that you don't growl.' If you think about it, that any trainer or practitioner out there is still doing this now—I don't know if malpractice gets much worse than that. It could not be more contraindicated, taking this approach . . . It's just boggling."

Several countries have already banned the use of shock collars—I hope it will one day happen where I live. Dog training organizations banning members or certificants from using them would significantly reduce the number of people using these devices where they're allowed, and would make it easier to find force-free trainers (see Chapter 14). Sadly, many ordinary dog guardians who would never think of using aversive devices end up buying them because a dog trainer has recommended them.

Puppy mills are another big issue that affects the prevalence of canine fears and anxieties. We've known for a long, long time that early experiences make a big difference to canine behavior. If your puppy has already had great socialization experiences at the breeder's home, it's much easier for you to continue with socialization; you already have a great starting point. When puppies have been raised in barns or cages and not had those early socialization experiences, they have already missed out on a lot by the time they get into your home. That's why finding a good breeder or rescue makes such a big difference.

The endless supply of social media videos of people doing things to dogs that you either shouldn't do to that particular dog at that time or shouldn't do to dogs, full stop, normalizes these behaviors. Sadly, many people find these videos cute. I'm not denying that cute animal videos are out there, but in general, if someone tells me they've seen one, my heart sinks. I don't want to know, because most of the time these videos show a dog who is unhappy or afraid and the person doesn't seem to realize it. Maybe the dog is turning their head away from the person's hand, licking their lips (and there's no sign of a treat), or tucking their tail and keeping their body low to the ground. When you see videos like this, don't share them. Even better, if they violate the guidelines of the platform they are posted on, report them.

People who work with dogs sometimes struggle with the things they see in their day-to-day lives. If this is you, take the steps you need to protect yourself. Don't be part of groups on social media that bring unwanted drama and unpleasantness to your life. Block or mute people who tag you in cases of animal cruelty and so on. Do what you need to do to protect yourself so you can continue to do the work that you love and that makes such a difference to people and their dogs.

As we've seen, fear, anxiety, and stress are complex issues, and we have to remember there are circumstances when fear is useful, even essential for survival. But it would be much, much better for dog welfare if so many of these issues didn't exist.

A SLOW APPROACH

I LIKE TO THINK that one thing I've learned from working with fearful dogs is how to pay very close attention to what they need. I've seen firsthand that trying to rush things or thinking that you "should" be going faster only slows down any progress.

Training a fearful dog will teach you patience if you don't have it already. While we often talk of going at the dog's pace, it can feel like a snail's pace to you . . . at least when you get started. The thing is, starting slowly makes the whole process go faster. If you ignore the pace at which the dog feels comfortable and do what you think you "ought" or "want" to do, progress will, at best, grind to a halt and, at worst, go into overdrive in the wrong direction. Having a fearful dog will teach you perseverance, because the route to a resolution is not exactly linear; learning happens at its own pace and there will always be setbacks along the way. Keep going and persevere, because better times await. Having a fearful dog will also teach you good problem-solving abilities, because of the way you need to think about breaking situations down into little bits that you can work on one at a time, and the way you have to think about changes you can make to help your dog feel safe. It also teaches you to have steak (or whatever your dog loves) on your person or nearby to be the unconditioned stimulus (US) whenever ad-hoc counterconditioning can occur.

This is what Bonnie Hartney told me about the pace of working with her dog, Dixie: "I never like to write any dog off. Dixie has taught me that. There's some dogs where, of course, it's harder. And I suppose we got lucky, because when she's afraid she runs away, she hides, she won't let you touch her. If she was coming forward and biting, that would be a different story. But I think if you have the patience and the time . . . You know, the one thing I've learned is that when you have a preconceived timeline, and you want to do something faster, it always sets you back; it almost never works out. And so it's a slow pace. That snail's pace really gets you to the end."

I would love it if more dogs became happy and optimistic, instead of shivering, shaking, and cowering from scary things. Knowing the right things to do makes such a big difference, which is why it's so important to understand the science behind these techniques. If you have found this book helpful, please let others know about it. You may also want to seek out my blog, *Companion Animal Psychology*, where I post regularly about canine and feline science and behavior. You can also listen to my podcast, *The Pawsitive Post in Conversation*, which I cohost with Kristi Benson. We chat about dogs and cats and interview scientists, authors, and pet professionals.

Writing a book is a long process that, although lovely, is difficult. In the final stages of working on this manuscript, when I could hardly bear to keep sitting down at my desk each day to keep on writing, when I badly needed a break not just from work but also from the difficulties that kept befalling our family, my husband made me a hazelnut cake. I love hazelnuts, and this wonderful sponge cake was a gift to help me through some hard days. I hope that you have a partner or friend who will make you a hazelnut cake when you need it. We all need people like that in our lives. And so do our dogs. We need to be the ones who will make a hazelnut cake for our dogs, or rather the canine equivalent. This metaphorical cake has layers, including the provision of a safe space, choices and control, and protection from stressful events; it involves management and training, and maybe one or more pet professionals; and it involves finding ways to nurture your relationship with your dog even when times are hard (see table below). And on the top of the cake, there's a generous sprinkling of unexpected cheddar cheese (or whatever makes a great unconditioned stimulus). Because even when you and your dog are finding things tough, your relationship is a special one. You're their provider of hazelnut cake—and they are yours.

The thing I love most about working with fearful and shy dogs is the way a feeling of trust grows between you. The dog learns that you will protect them from scary situations and act if needed to keep them safe. In exchange for all your hard work on whatever issues there are, you get the dog's real love. Not every situation has a happy ending, as rehoming or euthanasia are sometimes a necessity or inevitability. But there are also many happy endings, even if they are not the one you expected. Yours may involve grieving the life you thought you'd have with your dog, before realizing that, actually, things are pretty good. A fearful dog is no less of a dog than any other dog, and can still be a great friend.

Getting over my own fear of dogs, a long time ago now, felt like a great weight lifted off my shoulders. At the time, the process felt more like the removal of a series of small weights that added up to me losing an unnecessary fear—and ultimately opened up new possibilities for me. Helping your dog get over their fears can also feel like a weight is gone. I hope this book will help you see your dog in a new light, and I wish you many successes. Let me know how it goes!

"In our fast-paced, immediate gratification culture of instant downloads and overnight shipping, it can be hard to find moments of calm. However, many of my clients find surprising relief in the daily routines of living with a fearful dog. They report that it's the first time in a long time a situation has encouraged them to slow down and take a measured approach. Accepting that slow and steady is the best approach to help their dog brings unexpected, Zen-like patience and mindfulness to their lives. One client shared that the understanding, compassion, and patience she showed her fearful dog helped her extend the same to herself and others. There is no rushing a dog through their fears, so finding silver linings in unexpected benefits to our well-being can feel like a gift."

—LIZZY FLANAGAN, CTC, owner of Lizzy and the Good Dog People

Important tips for living with a fearful dog

- Understand that fear is a protective emotion; it's only in some circumstances that it becomes an issue.
- Above all, aim to help your dog feel safe.
- Remember that your dog is behaving this way (refusing to do something, hiding, growling, etcetera) because they are struggling.
- Establish a safe space for your dog and ensure all household members and visitors know to stay away from it.
- Take steps to ensure that your dog does not have to face anything they are afraid of (if this isn't possible, see your veterinarian).
- Give your dog choices whenever possible, such as whether to meet new people.
- Establish a routine for your dog.
- Keep a diary. When progress feels slow, you can look back and see how far you've come.
- Some setbacks are inevitable. Try to see them as learning opportunities.
- Pay attention to technique when you're training your dog, using the tips from this book.

- Follow a plan for your training (or work with a trainer who will develop one for you).
- Understand that training takes time, patience, and practice.
- Be generous with wonderful treats for your dog.
- If your dog has ever bitten someone (or seems like they might), prioritize muzzle training.
- Know that whether we're talking about muzzles, crates, harnesses, or jackets for your dog, you can't assume they will like them; you should expect to do some training.
- See your veterinarian as appropriate, to investigate potential medical issues and to see if medications may help.
- Seek help with behavior and training, if needed, from a suitably qualified trainer or behaviorist.
- Ignore well-meaning advice from people who don't really know what to do.
- Try to take pleasure in the small moments, and remember what you love about your dog.
- Lean on friends and family for support as needed.

ACKNOWLEDGMENTS

I'S A PLEASURE to be working again with everyone at Greystone Books. Many, many people are involved in making a book, and I am grateful to every one of them. Thank you in particular to my brilliant editor, Lucy Kenward. Thank you to Belle Wuthrich for designing yet another gorgeous cover. I am grateful to Fiona Siu, whose hard work on design and typesetting has made this book look amazing. And thank you to Megan Jones, Sydney Marchand, Corina Eberle, Andrew Furlow, Fiona Brownlee, Emily Cook, and Jill Owens Leigh for being such a great marketing and publicity team. Thanks, too, to Jennifer Croll, Jessica Sullivan, Andrea Damiani, Kathy Nguyen, and everyone else involved. And many thanks to Brian Lynch for a careful and collegial copy edit, and to Jennifer Stewart for thorough proofreading.

Special thanks to my agent, Fiona Kenshole, for all her hard work in helping this book come to fruition. Your guidance is much appreciated (as are the cat and dog stories!).

I've long admired Cat Warren's beautiful writing, and it's a dream come true that she agreed to write the foreword. Thank you, Cat.

I am grateful to all the scientists, veterinarians, and dog trainers who so kindly shared their expertise with me. Lizzy Flanagan, Bonnie Hartney, Erica Beckwith, Jean Ballard, and Bad Monkey Photography have kindly let me use their drawings and photos, which I appreciate very much. This book wouldn't have happened if I hadn't found Jean Donaldson's Academy for Dog Trainers all those years ago. Thank you, Jean, for your friendship, good humor, and intellectual curiosity. A huge thank-you to Kristi Benson, special correspondent to my blog, *Companion Animal Psychology*, and my cohost on the *Pawsitive Post in Conversation* podcast, for being so supportive of this book and so funny and honest in all our joint projects. Thank you to Tim Steele and Jessica Ring for their encouraging and helpful feedback on the outline for this book, and for all their support and kind words throughout the process. Coffees with and kind words from Bonnie Hartney have meant a lot. And thanks to Dr. Jill Bradshaw, Lindsay Dellas, Joan Forry, Sarah Futterman-Devies, Nick Honor, Kate LaSala, Ruby Leslie, Kaz Murakami, Lisa Skavienski, Dr. Rachel Szumel, Lyn Thomas, Marianne Wanderloek, and everyone in the writing group, for all your support.

I'm grateful to all the subscribers to my newsletter who answered my questions about what they'd like to see in a book about fearful and anxious dogs, including George Bolte, Jill Cote, Maureen Derseweh, Karen Draney, Marion Harper, Stella McVicker, Jean A. Paterson, Karen Shannon, and Gina Varrin. Thank you, too, to everyone who has bought me a coffee on Ko-fi to support my work on this book and my blog.

This book and my previous ones have included stories about my pets. I'd like to thank my incredible veterinarian, Dr. Adrian Walton, and everyone at Dewdney Animal Hospital for taking such excellent care of my pets and for always being so kind and compassionate.

Special thanks to Roy and Frankie Todd, Stef and Richard Harvey, Margaret and Alan Mace.

And to Al, for the hazelnut cake and for everything. This book couldn't have happened without you.

NOTES

Chapter 1: Understanding Your Fearful Dog

1. Luiz Pessoa, "How many brain regions are needed to elucidate the neural bases of fear and anxiety?" *Neuroscience & Biobehavioral Reviews* (2023): 105039.

2. Milla Salonen et al., "Prevalence, comorbidity, and breed differences in canine anxiety in 13,700 Finnish pet dogs," *Scientific Reports* 10, no. 1 (2020): 2962.

3. I. Meyer et al., "Behavior problems in dogs—An assessment of prevalence and risk factors based on responses from a representative sample of Danish owners," *Journal of Veterinary Behavior* (2023): 69–70:24–31.

4. Caitlin Boyd et al., "Mortality resulting from undesirable behaviours in dogs aged under three years attending primary-care veterinary practices in England," *Animal Welfare* 27, no. 3 (2018): 251–262.

5. Camilla Pegram et al., "Proportion and risk factors for death by euthanasia in dogs in the UK," *Scientific Reports* 11, no. 1 (2021): 9145; D.G. O'Neill et al., "Longevity and mortality of owned dogs in England," *Veterinary Journal* 198, no. 3 (2013): 638–643; Yan Yu et al., "Mortality resulting from undesirable behaviours in dogs aged three years and under attending primary-care veterinary practices in Australia," *Animals* 11, no. 2 (2021): 493.

6. James T. Todd and Edward K. Morris, "The early research of John B. Watson: Before the behavioral revolution," *Behavior Analyst* 9 (1986): 71–88.

7. Bram Vervliet and Yannick Boddez, "Memories of 100 years of human fear conditioning research and expectations for its future," *Behaviour Research and Therapy* 135 (2020): 103732.

8. Ben Harris, "Letting go of Little Albert: Disciplinary memory, history, and the uses of myth," *Journal of the History of the Behavioral Sciences* 47, no. 1 (2011): 1–17.

9. Russell A. Powell et al., "Correcting the record on Watson, Rayner, and Little Albert: Albert Barger as 'psychology's lost boy,'" *American Psychologist* 69, no. 6 (2014): 600.

10. Harris, "Letting go of Little Albert."

11. Elyssa Payne, Pauleen C. Bennett, and Paul D. McGreevy, "Current perspectives on attachment and bonding in the dog–human dyad," *Psychology Research and Behavior Management* (2015): 71–79.

12. Gal Ziv, "The effects of using aversive training methods in dogs—A review," *Journal of Veterinary Behavior* 19 (2017): 50–60.

13. For example: Nicola Jane Rooney and Sarah Cowan, "Training methods and owner–dog interactions: Links with dog behaviour and learning ability," *Applied Animal Behaviour Science* 132, no. 3-4 (2011): 169–177; Lucy China, Daniel S. Mills, and Jonathan J. Cooper, "Efficacy of dog training with and without remote electronic collars vs. a focus on positive reinforcement," *Frontiers in Veterinary Science* (2020): 508.

14. Daniel P. Todes, *Ivan Pavlov: A Very Short Introduction* (Oxford: Oxford University Press, 2022).

15. John O'Riordan and Lina S. V. Roth, "Rescue dogs show few differences in behaviour, cognitive abilities, and personality compared with non-rescue dogs," *Journal of Veterinary Behavior* (2023); Kate M. Mornement et al., "Evaluation of the predictive validity of the Behavioural Assessment for Re-homing K9's (B.A.R.K.) protocol and owner satisfaction with adopted dogs," *Applied Animal Behaviour Science* 167 (2015): 35–42; Deborah L. Wells, and Peter G. Hepper, "Prevalence of behaviour problems reported by owners of dogs purchased from an animal rescue shelter," *Applied Animal Behaviour Science* 69, no. 1 (2000): 55–65; Lauren Powell et al., "Characterizing unsuccessful animal adoptions: Age and breed predict the likelihood of return, reasons for return and post-return outcomes," *Scientific Reports* 11, no. 1 (2021): 8018.

16. Franklin D. McMillan, Deborah L. Duffy, and James A. Serpell, "Mental health of dogs formerly used as 'breeding stock' in commercial breeding establishments," *Applied Animal Behaviour Science* 135, no. 1–2 (2011): 86–94; Yasemin Salgirli Demirbas, Bahri Emre, and Mustafa Kockaya,

"Integration ability of urban free-ranging dogs into adoptive families' environment," *Journal of Veterinary Behavior* 9, no. 5 (2014): 222–227; Dorothea Döring et al., "How do rehomed laboratory beagles behave in everyday situations? Results from an observational test and a survey of new owners," *PLOS ONE* 12, no. 7 (2017): e0181303.

17. Karysa Britton et al., "Caregiving for a companion animal compared to a family member: Burden and positive experiences in caregivers," *Frontiers in Veterinary Science* 5 (2018): 325; Kristin Buller and Kelly C. Ballantyne, "Living with and loving a pet with behavioral problems: Pet owners' experiences," *Journal of Veterinary Behavior* 37 (2020): 41–47; Katherine J. Goldberg, "Exploring caregiver burden within a veterinary setting," *Veterinary Record* 181, no. 12 (2017): 318.

Chapter 2: Fearful Fido

1. M. A. Fullana et al., "Human fear conditioning: From neuroscience to the clinic," *Behaviour Research and Therapy* 124 (2020): 103528.

2. Lívea Dornela Godoy et al., "A comprehensive overview on stress neurobiology: Basic concepts and clinical implications," *Frontiers in Behavioral Neuroscience* 12 (2018): 127.

3. Godoy et al., "A comprehensive overview."

4. Michael B. Hennessy et al., "Plasma cortisol levels of dogs at a county animal shelter," *Physiology & Behavior* 62, no. 3 (1997): 485–490; Michael B. Hennessy et al., "Behavior and cortisol levels of dogs in a public animal shelter, and an exploration of the ability of these measures to predict problem behavior after adoption," *Applied Animal Behaviour Science* 73, no. 3 (2001): 217–233.

5. Godoy et al., "A comprehensive overview."

6. Yuncai Chen and Tallie Z. Baram, "Toward understanding how early-life stress reprograms cognitive and emotional brain networks," *Neuropsychopharmacology* 41, no. 1 (2016): 197–206.

7. Godoy et al., "A comprehensive overview."

8. Miho Nagasawa et al., "The behavioral and endocrinological development of stress response in dogs," *Developmental Psychobiology* 56, no. 4 (2014): 726–733.

9. Godoy et al., "A comprehensive overview."

10. Marc Bekoff, "Social play behaviour: Cooperation, fairness, trust, and the evolution of morality," *Journal of Consciousness Studies* 8, no. 2: 81–90.

11. Franklin D. McMillan, "Behavioral and psychological outcomes for dogs sold as puppies through pet stores and/or born in commercial breeding establishments: Current knowledge and putative causes," *Journal of Veterinary Behavior* 19 (2017): 14–26.

12. Federica Pirrone et al., "Owner-reported aggressive behavior towards familiar people may be a more prominent occurrence in pet shop-traded dogs," *Journal of Veterinary Behavior* 11 (2016): 13–17; Franklin D. McMillan et al., "Differences in behavioral characteristics between dogs obtained as puppies from pet stores and those obtained from non-commercial breeders," *Journal of the American Veterinary Medical Association* 242, no. 10 (2013): 1359–1363.

13. Christine Calder (originally by Sophia Yin), "Bite levels in dogs," Veterinary Partner (original 2012; revised 2020), veterinarypartner.vin.com/default.aspx?pid=19239&id=10004159.

14. Peter S. Tuckel and William Milczarski, "The changing epidemiology of dog bite injuries in the United States, 2005–2018," *Injury Epidemiology* 7, no. 1 (2020): 1–11.

15. Niamh Caffrey et al., "Insights about the epidemiology of dog bites in a Canadian city using a dog aggression scale and administrative data," *Animals* 9, no. 6 (2019): 324; Gary J. Patronek et al., "Co-occurrence of potentially preventable factors in 256 dog bite–related fatalities in the United States (2000–2009)," *Journal of the American Veterinary Medical Association* 243, no. 12 (2013): 1726–1736.

16. Find the official version at: apdt.com/wp-content/uploads/2017/01/ian-dunbar-dog-bite-scale.pdf.

17. Patronek et al., "Co-occurrence."

Chapter 3: Safety (for You and Your Dog)

1. Mary Cover Jones, "The elimination of children's fears," *Journal of Experimental Psychology* 7, no. 5 (1924): 382.

2. Ziv, "Using aversive training methods."

3. Emily J. Blackwell et al., "The relationship between training methods and the occurrence of behavior problems, as reported by owners, in

a population of domestic dogs," *Journal of Veterinary Behavior* 3, no. 5 (2008): 207–217; Rachel A. Casey et al., "Human directed aggression in domestic dogs (*Canis familiaris*): Occurrence in different contexts and risk factors," *Applied Animal Behaviour Science* 152 (2014): 52–63; M. E. Herron, F. S. Shofer, and I. R. Reisner, "Survey of the use and outcome of confrontational and non-confrontational training methods in client-owned dogs showing undesirable behaviors," *Applied Animal Behaviour Science* 117 (2009): 47–54.

4. A. C. V. de Castro et al., "Does training method matter? Evidence for the negative impact of aversive-based methods on companion dog welfare," *PLOS ONE* 15, no. 12: e0225023.

5. Rachel A. Casey et al., "Dogs are more pessimistic if their owners use two or more aversive training methods," *Scientific Reports* 11, no. 1 (2021): 19023.

6. China, Mills, and Cooper, "Efficacy"; E. F. Hiby, N. J. Rooney, and J. W. S. Bradshaw, "Dog training methods: Their use, effectiveness, and interaction with behaviour and welfare," *Animal Welfare* 13 (2004): 63–69; Rooney and Cowan, "Owner–dog interactions."

7. Ziv, "Using aversive training methods."

8. Ineke R. van Herwijnen et al., "Dog ownership satisfaction determinants in the owner-dog relationship and the dog's behaviour," *PLOS ONE* 13, no. 9 (2018): e0204592.

9. Ana Catarina Vieira de Castro et al., "Carrots versus sticks: The relationship between training methods and dog-owner attachment," *Applied Animal Behaviour Science* 219 (2019): 104831.

10. Christine Arhant et al., "Owner reports on the use of muzzles and their effects on dogs: An online survey," *Journal of Veterinary Behavior* 41 (2021): 73–81.

11. Finn Nilson et al., "The effect of breed-specific dog legislation on hospital treated dog bites in Odense, Denmark—A time series intervention study," *PLOS ONE* 13, no. 12 (2018): e0208393.

12. Caffrey et al., "Epidemiology of dog bites."

13. NHS England, "HES on . . . Dog bites," digital.nhs.uk/data-and-information/publications/statistical/hospital-admitted-patient-care-activity/hes-on-dog-bites.

14. Barbara W. Boat et al., "Pediatric dog bite victims: A need for a continuum of care," *Clinical Pediatrics* 51, no. 5 (2012): 473–477.

15. Molly Jakeman et al., "Pet dog bites in children: Management and prevention," BMJ *Paediatrics Open* 4, no. 1 (2020).

16. Mary D. Salter Ainsworth and Silvia M. Bell, "Attachment, exploration, and separation: Illustrated by the behavior of one-year-olds in a strange situation," in *The Life Cycle: Readings in Human Development* (Columbia University Press, 1981), 57–71.

17. József Topál et al., "Attachment behavior in dogs (*Canis familiaris*): A new application of Ainsworth's (1969) strange situation test," *Journal of Comparative Psychology* 112, no. 3 (1998): 219.

18. Pernille Darling Rasmussen et al., "Attachment as a core feature of resilience: A systematic review and meta-analysis," *Psychological Reports* 122, no. 4 (2019): 1259–1296.

19. Martin Pinquart and Dana-Christina Gerke, "Associations of parenting styles with self-esteem in children and adolescents: A meta-analysis," *Journal of Child and Family Studies* 28 (2019): 2017–2035.

20. Anouk Spruit et al., "The relation between attachment and depression in children and adolescents: A multilevel meta-analysis," *Clinical Child and Family Psychology Review* 23 (2020): 54–69.

21. Paula R. Pietromonaco and Sally I. Powers, "Attachment and health-related physiological stress processes," *Current Opinion in Psychology* 1 (2015): 34–39.

22. Rita Lenkei et al., "Adult, intensively socialized wolves show features of attachment behaviour to their handler," *Scientific Reports* 10, no. 1 (2020): 17296; Christina Hansen Wheat et al., "Human-directed attachment behavior in wolves suggests standing ancestral variation for human-dog attachment bonds," *Ecology and Evolution* 12, no. 9 (2022): e9299.

23. Payne, Bennett, and McGreevy, "Current perspectives."

24. Guy Bosmans et al., "A learning theory of attachment: Unraveling the black box of attachment development," *Neuroscience & Biobehavioral Reviews* 113 (2020): 287–298.

25. de Castro et al., "Carrots."

26. Giacomo Riggio et al., "Physiological indicators of acute and chronic stress in securely and insecurely attached dogs undergoing a strange situation procedure (ssp): Preliminary results," *Veterinary Sciences* 9, no. 10 (2022): 519.

27. Giulia Cimarelli et al., "Dog owners' interaction styles: Their components and associations with reactions of pet dogs to a social threat," *Frontiers in Psychology* 7 (2016): 1979.

28. Laurence Steinberg et al., "Over-time changes in adjustment and competence among adolescents from authoritative, authoritarian, indulgent, and neglectful families," *Child Development* 65, no. 3 (1994): 754–770.

29. Ineke R. van Herwijnen et al., "The existence of parenting styles in the owner-dog relationship," *PLOS ONE* 13, no. 2 (2018): e0193471.

30. Alexander J. German, "Style over substance: What can parenting styles tell us about ownership styles and obesity in companion animals?" *British Journal of Nutrition* 113, no. S1 (2015): S72–S77.

31. I. R. van Herwijnen et al., "Permissive parenting of the dog associates with dog overweight in a survey among 2,303 Dutch dog owners," *PLOS ONE* 15, no. 8 (2020): e0237429.

32. I. R. van Herwijnen et al., "Dog-directed parenting styles predict verbal and leash guidance in dog owners and owner-directed attention in dogs," *Applied Animal Behaviour Science* 232 (2020): 105131.

33. Morag G. Ryan et al., "Physiological indicators of attachment in domestic dogs (*Canis familiaris*) and their owners in the strange situation test," *Frontiers in Behavioral Neuroscience* 13 (2019): 162.

34. L. Brubaker, and M. A. R. Udell, "Does pet parenting style predict the social and problem-solving behavior of pet dogs (*Canis lupus familiaris*)?" *Animal Cognition* 26, no. 1 (2023): 345–356.

35. Sean Nealon, "Pet parenting style influences dog behavior, Oregon State University finds," Oregon State University Newsroom (October 10, 2022), today.oregonstate.edu/news/pet-parenting-style-influences-dog-behavior-oregon-state-university-finds.

36. Payne, Bennett, and McGreevy, "Current perspectives."

37. E. M. Payne, P. C. Bennett, and P. D. McGreevy, "DogTube: An examination of dogmanship online," *Journal of Veterinary Behavior* 17 (2017): 50–61; E. Payne et al., "Evidence of horsemanship and dogmanship and

their application in veterinary contexts," *Veterinary Journal* 204, no. 3 (2015): 247–254.

38. E. J. Blackwell et al., "The use of electronic collars for training domestic dogs: Estimated prevalence, reasons and risk factors for use, and owner perceived success as compared to other training methods," BMC *Veterinary Research* 8 (2012) PMID: 22748195; J. L. Woodward et al., "Factors influencing owner-reported approaches to training dogs enrolled in the Generation Pup longitudinal study," *Applied Animal Behaviour Science* 242 (2021): 105404; N. H. Dodman, D. C. Brown, and J. A. Serpell, "Associations between owner personality and psychological status and the prevalence of canine behavior problems," PLOS ONE 13, no. 2 (2018): e0192846.

39. N. Charles et al., "'Fulfilling your dog's potential': Changing dimensions of power in dog training cultures in the UK," *Animal Studies Journal* 10, no. 2 (2021): 169–200; Z. Todd, "Gender roles, dominance training, and caring for pets," *Psychology Today* (2022), psychologytoday.com/ca/blog/fellow-creatures/202203/gender-roles-dominance-training-and-caring-pets.

40. Biagio D'Aniello et al., "Interspecies transmission of emotional information via chemosignals: From humans to dogs (*Canis lupus familiaris*)," *Animal Cognition* 21 (2018): 67–78.

Chapter 4: Why Is My Dog Afraid?

1. Todes, *Pavlov*.

2. Michael Domjan, *The Principles of Learning and Behavior* (Wadsworth Publishing, 2020).

3. Domjan, *Principles*.

4. Jaak Panksepp, "Affective consciousness: Core emotional feelings in animals and humans," *Consciousness and Cognition* 14, no. 1 (2005): 30–80.

5. Christiane Hermann and Matthias F. J. Sperl, "Classical conditioning," in *Handbook of Clinical Child Psychology: Integrating Theory and Research Into Practice* (Cham: Springer International Publishing, 2023), 425–457.

6. Hermann and Sperl, "Classical conditioning."

7. Jenni Puurunen et al., "Inadequate socialisation, inactivity, and urban living environment are associated with social fearfulness in pet dogs," *Scientific Reports* 10, no. 1 (2020): 3527.

8. Christine Arhant et al., "Behaviour of smaller and larger dogs: Effects of training methods, inconsistency of owner behaviour and level of engagement in activities with the dog," *Applied Animal Behaviour Science* 123, no. 3–4 (2010): 131–142.

9. J. Friedrich et al., "Genetic dissection of complex behaviour traits in German Shepherd dogs," *Heredity* 123, no. 6 (2019): 746–758.

10. I. Zapata, "Genetic testing of dogs predicts problem behaviors in clinical and nonclinical samples," BMC *Genomics* 23, no. 1 (2022): 1–19.

11. N. R. Santos, A. Beck, and A. Fontbonne, "A review of maternal behaviour in dogs and potential areas for further research," *Journal of Small Animal Practice* 61, no. 2 (2020): 85–92.

12. Santos, Beck, and Fontbonne, "Maternal behavior."

13. E. E. Bray et al., "Effects of maternal investment, temperament, and cognition on guide dog success," *Proceedings of the National Academy of Sciences* 114, no. 34 (2017): 9128–9133.

14. L. Dietz et al., "The importance of early life experiences for the development of behavioural disorders in domestic dogs," *Behaviour* 155, no. 2–3 (2018) 83–114.

15. M. Morrow et al., "Breed-dependent differences in the onset of fear-related avoidance behavior in puppies," *Journal of Veterinary Behavior* 10, no. 4 (2015): 286–294.

16. Maike Foraita, Tiffani Howell, and Pauleen Bennett, "Environmental influences on development of executive functions in dogs," *Animal Cognition* 24, no. 4 (2021): 655–675.

17. J. H. Cutler, J. B. Coe, and L. Niel, "Puppy socialization practices of a sample of dog owners from across Canada and the United States," *Journal of the American Veterinary Medical Association* 251, no. 12 (2017): 1415–1423.

18. Puurunen et al., "Inadequate socialisation."

19. H. Vaterlaws-Whiteside and A. Hartmann, "Improving puppy behavior using a new standardized socialization program," *Applied Animal Behaviour Science* 197 (2017): 55–61.

20. L. Asher et al., "Teenage dogs? Evidence for adolescent-phase conflict behaviour and an association between attachment to humans and pubertal timing in the domestic dog," *Biology Letters* 16, no. 5 (2020): 20200097.

21. G. Caron-Lormier et al., "Using the incidence and impact of behavioural conditions in guide dogs to investigate patterns in undesirable behaviour in dogs," *Scientific Reports* 6 (2016): 23860.

22. Rowena M. A. Packer et al., "Pandemic puppies: Characterising motivations and behaviours of UK owners who purchased puppies during the 2020 COVID-19 pandemic," *Animals* 11, no. 9 (2021): 2500.

23. Claire L. Brand et al., "Pandemic puppies: Demographic characteristics, health and early life experiences of puppies acquired during the 2020 phase of the COVID-19 pandemic in the UK," *Animals* 12, no. 5 (2022): 629.

24. Dogs Trust, "Puppy smuggling: Puppies still paying as government delays" (2020), dogstrust.org.uk/downloads/2020%20Puppy%20 smuggling%20report.pdf.

25. J. Maher and T. Wyatt, "European illegal puppy trade and organised crime," *Trends in Organized Crime* 24, no. 4 (2021): 506–525.

26. Molly K. Houle, "Perspective from the field: Illegal puppy imports uncovered at JFK airport," CDC (2022), cdc.gov/ncezid/dgmq/feature-stories/operation-dog-catcher.html.

27. Dave Seglins and Carly Thomas, "Officials probe arrival of 500 puppies, 38 of them dead, aboard flight from Ukraine," CBC News (June 20, 2020), cbc.ca/news/canada/ukraine-flight-puppies-1.5620691.

28. T. Camps et al., "Pain-related aggression in dogs: 12 clinical cases," *Journal of Veterinary Behavior* 7, no. 2 (2012): 99–102.

29. D. S. Mills et al., "Pain and problem behavior in cats and dogs," *Animals* 10, no. 2 (2020): 318.

30. T. Camps, M. Amat, and X. Manteca, "A review of medical conditions and behavioral problems in dogs and cats," *Animals* 9, no. 12 (2019): 1133; L. Radosta, "Behavior changes associated with metabolic disease of dogs and cats," *Veterinary Clinics of North America: Small Animal Practice* 54, no. 1 (2024): 17–28.

31. N. D. Harvey et al., "Behavioural differences in dogs with atopic dermatitis suggest stress could be a significant problem associated with chronic pruritus," *Animals* 9, no. 10 (2019): 813.

32. Ahu Demirtas et al., "Dog owners' recognition of pain-related behavioral changes in their dogs," *Journal of Veterinary Behavior* 62 (2023): 39–46.

33. Daniel Mills and Helen Zulch, "Veterinary assessment of behaviour cases in dogs and cats," *In Practice* 45, no. 8 (2023): 444–458.

Chapter 5: Training a Fearful Dog

1. Ian R. Dinwoodie, Vivian Zottola, and Nicholas H. Dodman, "An investigation into the effectiveness of various professionals and behavior modification programs, with or without medication, for the treatment of canine fears," *Journal of Veterinary Behavior* 55–56 (2022): 1–6.

2. Tom Beckers et al., "Understanding clinical fear and anxiety through the lens of human fear conditioning," *Nature Reviews Psychology* 2, no. 4 (2023): 233–245.

3. Petfoodology available online at: vetnutrition.tufts.edu/petfoodology/. Checked on January 14, 2024.

4. M. E. Bouton, S. Maren, and G. P. McNally, "Behavioral and neurobiological mechanisms of Pavlovian and instrumental extinction learning," *Physiological Reviews* 101, no. 2 (2021): 611–681.

5. N. E. Keller, A. C. Hennings, and J. E. Dunsmoor, "Behavioral and neural processes in counterconditioning: Past and future directions," *Behaviour Research and Therapy* 125 (2020): 103532.

6. Hermann and Sperl, "Classical conditioning."

7. Keller, Hennings, and Dunsmoor, "Behavioral and neural processes."

8. K. A. Knowles and D. F. Tolin, "Mechanisms of action in exposure therapy," *Current Psychiatry Reports* 24, no. 12 (2022): 861–869.

9. Gaëtan Mertens and Iris M. Engelhard, "A systematic review and meta-analysis of the evidence for unaware fear conditioning," *Neuroscience & Biobehavioral Reviews* 108 (2020): 254–268.

10. Stefanie Riemer, "Effectiveness of treatments for firework fears in dogs," *Journal of Veterinary Behavior* 37 (2020): 61–70.

11. Riemer, "Effectiveness."

12. Ian R. Dinwoodie, Vivian Zottola, and Nicholas H. Dodman, "An investigation into the effectiveness of various professionals and behavior modification programs, with or without medication, for the treatment of canine aggression," *Journal of Veterinary Behavior* 43 (2021): 46–53; Dinwoodie, Zottola, and Dodman, "Canine fears."

Chapter 6: Exercise and Enrichment

1. N. S. Starinsky, L. K. Lord, and M. E. Herron, "Escape rates and biting histories of dogs confined to their owner's property through the use of various containment methods," *Journal of the American Veterinary Medical Association* 250, no. 3 (2017): 297–302.

2. C. Duranton and A. Horowitz, "Let me sniff! Nosework induces positive judgment bias in pet dogs," *Applied Animal Behaviour Science* 211 (2018): 61–66.

Chapter 7: Understanding the Role of Medications

1. M. Hammerle et al., "2015 AAHA canine and feline behavior management guidelines," aaha.org/aaha-guidelines/behavior-management/behavior-management-home/.

2. Maki Kato et al., "Effects of prescription diet on dealing with stressful situations and performance of anxiety-related behaviors in privately owned anxious dogs," *Journal of Veterinary Behavior* 7, no. 1 (2012): 21–26.

3. Gary Michael Landsberg et al., "Assessment of noise-induced fear and anxiety in dogs: Modification by a novel fish hydrolysate supplemented diet," *Journal of Veterinary Behavior* 10, no. 5 (2015): 391–398.

4. Amy L. Pike, Debra F. Horwitz, and Heidi Lobprise, "An open-label prospective study of the use of L-theanine (Anxitane) in storm-sensitive client-owned dogs," *Journal of Veterinary Behavior* 10, no. 4 (2015): 324–331.

5. Emmanuelle Titeux et al., "Effects of a new dietary supplement on behavioural responses of dogs exposed to mild stressors," *Veterinary Medicine and Science* 7, no. 5 (2021): 1469–1482.

6. Dinwoodie, Zottola, and Dodman, "Canine fears."

7. Katriina Tiira et al., "Environmental effects on compulsive tail chasing in dogs," *PLOS ONE* 7, no. 7 (2012): e41684.

8. D. Frank, G. Beauchamp, and C. Palestrini, "Systematic review of the use of pheromones for treatment of undesirable behavior in cats and dogs," *Journal of the American Veterinary Medical Association* 236, no. 12 (2010): 1308–1316.

9. C. Hermiston, V T. Montrose, and S. Taylor, "The effects of dog-appeasing pheromone spray upon canine vocalizations and stress-related behaviors in a rescue shelter," *Journal of Veterinary Behavior* 26 (2018): 11–16.

10. S. Taylor et al., "The behavioral and physiological effects of dog appeasing pheromone on canine behavior during separation from the owner," *Journal of Veterinary Behavior* 40 (2020): 36–42.

11. M. C. Osella et al., "Adaptive mechanisms in dogs adopted from shelters: A behavioral assessment of the use of a synthetic analogue of the canine appeasing pheromone," *Dog Behavior* 1, no. 2 (2015): 1–12.

12. N. R. Santos et al., "Influence of dog-appeasing pheromone on canine maternal behaviour during the peripartum and neonatal periods," *Veterinary Record* 186, no. 14 (2020): 449.

13. Miriam Rebecca Prior and Daniel Simon Mills, "Cats vs. dogs: The efficacy of Feliway Friends and Adaptil products in multispecies homes," *Frontiers in Veterinary Science* 7 (2020): 545329.

14. Camille King et al., "The effect of a pressure wrap (ThunderShirt) on heart rate and behavior in canines diagnosed with anxiety disorder," *Journal of Veterinary Behavior* 9, no. 5 (2014): 215–221.

15. Anne-Maria Pekkin et al., "The effect of a pressure vest on the behaviour, salivary cortisol and urine oxytocin of noise phobic dogs in a controlled test," *Applied Animal Behaviour Science* 185 (2016): 86–94.

16. Riemer, "Effectiveness."

17. Alessandra Di Salvo, Maria Beatrice Conti, and Giorgia della Rocca, "Pharmacokinetics, efficacy, and safety of cannabidiol in dogs: An update of current knowledge," *Frontiers in Veterinary Science* 10 (2023): 1204526.

18. Alysia B. G. Hunt et al., "A single dose of cannabidiol (CBD) positively influences measures of stress in dogs during separation and car travel," *Frontiers in Veterinary Science* 10 (2023): 153.

19. "Cannabis use and pets," American Veterinary Medical Association, avma.org/resources-tools/animal-health-and-welfare/animal-health/cannabis-use-and-pets.

Chapter 8: Social Wallflowers and Bashful Beasties

1. Rachel A. Casey et al., "Human directed aggression."

2. Marc Bekoff, "Play signals as punctuation: The structure of social play in canids," *Behaviour* 132, no. 5 (1995): 419–429; S. E. Byosiere, J. Espinosa, and B. Smuts, "Investigating the function of play bows in adult pet dogs (*Canis lupus familiaris*)," *Behavioural Processes* 125 (2016) PMID: 26923096; S. E. Byosiere et al., "Investigating the function of play bows in dog and wolf puppies (*Canis lupus familiaris, Canis lupus occidentalis*)," *PLOS ONE* 11, no. 12 (2016) PMID: 28033358; A. Horowitz, "Attention to attention in domestic dog (*Canis familiaris*) dyadic play," *Animal Cognition* 12, no. 1 (2009) PMID: 18679727.

3. A. M. Taylor, D. Reby, and K. McComb, "Context-related variation in the vocal growling behaviour of the domestic dog (*Canis familiaris*)," *Ethology* 115, no. 10 (2009): 905–915.

4. T. Faragó et al., "'The bone is mine': Affective and referential aspects of dog growls," *Animal Behaviour* 79, no. 4 (2010): 917–925.

5. A. Bálint et al., "'Beware, I am big and non-dangerous!': Playfully growling dogs are perceived larger than their actual size by their canine audience," *Applied Animal Behaviour Science* 148, no. 1–2 (2013): 128–137.

Chapter 9: Thumps, Bumps, and Bangs

1. Emily J. Blackwell, John W. S. Bradshaw, and Rachel A. Casey, "Fear responses to noises in domestic dogs: Prevalence, risk factors and co-occurrence with other fear related behaviour," *Applied Animal Behaviour Science* 145, no. 1–2 (2013): 15–25.

2. Salonen et al., "Prevalence, comorbidity."

3. Takuma Kurachi and Mami Irimajiri, "Preliminary study on the effects of attendance at dog training school on minimizing development of some anxiety disorders," *Journal of Veterinary Behavior* 34 (2019): 13–17.

4. Janet H. Cutler, Jason B. Coe, and Lee Niel, "Puppy socialization practices of a sample of dog owners from across Canada and the United States," *Journal of the American Veterinary Medical Association* 251, no. 12 (2017): 1415–1423.

5. A. L. Lopes Fagundes et al., "Noise sensitivities in dogs: An exploration of signs in dogs with and without musculoskeletal pain using qualitative content analysis," *Frontiers in Veterinary Science* 5 (2018): 17.

6. Stefanie Riemer, "Not a one-way road—Severity, progression and prevention of firework fears in dogs," *PLOS ONE* 14, no. 9 (2019): e0218150.

7. Eileen Anderson, "Sound masking to help dogs with a noise phobia or sound sensitivity," *Whole Dog Journal* (December 8, 2023), whole-dog-journal.com/behavior/noise-canceling-for-dogs/.

Chapter 10: Needles and Thermometers

1. Anastasia C. Stellato et al., "Risk-factors associated with veterinary-related fear and aggression in owned domestic dogs," *Applied Animal Behaviour Science* 241 (2021): 105374.

2. Ann-Kristina Lind et al., "Assessing stress in dogs during a visit to the veterinary clinic: Correlations between dog behavior in standardized tests and assessments by veterinary staff and owners," *Journal of Veterinary Behavior* 17 (2017): 24–31.

3. Petra T. Edwards et al., "Investigating risk factors that predict a dog's fear during veterinary consultations," *PLOS ONE* 14, no. 7 (2019): e0215416.

4. Edwards et al, "Investigating risk factors"; Stellato et al., "Risk-factors."

5. Stellato et al., "Risk-factors."

6. Erika Csoltova et al., "Behavioral and physiological reactions in dogs to a veterinary examination: Owner-dog interactions improve canine well-being," *Physiology & Behavior* 177 (2017): 270–281.

7. Lind et al., "Assessing stress in dogs."

8. Anastasia C. Stellato et al., "Evaluation of associations between owner presence and indicators of fear in dogs during routine veterinary examinations," *Journal of the American Veterinary Medical Association* 257, no. 10 (2020): 1031–1040.

Chapter 11: "Don't Leave Me!"

1. Salonen et al., "Prevalence, comorbidity"; J. W. S. Bradshaw et al., "Aetiology of separation-related behaviour in domestic dogs," *Veterinary Record* 151, no. 2 (2002): 43–46.

2. S. Cannas et al., "Video analysis of dogs suffering from anxiety when left home alone and treated with clomipramine," *Journal of Veterinary Behavior* 9, no. 2 (2014): 50–57.

3. Cannas et al., "Video analysis"; E. Blackwell, R. A. Casey, and J. W. S. Bradshaw, "Controlled trial of behavioural therapy for separation-related disorders in dogs," *Veterinary Record* 158, no. 16 (2006): 551–554.

4. Tia Meneses et al., "Review of epidemiological, pathological, genetic, and epigenetic factors that may contribute to the development of separation anxiety in dogs," *Journal of the American Veterinary Medical Association* 259, no. 10 (2021): 1118–1129.

5. Rebecca J. Sargisson, "Canine separation anxiety: Strategies for treatment and management," *Veterinary Medicine: Research and Reports* (2014): 143–151.

6. Barbara L. Sherman and Daniel S. Mills, "Canine anxieties and phobias: An update on separation anxiety and noise aversions," *Veterinary Clinics of North America: Small Animal Practice* 38, no. 5 (2008): 1081–1106.

7. Robert M. Christley et al., "Impact of the first COVID-19 lockdown on management of pet dogs in the UK," *Animals* 11, no. 1 (2020): 5.

8. Naomi D. Harvey et al., "Impact of changes in time left alone on separation-related behaviour in UK pet dogs," *Animals* 12, no. 4 (2022): 482.

9. Luciana S. de Assis et al., "Developing diagnostic frameworks in veterinary behavioral medicine: Disambiguating separation related problems in dogs," *Frontiers in Veterinary Science* 6 (2020): 499.

10. Chiara Mariti et al., "Effects of petting before a brief separation from the owner on dog behavior and physiology: A pilot study," *Journal of Veterinary Behavior* 27 (2018): 41–46.

11. Aaron R. Teixeira and Nathaniel J. Hall, "Effect of greeting and departure interactions on the development of increased separation-related behaviors in newly adopted adult dogs," *Journal of Veterinary Behavior* 41 (2021): 22–32.

12. V. Konok, A. Marx, and T. Faragó, "Attachment styles in dogs and their relationship with separation-related disorder—A questionnaire based clustering," *Applied Animal Behaviour Science* 213 (2019): 81–90.

13. Emily Jayne Blackwell, Rachel A. Casey, and John W. S. Bradshaw, "Efficacy of written behavioral advice for separation-related behavior problems in dogs newly adopted from a rehoming center," *Journal of Veterinary Behavior* 12 (2016): 13–19.

Chapter 12: "Grrr, Keep Away From My Stuff!"

1. Jacquelyn A. Jacobs et al., "Ability of owners to identify resource guarding behaviour in the domestic dog," *Applied Animal Behaviour Science* 188 (2017): 77–83.

2. Jacquelyn A. Jacobs et al., "Factors associated with canine resource guarding behaviour in the presence of people: A cross-sectional survey of dog owners," *Preventive Veterinary Medicine* 161 (2018): 143–153.

3. Jacquelyn A. Jacobs et al., "Factors associated with canine resource guarding behaviour in the presence of dogs: A cross-sectional survey of dog owners," *Preventive Veterinary Medicine* 161 (2018): 134–142.

4. Betty McGuire, "Characteristics and adoption success of shelter dogs assessed as resource guarders," *Animals* 9, no. 11 (2019): 982.

5. Betty McGuire et al., "Results of behavioral evaluations predict length of stay for shelter dogs," *Animals* 11, no. 11 (2021): 3272.

6. Karen E. Griffin et al., "What will happen to this dog? A qualitative analysis of rehoming organisations' pre-adoption dog behaviour screening policies and procedures," *Frontiers in Veterinary Science* 8 (2022): 1665.

Chapter 13: Turning, Turning

1. Valarie V. Tynes and Leslie Sinn, "Abnormal repetitive behaviors in dogs and cats: A guide for practitioners," *Veterinary Clinics of North America: Small Animal Practice* 44, no. 3 (2014): 543–564.

2. Andrew U. Luescher, "Repetitive and compulsive behaviour in dogs and cats," in Debra F. Horwitz and Daniel Mills (eds.), BSAVA *Manual of Canine and Feline Behavioural Medicine*, 2nd edition (Gloucester: BSAVA, 2017).

3. Jonathan Bowen and Jaume Fatjó, "Repetitive behaviors in dogs," *Veterinary Clinics of North America: Small Animal Practice* 54, no. 1 (2024): 71–85.

4. Luescher, "Repetitive and compulsive behaviour"; Tynes and Sinn, "Abnormal repetitive behaviors."

5. Belinda R. Walsh, "A critical review of the evidence for the equivalence of canine and human compulsions," *Applied Animal Behaviour Science* 234 (2021): 105166.

6. Tiira et al., "Environmental effects."

7. Walsh, "A critical review."

8. Bowen and Fatjó, "Repetitive behaviors."

9. Sini Sulkama et al., "Aggressiveness, ADHD-like behaviour, and environment influence repetitive behaviour in dogs," *Scientific Reports* 12, no. 1 (2022): 3520.

10. Luescher, "Repetitive and compulsive behaviour"; Nathaniel J. Hall, Alexandra Protopopova, and Clive D. L. Wynne, "The role of environmental and owner-provided consequences in canine stereotypy and compulsive behavior," *Journal of Veterinary Behavior* 10, no. 1 (2015): 24–35.

11. Karen L. Overall, *Manual of Clinical Behavioral Medicine for Dogs and Cats* (St. Louis: Elsevier, 2013),

12. Luescher, "Repetitive and compulsive behaviour."

13. D. S. Mills, F. M. Coutts, and K. J. McPeake, "Behavior problems associated with pain and paresthesia," *Veterinary Clinics of North America: Small Animal Practice* 54, no. 1 (2024): 55-69.

14. Mills and Zulch, "Veterinary assessment."

15. Mills and Zulch, "Veterinary assessment."

16. Tiira et al, "Environmental effects."

17. Tynes and Sinn, "Abnormal repetitive behaviors."

Chapter 14: Getting Help

1. Kristin Buller and Kelly C. Ballantyne, "Living with and loving a pet with behavioral problems: Pet owners' experiences," *Journal of Veterinary Behavior* 37 (2020): 41–47.

2. Kristin Kuntz et al., "Assessment of caregiver burden in owners of dogs with behavioral problems and factors related to its presence," *Journal of Veterinary Behavior* 64–65 (2023): 41–46.

3. Buller and Ballantyne, "Living with and loving a pet."

4. Emma J. Williams and Emily Blackwell, "Managing the risk of aggressive dog behavior: Investigating the influence of owner threat and efficacy perceptions," *Risk Analysis* 39, no. 11 (2019): 2528–2542.

5. Overall, *Manual.*

6. Anamarie C. Johnson and Clive D. L. Wynne, "Training dogs with science or with nature? An exploration of trainers' word use, gender, and certification across dog-training methods," *Anthrozoös* 36, no. 1 (2023): 35–51.

7. Pet Professional Accreditation Board, information retrieved from credentialingboard.com on August 29, 2023.

8. Eduardo J. Fernandez, "The least inhibitive, functionally effective model: A new framework for ethical animal training practices," *Journal of Veterinary Behavior* 71 (2024): 63–68; Zazie Todd, "Barriers to the adoption of humane dog training methods," *Journal of Veterinary Behavior* 25 (2018): 28–34.

9. Certification Council for Professional Dog Trainers, "Electronic training collars position statement," information retrieved from ccpdt.org/wp-content/uploads/2022/03/Electronic-Training-Collar-Position-Statement.pdf on August 29, 2023.

10. International Association of Animal Behavior Consultants, "IAABC statement on LIMA," information retrieved from iaabc.org/lima on August 29, 2023.

11. Certification Council for Professional Dog Trainers. "Least Intrusive, Minimally Aversive (LIMA) effective behavior intervention policy," information retrieved from ccpdt.org/wp-content/uploads/2015/01/LIMA-Policy-2019.pdf on February 18, 2024.

12. Carlo Siracusa, Lena Provoost, and Ilana R. Reisner, "Dog- and owner-related risk factors for consideration of euthanasia or rehoming before a referral behavioral consultation and for euthanizing or rehoming the dog after the consultation," *Journal of Veterinary* Behavior 22 (2017): 46–56.

13. Danielle N. Lee, "Diversity and inclusion activisms in animal behaviour and the ABS: A historical view from the USA," *Animal Behaviour* 164 (2020): 273–280.

14. National Association for Black Veterinarians, "Mission statement," information retrieved from nabvonline.org on October 17, 2023.

Chapter 15: Fearful Fido No More

1. Woodward et al., "Factors influencing owner-reported approaches."

2. AnimalKind, information retrieved from animalkind.ca on August 29, 2023.

3. Kristen Collins et al., "Behavioral rehabilitation of extremely fearful dogs: Report on the efficacy of a treatment protocol," *Applied Animal Behaviour Science* 254 (2022): 105689.

4. Zazie Todd, "England moves to ban electric shock collars for dogs," *Psychology Today*, April 28, 2023, psychologytoday.com/ca/blog/fellow-creatures/202304/england-moves-to-ban-electric-shock-collars-for-dogs.

INDEX

Illustrations and tables indicated by page numbers in italics

Also by Zazie Todd

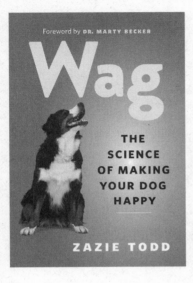

"The must-have guide to improving your dog's life."

MODERN DOG

Wag: The Science of Making Your Dog Happy

304 pages • Paperback

Winner, Best Book about Dog Behavior, Health or General Care, Dog Writers Association of America

What People Are Saying:

"If you've ever wondered what your pet is thinking and feeling, this book is a great place to start."

WUNDERDOG MAGAZINE

"Practical, compassionate, thorough—and based on science rather than wishful thinking—*Wag* is also a gift you should give to yourself and the dog or dogs in your life. I loved it!"

CAT WARREN, author of *What the Dog Knows*

"Well-written and packed with great advice, this book could fundamentally change the relationship between you and your dog."

DAVID GRIMM, author of *Citizen Canine*

"*Wag* will become a benchmark for the way that dogs need to be cared for: as sentient creatures experiencing emotions, just like us."

DR. PETE WEDDERBURN, veterinarian and author

Also by Zazie Todd

"Definitely a book your cat would want you to read!"

DR. SARAH ELLIS, coauthor of *The Trainable Cat*

Purr: The Science of Making Your Cat Happy

288 pages · Hardcover / Paperback

What People Are Saying:

"Enjoyable, approachable, easy to read. *Purr* is a must for anyone who shares their life with a cat."

KATE LASALA, certified trainer and behavior consultant, Rescued By Training

"An evidence-based guide . . . *Purr* is a welcome and exciting addition for every cat lover's shelf."

MIKEL DELGADO, PhD, certified applied animal behaviorist and cofounder of Feline Minds

"*Purr* covers all the essentials to ensure we are raising our cats right! From adoption to senior care, this book challenges the status quo."

INGRID JOHNSON, certified cat behavior consultant and founder of Fundamentally Feline

"Practical, entertaining, and thorough. Cat owners are in good hands with Zazie Todd."

LUCY JANE SANTOS, author of *Half Lives*